The Early French Novella

*An Anthology of Fifteenth- and
Sixteenth-Century Tales edited and
translated by Patricia Francis Cholakian
and Rouben Charles Cholakian*

*State University of New York Press
Albany 1972*

The Early French Novella

First Edition

Published by State University of New York Press
99 Washington Avenue, Albany, New York 12210

© 1972 State University of New York
All rights reserved

Printed in the United States of America
Designed by Richard Hendel

Library of Congress Cataloging in Publication Data

Cholakian, Patricia Francis, comp.
   The early French novella.
   Includes bibliographies.
   1. Short stories, French—Translations into English.
2. Short stories, English—Translations from French.
3. French literature—Old French—Translations into
English. 4. French literature—16th century—Transla-
tions into English. I. Cholakian, Rouben Charles,
1932–   joint comp. II. Title.
PQ1278.C5   843'.02   79-171179
ISBN 0-87395-090-9
ISBN 0-87395-190-5 (microfiche)

To the faculty of

Bates College

amore ac studio

Hommes pensifz, je ne vous donne à lire
Ces miens devis si vous ne contraignez
Le fier maintien de vos frons rechignez:
Icy n'y ha seulement que pour rire.

Laissez à part vostre chagrin, vostre ire
Et voz discours de trop loing desseignez.
Un autre fois vous serez enseignez.
Je me suis bien contrainct pour les escrire.

J'ay oublié mes tristes passions,
J'ay intermis mes occupations.
Donnons, donnons quelque lieu à folie,

Que maugré nous ne nous vienne saisir,
Et en un jour plein de melencholie
Meslons au moins une heure de plaisir.

BONAVENTURE DES PÉRIERS

Contents

List of Illustrations   11
Preface   13

Introduction   17

Les Quinze Joies de Mariage   75
"The First Joy of Marriage"   78
"The Fifteenth Joy of Marriage"   84

Antoine de La Sale: *Le Petit Jehan de Saintré*   93
"The Knight, the Lady, and the Abbot"   98

Les Cent Nouvelles Nouvelles   129
(9) "The Self-made Cuckold"   132
(19) "The Miracle of the Snow Child"   135
(34) "The Voice from on High"   139
(61) "Prisoner of Love"   142
(80) "Great Expectations"   147
(93) "Holy Pilgrimage"   148
(98) "The Lovers' Tragedy"   151

Philippe de Vigneulles: *Les Cent Nouvelles Nouvelles*   157
(4) "Modicum et Bonum"   160
(71) "The Peddler"   164

Nicolas de Troyes: *Le Grand Parangon Des Nouvelles Nouvelles*   167
(116, Mabille 22) "The Good Judge of Troyes"   170
(27, Mabille 39) "The Spell of the Ring"   173

Noël du Fail: *Baliverneries* 181
(3) "A Man's Best Friend" 183

Bonaventure des Périers: *Les Nouvelles
Récréations et Joyeux Devis* 186
(3) "The Cantor's Stew" 191
(9) "The Ear Specialist" 194
(34) "The Vicar of Brou and his Bishop" 196
(36) "Holy Excommunication" 199
(40) "In the Confessional" 200
(62) "Sister Thoinette" 201
(78) "The Italian Kiss" 204

Marguerite de Navarre: *L'Heptaméron* 206
(4) "A Bedtime Story" 211
(26) "The Wise and Foolish Ladies" 217
(29) "The Priest and the Plowman" 231
(40) "A Love Match" 233
(56) "The Tonsured Husband" 240

Illustrations

1. *Les Quinze Joies de Mariage*
   "The First Joy"   facing p. 78

2. *Le Petit Jehan de Saintré*   facing p. 127

3. *Les Cent Nouvelles Nouvelles* (34)
   "The Voice from on High"   facing p. 142

4. *Les Cent Nouvelles Nouvelles* (61)
   "The Prisoner of Love"   facing p. 146

5. The *Heptaméron*   facing p. 206

Preface

THE FRENCH NOVELLAS of the fifteenth and sixteenth centuries form a significant and large body of literature almost entirely unknown to the modern reader of English. To begin with, the language barrier is such that even students of French find this early prose difficult to read. Where translations of individual authors are available, they are often marred by archaisms or, in some instances, are simply incomplete and outdated.[1] What is more, outside of large university libraries, these texts are hard to come by.

In selecting these stories, we have tried to cull out of a vast and uneven literature those tales which seem best to exemplify the tradition. Since these writers used sexual situations and obscenity as the source of much of their humor, we have included here a fair sampling of that type of storytelling. For mature readers, however, all the texts have cultural value and offer insight into the literary tastes of the Renaissance reader.

It may appear somewhat arbitrary to specialists in the field that the translations stop with Marguerite de Navarre. It was our intention to suggest, however, that the queen of Navarre's use of the form marks an important high point in the evolution of the Renaissance novella, after which the genre suffers from an increasingly marked tendency toward discursiveness. It may also appear unwarranted to have excluded that master storyteller François Rabelais. If Rabelais is not, however, a part of our collection, it is not because he is unimportant to the novella tradition but because good and easily accessible translations are already available.[2]

The complex question of the origins and stylistic characteristics of the French novella and the specific contributions of each *novelliste* requires more space than can be reasonably provided in this anthology. Nonetheless, it has been our aim in both the general introduction and in our individual essays to help the nonspecialist to place these writers in their proper cultural context. For those who choose to pursue the subject further, we have prepared selected bibliographies.

The art of translation is of course full of pitfalls, especially when it deals with a language still in its formative stages. The principal rule observed here has been to steer an even course between linguistic accuracy and modernization. We have worked to create a style which seems faithful to the original without giving way either to distracting archaisms or to contemporary slang. As in the early days of printing, editors often inserted titles and summaries of their own invention, so we have taken the liberty of giving each story an English title.

We should like to express our gratitude to the staff of the Hamilton College Library and especially to Mrs. Eugenia W. King, for their invaluable assistance in locating materials. In addition, we should like to thank Norman Mangouni of the State University of New York Press and Professor Konrad Bieber of the State University of New York at Stony Brook for their help in the preparation of the manuscript for publication.

PATRICIA FRANCIS CHOLAKIAN
ROUBEN CHARLES CHOLAKIAN

Notes for Preface

1. Bonaventure Des Périers, the most neglected of all in this regard, was last translated in the sixteenth century. *The Mirrour of Mirth* (1583), an incomplete translation, has been reprinted by the University of South Carolina Press (1959).

2. Most recently, Professor Abraham Keller has examined the uses of short fiction in Rabelais in his study *The Telling of Tales in Rabelais* (Frankfurt: Klostermann, 1963).

The Early French Novella

Introduction

DEFINING THE NOVELLA is somewhat like trying to describe what a song is. Storytelling is so fundamental a part of human experience that for years the written tale disguised only faintly the presence of the oral narrator. What is more, the *novelliste*, whether like Des Périers he meant only to entertain or whether like Marguerite de Navarre he meant to use the story as a springboard for moralistic discussions, altered the form to suit his own particular purposes.[1]

It seems futile to attempt any definition which separates the *conte* from the *nouvelle*, or either of these from the *histoire*, when in fact, by the sixteenth century, these had become nearly interchangeable terms.[2] Yet some kind of simple definition will make the subsequent discussion more meaningful. In his study on French fiction, Henri Coulet suggests that the novella is the recounting of an event which is recent, true (at least according to the teller), and complete in and of itself.[3] If one adds to this that the story is fairly brief and in prose, one has a workable definition.

The Sources and Origins of the Novella

The ability to tell a good story is certainly not peculiar to any ethnic group.[4] The vast tables of folk-motives established by such scholars as Stith Thompson are evidence enough of that.[5] Nor can it be said that the pastime of storytelling is characteristic of any one class, for the novella literature springs from all the social levels.[6] When a literary phenomenon becomes so widespread, therefore, the critic in search of sources must be especially cautious about his inferences.

The question becomes further complicated when one realizes that during this period, the writer's originality was not measured by modern standards. An author like Nicolas de Troyes might very well "copy" from Boccaccio and think nothing of it—his reader still less!

In addition, one must ask what precisely is meant by "influences" and "borrowing." The question is both quantitative and qualitative. First, does influence apply to the thematic material of the novella, to the *idea* of a short piece of narrative prose, or rather to the concept of a collection of stories in the manner of Boccaccio's *Decameron?* Secondly, at what point and to what extent can one confidently assert that one author has consciously borrowed from another?

All the most recent scholarship attests to the complexity of this kind of *Quelle* research and how simplistic if not misleading some of the earliest work in the field has been. Pioneering scholars who first looked for *novelliste* sources seemed unable to remain totally objective. In 1895, Pietro Toldo's chauvinistic attempt to establish the predominant role of Italian literature in the rise of the French novella [7] elicited a no less nationalistic reply from the distinguished French medievalist Gaston Paris.[8] Paris's now-famous rebuttal, however, was important in underlining the need to distinguish between the form or idea of the story and its thematic content. Although a strict dichotomy is ultimately meaningless, for the purposes of our discussion here, we shall respect these two categories and review the sources from the point of view of the story itself and the themes.

Despite our definition that the short story is written in prose, the origins of the form must go back to verse-narratives of the Middle Ages, such as the Provençal *Novas* [9] and most especially to the *lais*, as exemplified by the poetry of Marie de France. Notwithstanding the handicaps of composing a tale in rhyme, this twelfth-century poetess showed evidence of being a remarkably gifted storyteller.[10] The conciseness and psychological penetration of a little tale like *Laostic* entitle her to a place among the important contributors to the development of fiction in France. In like measure, the anonymous *Châtelaine de Vergi* possesses many of the earmarks of modern narrative art.[11]

In the same courtly tradition must be included the numerous reworkings of classical stories such as the *Roman de Thèbes,* the *Roman d'Enéas,* and the *Roman de Troie,* which Gustave Cohen calls the "triade classique." [12] Their recounting of the touching and dramatic love-episodes of Dido and Aeneas and

Lavinia and Aeneas, as well as the love story of Troilus and Cressida are further proof of the abiding interest in psychological realism which predominates in all of French literature, and their frequent adaptations attest to their lingering popularity among the French aristocracy.[13]

Noteworthy in the courtly literature also is the famous *chantefable*, *Aucassin et Nicolette*. Part verse and part prose, this half-serious tale of love marks a notable intermediate stage in the evolution from narrative verse to prose.[14] But aside from this, *Aucassin et Nicolette* is important to our study to the extent that it reflects the tastes of a new class, critical of the exaggerations of the courtly ethic. The anonymous poet satirizes the Arthurian never-never world so dear to the nobility. He joins bourgeois realism with ironic wit to create a humorous parody of all the clichés of the *amour courtois* tradition. Were it only for the extraordinary, true-to-life details in the famous forest scene (where Aucassin goes in search of his beloved Nicolette and meets with the local peasantry), this unique story would deserve mention in a review of French medieval narrative art.

This same need for a more sensible, if not cynical, view of life gave birth to the *Roman de Renart*, the first "branches" of which date from the second half of the twentieth century. The symbolic animals of these clever stories, like those in the fables of about the same period, amused a wider and more down-to-earth audience, which seemed to enjoy laughing at itself as well as at the rest of the world. Though still in verse, Marie de France's *Isopet* (late twelfth century) contributed significantly to the trend towards realism by replacing the animals with people. By the next century, the transition away from animals was complete with the creation of the fabliau, whose name is really a diminutive of the word "fable." [15] The increased use of realistic dialogue, the concern with events of daily life, and the descriptions of the characters like the cuckolded husband and corrupt monk make the fabliau still another salient link in the growth of narrative art.

Contemporaneous with this bourgeois tradition is that of the oriental tale. Two striking features make these stories relevant to our analysis. They are relatively short, and they are usually part of a frame structure. Most of them came into France by way of Latin prose versions and were soon translated into the vernacular. The first translation was probably *Li Romans de Dolopathos* (1210) followed toward the end of the thirteenth century by the *Estoire des Sept Sages*. Though the details are somewhat different in each, both are based on Latin originals and both tell the same frame story. During the absence of her husband, a wicked stepmother, rebuffed by her stepson, accuses the latter of making advances and condemns him to death. A series of tales spread out over a week's time delays the execution until the father is able to return and correct the wrong that has been done.

Lacking the frame and more emphatically didactic are the collections of Latin tales called *exempla*, which, during most of the Middle Ages, served men of the church as pedagogical tools in their sermons.[16] The earliest of these seems to have been the *Disciplina clericalis* composed at the close of the eleventh century by a converted Spanish Jew, Petrus Alfonsi. In the next century these thirty-four Latin stories were translated into Old French verse under the title of *Castoiement d'un père à son fils*. In the same didactic vein, but in prose, the Chevalier de La Tour Landry composed for his own daughters a catechism of good manners, which he sprinkled liberally with edifying anecdotes.[17]

The idea of the *exempla* spread among churchmen very quickly. Numerous collections appeared, the most famous being those by Jacques de Vitry, Étienne de Bourbon, Arnold de Liège, and Jean Gobi. These writer-clerics drew their material from oriental sources, fables, and fabliaux. They frequently used popular themes which would appeal to their heterogeneous audience. Whatever the source, however, the stories had to be brief and very much to the point, inasmuch as they existed only as illustrations to moral lessons. By the fourteenth century perhaps the best-known collection was the compilation known as the *Gesta Romanorum*, which clerics and storytellers alike found a useful source book for themes.[18] It was at the close of the century that Nicolas Bozon finally made his famous prose compilation in the vernacular, the *Contes moralisés*.

Helped by the impetus of prose chronicles like those of Villehardouin and Joinville, the preference for prose as a vehicle for storytelling became more commonplace by the beginning of the thirteenth century. Aside from the countless prose adaptations of the already well-known Arthurian and Greco-Byzantine tales, there appeared a number of shorter prose pieces which deserve special mention. Though the story of *L'Empereur Constant* is yet another reworking of an earlier verse romance,[19] *Le Conte du Roi Flore et la belle Jeanne* seems to be entirely original and noteworthy both for its realistic details of custom and manners and for its intelligent manipulation of dialogue.[20] Notwithstanding a rambling plotline, *La Fille du Conte de Ponthieu* suggests the narrative possibilities of this still young art form.[21] Finally, we must mention briefly two fourteenth-century works, the biblically inspired tale of *Asseneth* and the *Histoire de Foulques Fitz Warin*, which the English critic George Saintsbury considers to mark the beginnings of French historical fiction.[22]

As we approach the fifteenth century,[23] therefore, we must return to the question we set out to answer: where, in fact, must one look for the origins of the French novella? Incontestably, the researcher who goes back to medieval French literature, will discover there impressive numbers of narrative antecedents. Though still too much a part of an unreal world, the courtly romances did make their contribution to the development of fiction. The *Petit Jehan de Saintré* grows, in good measure, out of this tradition.[24] In like manner, the didactic story undoubtedly left its mark on the embryonic novella, notably on the *Quinze Joies de mariage*.[25] The single over-all influence of any consequence, however, is that of the *gaulois* or bourgeois literature of the Middle Ages. Indubitably, a growing middle class was instrumental in helping to make the transition from verse to prose and in introducing realistic details into the artist's world of fiction.[26]

Still, we must be careful not to confuse literary antecedents with catalytic influences. Though it was not until 1545 that Le Maçon prepared his translation of the *Decameron* for Marguerite de Navarre, Boccaccio's stories were certainly already known in France as early as 1415.[27] What is more, by his own avowal, the "acteur" of the *Cent Nouvelles nouvelles* models his work on that of the great Italian storyteller. Therefore, simply because the idea of the frame is inherent in the oriental tale (already popular in medieval France) long before Boccaccio thought of it, there is no reason to assume a causal link between these stories and their French counterparts of the fifteenth century.[28] Because French medieval writers displayed considerable narrative skill in both the chivalric romance and the realistic fabliaux is no reason to assume these works had any *direct* influence on the novella. In any discussion of "influences," time and proximity are always relevant factors, and to locate literary similarities in the remote past (even fifty years can be a long time in these matters) proves very little. The simple fact is that the Italian works were already being circulated in France during the fifteenth century when the concept of short narrative prose was at an important stage in its development.[29]

In brief, therefore, the answer to our question would seem to be this: it is not so much that the Italians "invented" the novella, but rather that the appearance of Boccaccio's work in France came at a crucial moment in the history of French fiction, when it was able to exercise substantial influence on the novella. Whereas the French writers might have continued to compose works whose narrative elements were subordinated to didactic and courtly considerations,[30] Boccaccio's *Decameron* gave them a model which achieved a high level of artistic expression and which had no other ostensible purpose than to tell a good story.[31]

The problem of thematic borrowing, with its countless imponderables, requires even greater circumspection. First, one must examine all possible written sources, a task which, in itself, assumes a considerable amount of reading. Next, one must be scrupulously careful about the chronology of publications, so as to judge accurately whether texts were actually available and, if so, in a language accessible to the "borrower." [32] And even then, one can only make hypotheses with varying degrees of certainty, for a resemblance is no assurance of borrowing one way or the other, inasmuch as the authors may have simply used a common source, written or oral.

Here too, Toldo's conclusions seem simplistic in their zealous attempt to establish Italian influence. The problem calls for more scientific and prudent methods of study. Sozzi, in his recent work on Bonaventure Des Périers, exemplifies the kind of caution required in this field, when he divides the "evidence" of Italian sources into three distinct categories: 1) interesting analogies, 2) certain or probable sources, and 3) improbable sources.[33]

In order therefore to avoid hasty generalizations, we shall only review here themes as they appear in the stories chosen for this collection. Such a step-by-step procedure ought to underscore how frequently enigmatic are the thematic sources for the French novella.

The first two selections in our anthology, taken from the *Quinze Joies de mariage,* are a good case in point. One can speak of the possible theatrical influence on the author's use of dialogue. It is also easy enough to talk in very general terms about the anti-feminist traditions in medieval literature, especially as manifested in the popular fabliaux; but when one is obliged to be more specific, the evidence of real influence is problematic at best. To begin with, by the early fifteenth century, when our anonymous author was composing his satire on marriage, the fabliau as a genre had already disappeared. Thus, whatever influence there might have been was probably oral in nature. On the other hand, closer examination offers some more reliable and tangible evidence of borrowing. The title itself, for example, is quite clearly a parody on the prayer to the Virgin, the *Quinze Joies de Notre Dame.*[34] In fact, the syntax of each opening sentence also suggests a borrowing from this religious source. As for the antifeminist elements, Rychner lists the *Roman de la rose* of Jean de Meung, from which comes, no doubt, the image of the net, the *Lamentations* of Matheolus, and the *Miroir de mariage* of Eustache Deschamps.[35] Having said all this, however, one must still recognize the fact that the author's personal style, his special handling of comic dialogue, and his choice of telling details make him the creator of a work which is essentially his own.

Much the same kind of conclusion can be reached regarding Antoine de La Sale's *Petit Jehan de Saintré.* In her study on the development of fiction, Andrée Bruel would like to have us believe that Antoine de La Sale borrowed heavily from the Italian conteurs.[36] On closer inspection, however, one discovers that this is more an assertion than a proof. Indeed, the *Petit Jehan de Saintré* seems to owe far more to the courtly traditions of French literature. Belles Cousines and her idealized pupil-hero could easily appear in any number of courtly love stories. As for the lascivious monk, Lord Abbot, his prototype abounds in the fabliaux of the thirteenth century. But here, as in other instances, the influences seem to reflect in a general way a common body of literary clichés rather than concrete and precise borrowings to which one can point with confidence. What is more, Antoine de La Sale stands out among these precursors of modern fiction as one of the more acute observers of human psychology. His persuasively realistic portraits have even led some to try to prove he was composing a *roman à clef*. Scholars have found that a real Jehan de Saintré existed, and Belles Cousines has been likened to a number of historical figures, not least among them Marie de Clèves, third wife of the poet, Charles d'Orléans. But the student of literature and not of history will rightfully contend that this kind of "borrowing" is at the heart of the creative process. Antoine de La Sale is no different from any artist in any period who gathers his material from many sources, including his own personal insights into the people around him, and creates from these a coherent and original work of art.

As for the anonymous compiler of the *Cent Nouvelles nouvelles,* he would seem to be simplifying our task when in his prologue he himself confesses to modeling his work after the *Decameron.* But it is quite certain that he is speaking of the form that collection of stories takes rather than its contents.

The possibilities of discovering parallel texts in a group of one hundred different tales are all too enticing, and once again a great deal of caution must be exercised. At least until a more thorough and up-to-date study on the sources of the *Cent Nouvelles nouvelles* has been made, it is safer to speak only in terms of noteworthy similarities.

An excellent case in point is the popular theme of the "Self-Made Cuckold" (9), variations on which are to be found among the fabliaux,[37] and in numerous Italian collections.[38] Suffice it to say, however, that any causal relations would be extremely difficult to prove, and the more prudent supposition is to believe the author simply heard the story somewhere, a fact which is borne out by the popularity of the theme.

Parenthetically, we might note that in some cases the number of analogues is so great that the same story occurs in practically every collection. For example, the tale of the one-eyed husband, *Cent Nouvelles nouvelles* (16), appeared not only in the *Decameron* (VI, 6), and the *Heptaméron* (6), but also in Latin collections such as the *Disciplina clericalis* (fab vii) and in Thomas Wright's collection of thirteenth- and fourteenth-century Latin stories.[39] This story, whose theme is one of the most interesting to trace, was not included here, because it is so often reproduced elsewhere.

The subject matter of "The Miracle of the Snow Child" (19) also enjoyed widespread popularity during the Middle Ages. Attested to in the folk literature of Scandinavian countries and in the collections of fifteenth-century Italian writers as well, its earliest French form would appear to be the fabliau, "L'Enfant qui fu remis au soleil." Since this genre had fallen into disuse, however, an oral retelling seems the most probable inspiration for our tale.

"The Voice From on High" (34) would appear to have at least one antecedent in the fabliaux literature.[40] Once again, however, there are no grounds for asserting a definite conscious borrowing and an oral source seems as plausible an explanation as any.[41]

No source is listed for story 61, but Champion compares "Great Expectations" (80) to one of the *Facéties* of Poggio (43).[42] The attribution is reasonable, since it is generally believed that Poggio's influence on the thematic material of the *Cent Nouvelles nouvelles* is quite extensive.[43]

As for the last two stories, no source is listed anywhere for "The Holy Pilgrimage" (93), but "The Lover's Tragedy" (98) is unquestionably a reworking of Rasse de Brunhamel's French version of an original Latin story by Nicolas de Clamanges. It might be mentioned in passing that the publication of this story in the 1518 edition of the *Petit Jehan de Saintré* and the fact that Rasse de Brunhamel had dedicated it to Antoine de La Sale has caused some critics to argue for La Sale's authorship of the *Cent Nouvelles nouvelles*.[44]

In the few places where one can speak of written sources, the author of the *Cent Nouvelles nouvelles* has often produced a work which is a decided improvement over other versions.[45] In addition, this review of possible borrowings would seem to lend further support to the theory of oral sources and their important role in the development of the novella. It is certain that a good many of these tales, though artfully told, possess a distinct flavor of the spoken language. Perhaps the author's claim that his material is of "fresche memoir" ought to be considered in that light.

In the case of the second *Cent Nouvelles nouvelles* (1505–15) it is nearly certain that its author, Philippe de Vigneulles, knew at first hand the works of the Italian storytellers. In his autobiography, Philippe informs us that he lived four years in Italy and returned with a sack full of Italian books.[46] What is more, his references to the *Decameron* indicate that he knew this work especially well. Story 71 has an indisputable parallel in a tale by Boccaccio,[47] but the tone has been appreciably altered through the author's use of local color. Carlungo has become a town near Metz, the unscrupulous priest a conniving merchant, and the coat left as collateral a comb-like instrument used in the preparation of wool. If Philippe de Vigneulles did know the Boccaccio story, he had no scruples about changing it to suit his own bourgeois tastes and those, no doubt, of his audience.

However much he may have borrowed from the Italians, Philippe de Vigneulles, like so many other French writers of the novella, was steeped in the narrative traditions of his own country. He was familiar with the first *Cent Nouvelles nouvelles* but, more significantly, had heard itinerant entertainers as well as local citizens retell the well-known tales based on the fabliaux and the didactic traditions. Story 24, for example, has equivalents in both.[48] Philippe insists, however, that he heard the story told. Perhaps these recurrent allusions to oral sources are more than a mere literary device used to establish veracity. It is quite evident, at least, that either he or his immediate predecessor imposed upon the familiar plots, the dialectical turns of phrase and the social characteristics of the people of Metz.

According to the most recent study on Nicolas de Troyes,

only 11 of the 180 known stories have no traceable antecedents or parallels.[49] Miss Kaspryzk's research has uncovered at least 9 written sources for the *Grand Parangon*, notably the *Decameron* and the fifteenth-century *Cent Nouvelles nouvelles*. With the caution which has more and more characterized researchers in this field, she concludes, however, that to speak of direct literary influences is extremely hazardous.[50] It is far more suitable to think in terms of a common oral base or "matériel roulant." Of 59 distinguishable themes, 48 seem to be of oral origin, she decides; 34 percent of the stories in the *Grand Parangon* are attributable to popular or folk sources, not all, by any means, Italian.

Though the "Spell of the Ring" (27) has an antecedent in a thirteenth-century fabliau, "De l'Anel," it probably came down to the author through oral transmission. Retaining much of the vulgarity of the earlier telling, the sixteenth-century version is longer and more fully developed. In like manner, the "Good Judge of Troyes" finds a parallel in Petrus Alfonsi's collection of *exempla*, the *Disciplina clericalis*, but is different enough to suggest that the author had heard another version or changed his source, either written or oral.

In his study on Noël du Fail, Emmanuel Philipot accepts the theory that emphasis on authenticity is a literary pose, that in fact the author of the *Propos rustiques*, the *Baliverneries*, and the *Contes d'Eutrapel* owes much to his predecessors and contemporaries.[51] The first reflects the *Evangile des quenouilles*, and all the works show the influences of the *Quinze Joies de mariage* and the early books of Rabelais. It cannot be denied that Noël du Fail's style possesses the same verve, richness, and penchant for obscurantisms which are so prevalent in *Pantagruel* and *Gargantua*. In addition, Noël du Fail knew the writings of at least one Italian, Poggio. Nevertheless, his realistic depiction of the French peasantry and the piquant flavor of the dialogues are his own. Philipot himself points out the author's unusual gift for recreating a specific social milieu.[52] The character delineations, clear and consistent, are also native to his own genius. Suffice it to say that stylistic influences are the most difficult to prove.

It becomes increasingly apparent how complex it is to define literary sources and how little the earliest scholars of the novella valued the role of oral origins. Even so well-read and humanistic a writer as Bonaventure Des Périers defies the critics' attempts to establish ties between the tales of his *Nouvelles Récréations et joyeux devis* and other novellas. In addition, his nationalistic emphasis on local inspiration and his disavowal of the authenticity of his stories argue against conscious borrowing. It is not improbable that the learned author of the *Cymbalum mundi* was taking a holiday from his more serious work. In any event, Bonaventure Des Périers' attitude toward the stories he was telling gives credence to the assumption that taletelling was a very popular form of entertainment and that its participants certainly worried little about their literary sources. But Des Périers could not escape from his own education and humanistic tastes. No one, after all, creates in an intellectual vacuum. So however we define sources, or however conscious the borrowing, we must continue to look for influences on the writer's imagination.

In reviewing the themes of the *Nouvelles Récréations*, Sozzi establishes some forty probable literary influences, including the works of both French and German writers. As for the Italians, he concedes to Poggio the first place, for furnishing Des Périers with eight themes. What is more, not all the sources are narrative ones. The author of the *Nouvelles Récréations* leaves numerous telltale indications that he was familiar with humanistic traditions. Erasmus, Bebel, Castiglione, and Abstemius, among other distinguished men of the Renaissance, all contributed to his literary heritage.

Nevertheless, Sozzi, like Hassell before him,[53] judges that the main influences on Des Périers were oral. In fact, of the seven stories included in this anthology only one, according to Sozzi, reflects a "probable" source. "The Cantor's Stew" (3) has some resemblance to a tale by Bandello (III, 26), but nothing can be asserted with assurance.[54] The character of the "Vicar of Brou" (34) has as his prototype some celebrated quasi-legendary personality rather than any literary source.[55] Other literatures suggest examples of these wise-fool types, mischievous but likeable. One can point to at least one other parallel in French literature, the legendary Pierre Faifeu, hero of the sixteenth-century comic poem by Charles de Bourdigné.[56]

The first two anecdotes of "In the Confessional" (40) appear to be original although there are a number of parallels for the third story.[57] In any event, insincerity in the confessional is a fairly common theme and Bonaventure Des Périers seems to suggest, what is more, an oral source for his story when he says it is "as old as the hills." To the possible Italian sources which Toldo has already cited for "Sister Thoinette," Sozzi adds the names of Francesco da Barberino and Sercambi,[58] as well as an anonymous fifteenth-century tale.[59] But he concludes nothing certain. As for numbers 36 and 78, "Holy Excommunication" and "The Italian Kiss," he finds no source whatsoever.

Only in the case of "The Ear Specialist" (9) does he hazard more concrete conclusions, pointing to Poggio as a *probable* origin for the theme.[60] But even here he admits that the story line is very widespread, with parallels in many different places.[61] In brief, therefore, Bonaventure Des Périers demonstrates once more how difficult it is to speak in terms of written sources and conscious imitation, and how much an author necessarily brings to his stories from his own personal experiences and outlook on life.

Perhaps more than any other writer in this anthology, Marguerite de Navarre emphasized the historical authenticity of her tales. She did so, however, to give support to the philosophical analyses which followed them. It is generally conceded, for example, that her ten *devisants*, or storytellers, were all inspired by real persons. The question is whether or not the same can be said of the characters in the stories themselves.

Jourda's extensive examination of the *Heptaméron* reveals many similarities between its thematic content and that of earlier French and Italian collections.[62] When one considers the intellectual climate of the court which surrounded this cultured woman, and her own patronage of authors like Rabelais, Marot, and Des Périers, it seems altogether natural that she should have been close to both the literary and oral traditions of her times. It is no wonder, therefore, that Jourda's inquiry uncovers parallel texts in the works of Poggio, Morlini, Masuccio, Fortini, Arienti, Sercambi, Brevio, and Bandello,[63] to say nothing of Boccaccio, whose *Decameron* Marguerite ordered translated, and whose frame unquestionably inspired the setting of her own collection of tales. To this list of Italians must be added the name of Castiglione, whose *Il Cortigiano*, translated in 1537, inspired in some measure the language and style of the dialogues. Yet Jourda wisely cautions against hasty assumptions, for he too recognizes the difficulty of establishing direct borrowing on the basis of apparent similarities.[64]

The five stories included here are quite indicative of Marguerite's techniques and preferences. The tale of "The Priest and the Plowman" (26) and that of the "Tonsured Husband" (56) both represent her concessions to popular Gallic tastes.[65] Although the economy of words and comic exchanges show that she can tell this kind of story exceedingly well, her natural penchant is for the subtler intrigues, to which she can add realistic psychological dimensions, based on personal observations, and from which her storytellers can draw material for their protracted analyses. "The Wise and Foolish Ladies" (26) is just such a story, for even if one were to question whether the principal characters are indeed the real persons attested to by Brantôme,[66] the reader feels them to be of flesh and blood, their sufferings and vacillations very true to life.

In the same manner, "The Love Match" (40) goes far beyond the known plot line, since Marguerite does not content herself with a simple retelling of the story as she may have heard it, but introduces events from the lives of real people of whom she knew.[67] But the best example of this creative process is "A Bedtime Story" (4), in which Marguerite herself becomes the heroine.[68]

No doubt it is this technique of subtly blending truth and fiction which makes the *Heptaméron* appear more modern than the other works of the novella tradition. Marguerite was not, however, the only artist to do this; she was simply more adept at it, which is, in good part, the reason this anthology concludes with her work.

In her analysis of the origins and development of the French novella, Janet Ferrier leads one to believe that the French need only look to their own literary past to find the origins of the novella.[69] On the other hand, Kasprzyk, though dubious about the importance generally attributed to Italian writers as a source of thematic material, is clear-cut about their preeminence in the creation of the frame and the story which purports only to entertain.[70] How do we reconcile these seemingly contradictory conclusions of two such eminent specialists in the field?

In the first instance, storytelling, we have seen, is a universal experience and oral traditions preceded everywhere the idea of the written tale. In addition to the professional recitations of traveling jongleurs,[71] there existed the practice of storytelling which occupied the leisure time of all people. The *veillée*, a tradition hoary with age, brought friends and neighbors together on any occasion which justified merrymaking. During these festive hours, amidst eating and drinking, the exchange of a few good stories was considered a vital part of the entertainment. The young admired the old for their rich store of tales, many of them based on the well-worn themes familiar to all, but duly embroidered with elements from that other convenient store of creative materials, personal experience.

It is thus difficult to speak accurately about thematic borrowings, and the idea of the "matériel roulant," a common literary grab bag out of which writers could draw their plots and characters, seems more and more the best explanation for so many similarities. From this point of view, Ferrier's statement would seem justified. But if our discussion narrowed itself to the novella as a written art form, then we should be forced to modify our position. Ferrier is quite right in pointing out the important antecedents of French medieval literature, but, as our previous analysis has tried to make clear, it is not until the anonymous writer of the *Cent Nouvelles nouvelles* penned his tales in conscious imitation of his predecessor Boccaccio, that the collection of short fiction, unfettered by didactic overtones, came into existence in France. In conclusion, therefore, neither of these explanations is contradictory, but in the broadest sense, each tells a different truth about an extremely complex question.[72]

Formal Aspects of the Novella

The thirteenth-century writers who began adapting popular verse romances into prose were making a significant comment on the French cultural life of the time. Preoccupied with the things of this world, the emerging bourgeoisie demanded a new kind of art form, one which was based on the events of everyday life rather than on the idealized world of aristocratic literature. They therefore began to reject poetry, which places an undue emphasis on form and creates an unnecessary obstacle between the idea and its literary expression. It was, in brief, this conception of art and life which gave rise to the development of realistic literature in France. Stylistically, this meant that several generations of prose fiction had to evolve before the artist could place expression on a par with content.[73]

Prose of the preclassical era suffered from at least two general stylistic handicaps. So long as there was no sense of a unified language, a phenomenon which came about with the rise of the literary salons in the seventeenth century and their corollary literary-linguistic manifestations, authors allowed their style to be governed by the colloquialisms of local dialects. It is true that in the novella, regional dialects were sometimes used for consciously comic effects; but the fact is that no clear-cut distinctions between good and bad usage and no general rules relating to syntax had as yet come into being. The French vernacular was still considered to be an illegimate heir to the Latin language, and it was Latin, not French, grammar which was taught to schoolboys. In addition, prose still ranked far below poetry as a vehicle of expression. When the artist became self-conscious about what he wanted to say, he naturally thought in terms of verse. Prose was used for the communication of facts and events; poetry for the stylization of those events. Therefore, prose writers did not often labor to polish their works as did their poetic colleagues; and this was especially true in the case of the novella which was never considered a serious form of literary endeavor. It was practiced by men of no great literary pretensions, such as Philippe de Vigneulles and Nicolas de Troyes, and as a frivolous pastime by a serious humanist like Des Périers or a man of law like Noël du Fail. In many cases the author thought so little of his own work that he never made any serious attempt to get it published, even after the advent of the printing press, but contented himself as had his forefathers with a handwritten manuscript, which was passed from hand to hand.

For those writers whose education brought them into contact with the Latin of officialdom, there is a measurable influence of the so-called "curial" style, in which legal and ecclesiastical business of the time was conducted.[74] This style is characterized first of all by Latinic turns of phrase such as "ledit" or "ladite" (literally, the said). It also tends towards tautology.[75] Thus where one adjective might have sufficed, the author often feels called upon to add two, three, or even four, all of which repeat approximately the same idea. A man is, for example, "happy, content, and joyous," or he "says and remarks."

In evaluating the style of these early prose works, however, one must consider above all else the effects of the oral tradition.[76] Poetry was of course intended for recitation or perhaps even for music; and after the gradual changeover to prose declamation, the idea of a present audience was very much a part of the storytelling experience. Signs of this relationship between narrator and listener are prevalent everywhere in these works. As relatively refined a stylist as Bonaventure Des Périers had no real sense of formal beginning or end in his stories, partly because of this oral influence. One story frequently followed fast upon another, even to the structural and psychological detriment of the first. Transitions were made with no more than a "Mais pourquoi ne vous conterai-je bien encore un?" (Why not tell you still another?) In general, transitions lack the subtlety of a reader-oriented style. One encouters clumsy linking expressions like "comme avez ouy" (as you have heard) or "ainsi que dit est" (as it has been said). Monotonous repetitions are another characteristic suggestive of recited literature. In the *Quinze Joies de mariage* they serve a didactic purpose as well, but elsewhere in this literature, they are simply holdovers of a form which needed periodically to stir the listening audience into attentiveness: "Oez comment" (Hear . . .), "veez cy" (Look at this). This prose abounds in expressions like "bref" (in brief), or "que vous dirai-je plus" (what more can I tell you), which underscore the listener's impatience with ornamentation and stylistic niceties, and the teller's willingness to comply. Yet another mark of the oral style is the run-on sentence, which hardly takes into account any formal consideration for the end or beginning of logical ideas. What is more, such exaggerated adverbial forms as "trèsfort" and "moult" appear in staccato effect throughout the stories to mark a hasty emphasis. Ungainly paraphrases like "comme l'autre dit" (as the other said) betray an unwillingness to dawdle over clear-cut references. The listener's impatience to hear what happens next leads the author to attribute stereotyped reactions to his characters, constantly repeating such words as "ébahi" (dumbfounded), "étonné" (astounded) instead of searching for less trite qualifiers. Finally, with phrases like "notre bon bourgeois" (our good townsman) the writer establishes a close rapport with his listeners, as if storyteller and audience formed an integral collaborative unit, as in fact they did.

Perhaps the greatest refinement of style present in these stories is the use of verbal irony and understatement. The droll euphemism has always had its place in Gallic humor and writers like Des Périers were past masters at inventing a vocabulary pertaining to the sex act and the sexual organs which was both bland and hilariously gross. Another example of the same technique may be found in the "confession" scene between Lord Abbot and Madame, in which the words of the text give an ostensibly innocent version of the events, while at the same time the author makes it quite clear to the reader what is actually going on.

It should be added here that the nature of this irony varies with the author's intentions. In comparing the *Quinze Joies de mariage,* for example, with the fifteenth-century *Cent Nouvelles nouvelles,* we see that the former has the more "serious" objectives. In this work, therefore, irony becomes a tool of the author's didactic antifeminism; and as a direct result, the style becomes somewhat flat-footed and banal.[77] On the other hand, the *Cent Nouvelles nouvelles* were written from purely literary motives. Its antifeminism is no more than a cliché, one of several medieval devices sure to make people laugh. As a result its irony is light-hearted and detached, rather than heavy-handed and subjective.[78]

It is plain that the writers of these early novellas were not great stylists. They were more concerned with what they were saying than with how they were saying it. This very lack of self-consciousness, however, lends a certain naive freshness and charm to their works. What is more, they knew how to spin out a tale which would capture the interest of their readers, and in the last analysis, it is the ability to narrate effectively which distinguishes all great masters of prose fiction.

One result of the close identification between the story itself and the *act* of storytelling was the use of a frame in order to create the traditional oral situation, in which stories were told by a narrator to a group of listeners. In the fifteenth-century *Cent Nouvelles nouvelles* and the *Grand Parangon*, however, this frame is not developed. Only the names of the storytellers are given, but this information has little bearing on the stories themselves. By including the names of the "original" narrators, the authors in effect relegate themselves to the role of recording scribes, whose task it was to transmit the tales of others for the benefit of those not present at the first telling. That their readers shared this view of their art is evidenced by Philippe de Vigneulles' introduction to his collection of tales. In it he states that the stories in the first *Cent Nouvelles nouvelles* were actually told by a group of gentlemen in garrison, during a truce, and were later written down by a "vaillant acteur" (bold author).[79] The earlier stories must thus have been retold and discussed as late as 1515, and the circumstances of their first telling continued to occupy a prominent place in the minds of those who read or heard them.

In the *Heptaméron*, this primitive idea of a framework was developed and amplified into a full-fledged literary device, which gave coherence and depth to a collection of miscellaneous tales. Consciously imitating Boccaccio's use of the frame, Marguerite de Navarre characterized her ten narrators or *devisants* in some detail; but whereas Boccaccio's setting enhanced his work esthetically and artistically, the French collection used the frame to emphasize the moral and didactic aspects of the tales. Each of the narrators displays a distinct moral bias in his reactions to the stories and tends to tell stories which illustrate or support his own point of view. Furthermore, in many instances, the stories serve as points of departure for lengthy conversations which are in reality small essays.[80]

This tendency to enlarge the frame into a forum for the

protracted discussion of ideas came to dominate the prose narratives of the later sixteenth century. Already in the early works of Noël du Fail, frame and narrative have become so entangled that it is often impossible to distinguish one from the other. The three protagonists of the *Baliverneries*, Polygame, Eutrapel, and Lupolde, are more dialoguists than narrators. They discuss their own exploits, both past and present, or comment on the experiences of others. Sometimes their divagations can be termed tales, as in the example translated here, but more often they are merely anecdotes, examples, or recollections. In the later *Contes et discours d'Eutrapel*, the tendency becomes even more marked. The old tales are often reduced to a few lines and grouped together in a series. The art of storytelling has been replaced by that of conversation. The gradual decline of the narrative form at the end of the sixteenth century thus parallels in a sense the new interest in a more discursive form of prose, best exemplified in the essays of Montaigne, and prefigures the rise of the literary salon in the seventeenth century.[81]

Not all of these authors felt the need of placing their stories in a frame. A bookish pedagogue like Antoine de La Sale had no difficulty in conceiving of himself as an "acteur," who addressed himself directly to his reader. Even when the idea of a frame was not consciously expressed, however, the habits of thought engrained by the oral tradition persisted, and the author betrayed by his style that he still thought of himself as addressing an imaginary listener, whose attention he must continually solicit.

Another characteristic of oral literature is its tendency to oversimplification and repetitiousness, for the inattentive listener cannot return to portions of a story which he may have missed or misunderstood. For this reason, the same stock situations and easily recognizable characters tend to recur: the corrupt or lecherous priest, the unchaste wife, the lover, the cuckold, and the wise fool. Since such characters are stereotypes, the interest of the stories lies not in them, but in the situations they get themselves into and the conflicts which arise among them.

It is in the *Cent Nouvelles nouvelles* that this type of story occurs in its purest form. "Prisoner of Love" serves as a good example. In it we find the classic triangle: unfaithful wife, lover, and suspicious husband. The story does not revolve around the emotions resulting from this situation, however. Rather it centers on an amusing incident in which the husband tries to prove his wife's guilt, but is foiled in the attempt, thanks to her resourcefulness. The substitution of the donkey, (of all animals the surest one to evoke a humorous response), for the lover, who has been locked into the chest, prepares for the climax of the story when the husband is humiliated before his wife's relatives, whom he has convoked to witness her downfall. This scene is the true *raison d'être* of the story, and the author exerts all his skill to lead up to it and to present it as dramatically as possible. He has no other interest in these characters or their lives, beyond the fact that they were the actors who participated in this amusing confrontation.

In order to extract the greatest amount of entertainment from his denouement, the author has developed a set pattern which subordinates all other literary considerations in order to focus exclusively on the dramatic incident which forms the heart of his tale. The opening paragraph of such a story presents the leading characters and their situation in life as succinctly and compactly as possible. It will provide only such facts as will enable the reader to recognize the milieu of the story and to identify the stereotypes. So eager in fact is the author to get on to his story that he is often wont to cram all his information into one or two hopelessly complex sentences. After this, the author proceeds immediately into the circumstances leading up to the main event in the story. In the best of these stories, then, the exposition is kept to a bare minimum while the main scenes are presented in dramatic form. Thus the action of "Prisoner of Love" does not really begin until the wife discovers her lover locked up in the chest. At this point the author switches from narrative to dialogue in order to savor fully the distress and apprehension of the two guilty parties, seemingly caught in a hopeless trap. By prolonging this scene, the author arouses and maintains the reader's suspense, which eventually changes to anticipation as he awaits the husband's discovery of the trick which has been played on him. This he maintains once again by lengthening out his narrative with dialogue. The husband denounces his wife publicly, and she falls to her knees protesting her innocence and making references to the contents of the chest, thus heightening the humorous effect of the scene for the reader, who is already in on the joke. Naturally, once the donkey has emerged from the chest, all dramatic excitement is at an end, and the tale closes swiftly with a sentence or two outlining the repercussions of this happening.[82]

The only purpose of such a story is to lead up to an amusing situation as skilfully and humorously as possible.[83] To do so, it makes use of all the resources of low comedy: disguises, mistaken identity, concealed hiding places, practical jokes, and the rest. Stories of this kind can succeed only if the storyteller is master of his art. All depends on his ability to choose the moment of highest interest and to arrange all his materials in such a way that the climax will appear at peak intensity. Should he fumble or digress, all the inconsistencies, inadequacies, and superficialities of his art will become immediately apparent.

Such a concept of fiction may imply a world view which is somewhat superficial. In addition, such a pattern, repeated endlessly with only slight variations, eventually becomes monotonous and bereft of the element of surprise which is its only real virtue. Nevertheless, for all its shortcomings, this type of story is to be found in all the collections presented here. "The Spell of the Ring," "The Cantor's Stew," "The Ear Specialist," and the "Priest and the Plowman" all use the same narrative techniques: the brief, concise exposition; the humorous denouement, dependent upon a surprise twist, a piquant situation, or a "bon tour" (trick); and the swift conclusion. They are purely narrative in intent and desire only to amuse, not to analyze or instruct.

The more subtle writers, however, were able to vary, enlarge, or enrich this basic form with other elements which added to its subtlety and interest. Our excerpt from *Les Quinze Joies de mariage* begins with a situation identical to that found in "Prisoner of Love": a deceived husband who catches his wife red-handed. The story does not turn the tables on the hapless cuckold by means of a mechanical device, such as the donkey in the chest, however. The guilty parties are extricated from their predicament by a brand of psychological warfare which literally brainwashes the victimized husband into believing that *he* is the guilty one. What is more, the reader's attention is diverted from his anticipation of the final outcome, the only element capable of maintaining his interest in the former tale, to absorption in the process involved. It is not the husband's defeat which is funny, but the outrageously wicked machinations of his wife's female allies. Once again, the author places these in relief by the adroit use of dialogue: the women are condemned out of their own mouths, by their illogicality, hypocrisy, and shameless cunning, but here, the dialogue becomes an end in itself rather than a means of arousing and prolonging suspense. As a result, the denouement is relegated to a position of lesser importance, as the reader becomes more interested in the process than in the end result.

Since the *Petit Jehan de Saintré* uses a longer narrative form than either of the other two fifteenth-century works, it is able to explore more fully the causes and results of the triangular relationship, which serves as the point of departure in both the "Fifteenth Joy" and the stories from the *Cent Nouvelles nouvelles*. Rather than simply presenting the relationship between the Abbot and Madame as a *fait-accompli*, some attempt is made to show the genesis of the affair and to trace its successive stages. The effects upon Madame's character, the evolution of Jehan's reactions, from hurt bewilderment to determined vengefulness, are also sketched in. The final confrontation between the three protagonists blends the surprise element of the traditional trick (the device of the armor) with a study of their psychological reactions: Madame's disarray, Lord Abbot's cowardice, and Jehan's icy dignity. Once again the mechanical device does not provide the main interest of the story. Here it is used as a catalyst which forces the characters to reveal their true natures. The skeleton of the simpler narrative form remains clearly visible, but it has been fleshed out and clothed by the emotional and psychological ramifications inherent in the conflict between the three main characters; and the emphasis has been shifted from the events themselves to the reactions to these events.

Stories based on the same pattern and using the same situations and characters continued to be told and retold well into the sixteenth century, but less rigid forms were also used, especially by Bonaventure Des Périers. He was capable of beginning a story *in medias res*, with no exposition whatsoever, or of stringing together a series of anecdotes without taking any great care to build up to the denouements of each separate incident.[84] In many of his stories, the outcome or final confrontation is relegated to a position of secondary importance. What interests him is human eccentricity in action. He loves to show how this or that "character" acts or talks. He will tell a rather pointless story about an old woman and a bishop simply in order to poke fun at provincial pronunciation, grammatical errors, and dialectical oddities. For obvious reasons, we have not been able to provide satisfactory translations of this type of story, but it does occur frequently in the *Joyeux Devis*. A similar interest in verbal eccentricities and the resulting confusion is the main theme of Philippe de Vigneulles' story "Modicum et Bonum."

As we have already seen, Noël du Fail displays an even greater tendency to renounce the formal novella in order to pursue the meanderings of conversation. He has a strong predilection for description, and as a result, his narratives tend to break down into a series of static tableaux. For instance, in the selection we have presented here, the bulk of the story enumerates the household articles which the panicky villagers attempt to take with them in their flight. The expected confrontation with the brigands never takes place, nor are we informed of the final outcome. Instead the story veers off into a dialogue reminiscent of those in the *Quinze Joies* and ends with a humorous jibe at the mores of the fairer sex.

Both Des Périers and du Fail develop certain aspects of the story which were neglected by the *Cent Nouvelles nouvelles*, but in general they do so at the expense of the formal narrative pattern which was its greatest achievement. The more anecdotal stories which began to appear in the sixteenth century nevertheless remained essentially superficial, making use of stock characters and situations and maintaining as their primary goal the amusement of the reader.

With the possible exception of Antoine de La Sale, Marguerite de Navarre is the only raconteur who saw the serious possibilities of narrative fiction and made a real effort to examine the psychological mainsprings of human behavior.

She developed the discussions surrounding her stories and lengthened the story itself in order to have space in which to explore more fully the backgrounds and motivations of her protagonists. In addition, she frequently introduced long monologues or soliloquies, during which the characters reviewed past events and justified their own acts and decisions. Such monologues had been frequent in medieval literature of the courtly type, and by reviving them, Marguerite took an important step towards transforming the novella into a form capable of analyzing human emotions.

In general, however, the main goal of these storytellers was to provide entertainment, and they bent all their narrative skill to this purpose; only gradually and incidentally did they realize the serious possibilities of the form they had chosen to practice.

Characterization

It may be seen from this brief summary of the formal aspects of narrative fiction during the fifteenth and sixteenth centuries that the forms were expanded or altered as a result of differing concepts of human behavior. The simpler stories, and especially those from the *Cent Nouvelles nouvelles* were based on a static and essentially pessimistic view of human nature, which tended to divide people into categories. The typical character was portrayed as cunning, proud, sensual, and incapable of understanding any of the finer or nobler instincts. He was a stock character, a stereotype, who behaved like a puppet in a preordained manner. What he thought was therefore much less important than what he did.

Furthermore, the great majority of the French stories of this period were influenced by the antifeminism which had been prevalent since the Middle Ages and which held that women were *prima facie* unfaithful.[85] Thus one of the characters most frequently portrayed was the inconstant wife. In the *Cent Nouvelles nouvelles*, she was usually presented as such without prelude or explanation, except perhaps for a brief exposition of the circumstances which made her infidelity practically possible. The author seems to assume that faithlessness is a kind of profession, like law or medicine, which carries with it a certain life style and requires no further justification. The natural corollary to the inconstant wife is the jealous husband, who reacts to his wife's infidelity in all the predictable ways and causes thereby the conflict or crisis which becomes the focal point of the story.[86]

Even when marital discord is not the subject of the stories, however, the stereotyping of characters tends to persist. In the story of the "Good Judge of Troyes," for example, there are two main characters, the good judge and the rich man, each of whom plays the role assigned to him without ever departing from it or exhibiting any other sidelights on his personality. Likewise the Vicar of Brou is immediately established as the "wise fool" and the stories about him illustrate this single trait. But although none of these characters is developed into a real person, they do become central to the story and are not just used as a means to an end. Thus an interest in the variety and eccentricity of human behavior, even when only a single trait is assigned to each character, does tend to modify the form of the story and to make it less dependent on the denouement for its final effect.

Antoine de La Sale's approach to the problem of characterization is more sophisticated than that of the *Cent Nouvelles nouvelles*. This is especially true in the case of Madame, for although she follows the general rule for feminine misbehavior, her attitudes and actions remain ambiguous and contradictory. In the opening portion of the novel, she is portrayed as the very incarnation of wisdom and virtue, and it is from her erudite lips that Jehan learns the principles of courtliness and chivalry which are to mold all his thought and conduct. Nevertheless, even in these early pages, she gives evidence, by her coy treatment of the young page, of a certain capriciousness and taste for intrigue. This becomes marked, however, only after Jehan's departure for Germany, against her will. Then in her dealings with Master Hugh she betrays for the first time the possible extent of her cunning. The moment she comes into contact with Lord Abbot, however, the baser aspects of her nature begin to assume ascendancy and eventually gain complete mastery of her. It is only then that she shows herself to be ungrateful and disloyal to her former friends, as well as cynically vulgar and hypocritical. At the end of the book, she exhibits all the characteristics traditionally attributed to women, but she arrives at this stage only by a gradual process of transformation and self-revelation. And it is due to this method of presentation that Madame's character takes on the air of paradox and mystery which surrounds the human personality in real life.

In general, it is safe to state, however, that with one exception, all the authors discussed here present their characters as stereotypes of one kind or another. That exception is Marguerite de Navarre, who bases her characterizations on a completely different philosophical interpretation of human behavior. For her, human beings are not simple, but terribly complex. They do not act or react automatically in a given situation, rather they choose, after tremendous moral struggles, an individual course of action. She too is pessimistic in regard to man's moral nature, but she places his wickedness in a theological context. The traditional *novelliste* is essentially materialistic and even deterministic in his view of man. He depicts a "dog-eat-dog" universe in which one must fool or be fooled, but he makes no reference to ultimate Justice or Final Causes. Possessed of the true intellectual's active mind, however, Marguerite interpreted man's shortcomings as proof of his basic sinfulness and his consequent need for grace. She had of course been influenced in her thinking by the evangelists and reformers to whom she often looked for advice and to whom she often offered her protection. To these thinkers, man was not merely cunning, mischievous, or dishonorable, he was depraved, and Marguerite often depicted characters who were diabolically wicked. Such a character is the Count Jossebelin. Too avaricious to offer a dowry from his sister's inheritance, he amuses himself by encouraging her inclination for a lowborn favorite. Then upon discovering that the alliance between the two has become a fact, he orders the man to be slain on the spot, without waiting to hear the facts of the case; and instead of repenting his ill-considered deed, he shuts his sister up in a tower in order to prevent her from seeking redress of her grievances. Vicious, cruel, utterly devoid of mercy or compassion, Jossebelin seems the embodiment of human wickedness. Yet he is by no means a cardboard villain. Indeed, he is both ingenious and complex in his wickedness, which is composed of not just one vice but many.

Less far advanced in sinfulness, but displaying already many of its earmarks is the Lord of Avannes, who despite his tender years will stop at nothing to gain his ends. He combines the ruthlessness of the Count, however, with great personal charm and what seems to be an intermittent but sincere desire to triumph over his own baser instincts.

The doctrine of grace to which Marguerite adhered did not condemn mankind to everlasting depravity, but offered hope for salvation, and she believed that men are capable of being either good or bad, or of combining elements of both good and bad in their own lives. This is obviously a much more advanced view of human nature than that met with in the other authors. Naturally such a view, not to mention her own feminism, made Marguerite reject the generally accepted idea that women are born deceivers. She therefore told many stories which prove that just the opposite is often true, that it is the women who are virtuous, while the men are completely lacking in any sense of decency. Indeed, she puts the record straight and proves that women are often innocent victims, while society through its double standard permits in men what it castigates in women.

As is shown by the story of the "Wise and Foolish Ladies," however, she does not go so far as to claim that all women are guiltless. Perhaps one of her greatest contributions is her attempt to give reasons for the behavior of her characters. She takes care to show the unsatisfactory relationship between the foolish lady and her husband, who cares more for his horses than he does for his wife, and to contrast them with the complete trust and understanding between the wise woman and her husband. Thus, as she shows in the discussions, although much mystery surrounds human behavior, there are reasons for the way people act.

Because of this interest in psychological analysis, her stories follow a much less rigid pattern and are less dependent on external acts for their interest. She does retain the older type of novella, but a careful analysis reveals that there is a direct relationship between the type of story and the character of the *devisant* who is taking his turn as narrator. For instance, "The Priest and the Plowman," the story which follows most closely the traditional narrative pattern, is narrated by Nomerfide, who has been presented in the conversations as the youngest and silliest member of the group. In many other cases, stories obviously growing out of the antifeminist *Querelle des Femmes* are narrated by Hircan, in real life Marguerite's husband, or other male members of the party who display a strong antifeminist bias. Almost no frivolous or scabrous tales are contributed by the more serious members of the group. Thus Marguerite correctly related the simplistic story made popular by the *Cent Nouvelles nouvelles* to a certain attitude towards sexual behavior and placed it in this context within the *Heptaméron*. At the same time she made the form more elastic in order to allow for greater latitude in the depiction and interpretation of human behavior. The *Heptaméron* contains both types of story—the simpler and more direct form, whose main intent was to amuse, and the longer and more complex type, which gave new dimensions to the conventional characterizations.

Realism

The French novella placed great emphasis on realism, that is to say on *vérité* or truthfulness. It was common practice to introduce a story with the assertion that it had really happened. Most interesting in this respect are the introductory remarks of Philippe de Vigneulles, in which he stated that it was a matter of common debate whether or not the stories of the *Cent Nouvelles nouvelles* were true. He went on to say that in his opinion there was no reason why such things could not really happen and that he had put together the present collection of "true" stories in order to prove that such happenings were still possible in modern times. Although there is no such blanket statement at the beginning of the *Cent Nouvelles nouvelles*, the stories often open with an assertion that they are based on good authority, and therefore may be accepted as true. It is the *Heptaméron* which goes farthest in this direction. Marguerite de Navarre writes in her prologue that the collection is based on the plan originated by Boccaccio in the

Decameron, that is, ten stories told by ten narrators on ten successive days, with the notable exception that all the stories shall be "véritables." Antoine de La Sale makes no such general claim, but his notice to the reader that he is withholding the real identities of Lord Abbot and Madame implies that he too is relating a true sequence of events. Only Des Périers refuses to vouch for the historical accuracy of his tales, saying that he may have mixed up the names and places, or that the reader may have heard other versions which do not agree with his, but that such details are of no importance, since his stories are only meant to amuse, not to instruct. He does not, however, deny that his tales have some basis in fact.[87]

Scholars agree that these protestations of veracity are a literary device, which in most cases should not be taken literally.[88] Most of the so-called true stories can be traced back to their sources—fabliaux, *exempla,* etc., which frequently were laid over with a thin veneer of realistic detail: a reference to a town or a province in which the events were supposed to have taken place, or a mention of the monarch in whose reign they occurred. Even the *Heptaméron,* which places such emphasis on truth, uses this same device and includes many stories which are obviously derived from literary or oral sources.

It is not clear whether or not Marguerite de Navarre was herself aware of the literary antecedents of some of her tales, since it is possible that she had gathered them from oral sources which she trusted to be authentic. It is worth noting, in this regard, that she did admit scrupulously to having taken the story of the "Dame du Vergier" (number 70) from a written source. It is also true that many of the stories in the *Heptaméron,* including two of those which we have offered here, were based on historical events; and this fact in itself is ample proof that the author took the pledge of veracity seriously, even if she did not consider it completely binding.[89]

With the notable exception of the *Heptaméron,* however, most of these stories had their basis not in fact but in fiction. Why then did their authors place so much emphasis on veracity? The answer must be that they intended to create fiction which was true to life, believable, and solidly realistic. The marvelous, the miraculous, the supernatural, the exotic, the "long ago and far away" had almost no place in their works.

On the contrary, they confined themselves to familiar settings, everyday situations, and contemporary times. They dealt with the world in which they lived and which they knew intimately.

In addition, they wrote tales which were self-consciously French. The author of the *Cent Nouvelles nouvelles* stated specifically that he was including no stories which took place in Italy, only ones from France and the other northern provinces then under the control of the Dukes of Burgundy. Des Périers likewise expressed his determination to recount events which had happened in his own country, because, in his opinion, imported tales lost half their spice before arriving at their destination. And Marguerite de Navarre wrote in her prologue that she was fulfilling a dream of many years' standing by creating a French counterpart to the *Decameron*. Thus these works grew out of a sense of national pride, a determination to found and continue a national literary heritage, and most important, an appreciation of the wealth of fictional material available in French life and French institutions.

There are many kinds and qualities of realism, and this literature certainly does not explore all of them to their logical conclusions. Nevertheless, by its unblinking portrayal of human weaknesses, by its determination to depict honestly the world of its own time and place, and by its avowed wish to remain within the limits of credibility, the prose fiction of the French Renaissance aligned itself unequivocally with the methods and aims of realism.

Nearly all the stories take place within the most familiar of all settings, the home. As a result, they contain a wealth of realistic documentation on the living arrangements, domestic routines, and customs of the times. In fact, they provide one of the more reliable sources of information on how people lived in the late Middle Ages and early Renaissance. Antoine de La Sale depicts in elaborate detail the physical comforts which made life pleasant for the rich and well-born such as Lord Abbot and La Dame des Belles Cousines: the blazing fires, fine linens, groaning boards, tapestried and curtained rooms, attentive servants, and vigorous outdoor pastimes.[90] Although he is one of the few to practice formal description, all the authors have a quick eye for the realistic touch which will render their story true to life. The author of the "Fifteenth Joy" emphasizes the greedy duplicity of the women friends by telling how they warm themselves by the fire and eat and drink the best the house has to offer, while they plot against the poor husband. In "Holy Pilgrimage" we see the various preparations the guilty housewife must make before absenting herself from home for a day. The list of ingredients in the cantor's stew is a lesson in sixteenth-century cuisine as well as an explanation for the reaction of the guests. The pictures of the young Lord of Avannes jumping and cavorting at a dance, or shivering in his nightshirt while his house goes up in flames, of the rich man accompanying him home on his donkey, of the group of servants weeping in the courtyard as their mistress lies dying, all show the skill with which Marguerite de Navarre sketched in a realistic background and gave life and substance to her stories. Colorful scenes drawn from everyday life abound in all the collections: a bishop making his ceremonial entrance into a town, while the townspeople come out to greet him and kneel down at the sign of the cross; a group of relatives venturing forth late at night armed with flambeaux, a man returning home after a long journey, gathering his family around him, and eagerly inspecting the children whom he has not seen for many months. Without exception, the stories move naturally against real-life backgrounds, which form a coherent, believable, and vivid setting for the events they relate.

In addition to placing their characters in a familiar and realistic setting, many authors of this period noted with exactitude the patterns of speech habitual to people in various walks and conditions of life. The *Quinze Joies* and the *Cent Nouvelles nouvelles* were permeated with the rhythms of everyday conversation—the expletives and exclamatory oaths, with which the common folk were wont to preface their remarks, the pungent proverbs, and most of all, the garrulous rhetoric of a people who loved to hear themselves talk. Antoine de La Sale contrasted the rather stilted style of the court with the hearty openness of a man from bourgeois beginnings, like Lord Abbot. Des Périers took pleasure in imitating the various dialects of the lower classes and drew humor from the peculiarities of the regional *patois*. Vigneulles mocked the snobbish tendency among clerics to substitute Latin for French, even at the risk of being misunderstood. In her frame, Marguerite de Navarre captured the flow of cultured conversation: the swift retorts, the tendency to pursue one's own train of thought, to go off on tangents, and to turn a serious question into a joke. Persuading, arguing, cajoling, the characters of the French novella literally talk themselves alive.

The great majority of these stories are based on an oversimplified, materialistic view of human behavior. Yet within this limited framework, they display considerable psychological acumen, especially in their analyses of the predictable reactions of men and women to certain situations, and in their portrayal of anger, jealousy, and the desire for revenge. There is also considerable knowledge of the subtle art of psychological manipulation, whereby one person maneuvers another into becoming his dupe. Such is the case, for instance, in the story, "The Ear Specialist," in which the clever Sir André deceives the gullible mother-to-be. Likewise, the story of the "Fifteenth Joy" shows the stages by which mass psychology progressively breaks down the moral commitment of the group of women.

Nevertheless, the view of human nature implicit in so many of these stories leads to situations which are ultimately unrealistic; and more often than not, caricature and exaggeration replace the true study of human behavior. Thus although the author of Les Quinze Joies leads us by progressive stages to accept the outrageous behavior of the guilty wife's friends and relatives, it is hard to believe that such a complete turnabout could ever happen in real life. In the same way, it is not credible that a group of women would seriously consider exposing themselves to the lusts of a band of brigands ("A Man's Best Friend"). Such acts are predicated not on reality but on the malicious antifeminism perpetrated by the Querelle des Femmes.

Especially in the case of the Cent Nouvelles nouvelles, the situations themselves stretch the imagination to the very limits. It does not seem likely that a husband would summon his friends to the scene of the crime, as one does in "Holy Pilgrimage," or convene a family council for so delicate a matter as that forming the subject of "Great Expectations"; nor do the reactions of either the husband or the wife in "The Snow Child" ring true. In the same way it seems unlikely that any woman would know so little about the reproductive processes as does the wife in "The Ear Specialist," or that any farmer, no matter how benighted or exhausted would accept without question his wife's explanation of the appearance and disappearance of the priest in "The Priest and the Plowman." In such stories, the reactions of the characters are obviously manipulated to fit the exigencies of the plot, and realism is accordingly sacrificed in order to create an amusing situation for the benefit of the reader. The nuances and complexities of human relationships are not studied. Instead, behavior is viewed externally and without care to inquire into its sources.

There are exceptions to this general tendency towards stereotyping and overgeneralization, especially in the *Heptaméron* and the *Petit Jehan de Saintré*, but on the whole, psychological realism is not so fully developed as the more external forms of realism noted above. Despite their lapses into incredibility, (lapses which are common to all forms of farce and which are often found even in high comedy), however, these stories do provide penetrating vignettes of human behavior, limited and miniaturist perhaps, yet striking in their detail, their movement, and above all, in their vivacity.

Themes

Romantic love has always occupied a central place in literature, whereas marriage has been relegated to a secondary place. In these stories just the opposite is true; here attention is focused not on the transports of lovers, but on the social repercussions of adulterous love within the institution of marriage.[91] What is more, the general outlook is decidedly antiromantic. Love is depicted as cynically sensual in nature, and the tender emotions which it traditionally evokes receive little attention or commendation.

The antifeminism of the times was of course in large measure responsible for this preoccupation with adulterous relationships, but behind the emphasis on feminine infidelity lay the ambivalence of medieval thought towards sexual love. On the one hand, the Christian religion had given its blessing to monogamous marriage, but at the same time, it had imposed celibacy on its clergy, thus seeming to relegate those bound by matrimonial ties to an inferior spiritual status. Society had further complicated the situation by making of marriage a political and economic tool, often marrying women at a very early age to men whom they did not even know, and who were often on the verge of senility. The result was that over the centuries, married men, many of whom had spent their youths sowing wild oats and had postponed matrimony until they could accumulate enough wealth to support a household, developed a terror of cuckoldry which amounted to an obsession. It is not difficult to understand the psychological suffering involved in discovering that one's mate has been unfaithful, but it is harder to account for the exaggerated reaction to such a misfortune, which made of it a major literary theme.[92] This preoccupation with cuckoldry seems to have stemmed in part from the fact that the transmission of family wealth was through the male succession. Since marriages were arranged not for love, but to assure the continuance of the line, the slightest suspicion of the wife's unchastity placed in jeopardy the just claims of the heirs, and by extension, that of the whole house. This is why the wandering husband found it so essential to dispose of the ill-begotten "snow-child."

As a footnote to these remarks on the prevalence of cuckoldry as a theme, we may note the widespread use of scabrous detail and gross sexual exaggeration in this fiction. It is a curious paradox that an openly ribald approach to sex may seem obscene in an age whose literature abounds in graphic descriptions of erotic adventures. The fact is that although our attitude towards sex has become increasingly serious and even clinical, we still do not share the frank, open, and often coarse enjoyment of it which was to be found in all levels of society during the French Renaissance. No prudery, delicacy, or refinement prevented these authors from laughing raucously at the grotesque and bizarre aspects of essentially biological functions. Nor was any subject considered too intimate or too sacred. At their lowest, they did not hesitate to snicker over the end products of the digestive system, and even the highborn Marguerite de Navarre saw nothing wrong in including several literally filthy tales in her collection. All was grist to the mill, and a resounding guffaw seems to have been the only justification needed. Such subject matter has long since passed out of our formal litertaure, but a bit of reflection reveals that it still persists in a vigorous oral tradition of jokes, riddles, limericks, and bawdy stories which are the direct descendants of those printed here.

When characterizing the coarser attitudes of our fathers towards sex, it is not necessary to castigate our own culture for its puritanical Victorianism, but it is essential to recognize that in a time far removed from our own, when people lived closer to nature and were often deprived of the privacy which modern man takes for granted, standards of taste were vastly different from our own. Ribald vulgarity was an integral part of medieval and Renaissance fiction, and no study can ignore the important role it played.

The novella tended to debase human nature and to show it at less than its best. It did not, however, entirely exclude the strains of another tradition which interpreted the relationship of man to his mate from an entirely different set of prejudices. Likewise confronted by the inadequacies of marriage as an institution, the aristocratic writers of the Middle Ages had worked out a kind of compromise between the demands of unhappy monogamy and the dishonor of infidelity. The proponents of this "courtly" love held that woman was an object of veneration, who should be served by her admirers with humility. As the theory seems to have evolved in the late Middle Ages, a man who "served" a lady was entitled only to converse with her in some more or less public place and to accept from her a token which he could wear in combat.[93] In practice, such relationships usually went beyond mere conversation, but they did elevate love by viewing it as a sacred compact and by imposing on it a set of rules designed to insure the dignity and honor of the lady.

As a theme, courtly love appears less frequently in these stories. As it is decidedly aristocratic in orientation, the two authors who introduce it into their works are those who were intimately involved in court life, Antoine de La Sale and Marguerite de Navarre. In the first half of the *Petit Jehan de Saintré*, Madame plays the role of the courtly lady and Jehan that of her servant. The relationship evolves according to the strictest rules and there is no indication whatsoever that it surpasses the bounds of chastity traditionally imposed. In the second part of the book, that given here, Madame betrays her love for Jehan and enters into a sensual relationship with Lord Abbot. The essential conflict of the story thus lies between the courtly idealism of her relationship with Jehan and the cynical materialism of her affair with the abbot. Her faithlessness is all the more reprehensible because she has betrayed not a husband, but a "servant" to whom she had bound herself of her own free will.[94]

The influence of the courtly tradition may also be seen in the story "The Lovers' Tragedy," which depicts a noble knight and his tragically virtuous fiancée. The story makes clear the class distinctions which separated this type of literature from less rarefied forms of popular fiction. The two lovers are confronted by a group of drunken, brutish ruffians, who are incapable of accepting or even understanding the pure and honest relationship between them. As a result, the two must die in order to preserve their honor and fidelity. The courtly literature is rooted therefore in a sentimental and tragic view of life, which is irreconcilable with the earthy cynicism of the bourgeois tradition.

During the Renaissance, a renewed interest in platonism led to yet another attempt to justify romantic attachments between the unmarried. The platonists held that by fastening his affections on a woman, whom he took to be the incarnation of divine goodness, a lover would eventually attain mystical enlightenment and a perfect love of God. The theory greatly interested Marguerite de Navarre, and it appears frequently in the *Heptaméron*, for instance in the long conversation between the Lord of Avannes and the wise lady. In general, however, Marguerite felt that love could be properly expressed only within the sacrament of marriage. She is therefore the only one of these writers who takes the institution seriously. Constancy, mutual respect, and the traditional Christian virtue of self-denial offered the only real hopes for solving the sexual dilemmas imposed by society. In her more serious novellas, therefore, she studied with sympathy and realistic insight the conflicts and problems arising out of the institution of marriage. From her objective and impartial presentation of the situation as it existed in her day, the modern reader can gain greater insight into the whole theme of sexual relationships in the literature of the fifteenth and sixteenth centuries.

The second major theme, the corruption of the clergy, is closely allied to the first. As marriages were arranged out of expediency, so were religious vows imposed for the same reason; and often young children, whose families could not or would not provide for them, were delivered over to the church when they were still practically babes in arms. Possessing great material wealth and political power, peopled by numerous members who had no true religious vocation, the convents, monasteries, and parish churches fell into decadent and even scandalous practices. Even more debauched were the so-called "cordeliers" or mendicant friars, who wandered from town to town, preying on the credulous piety of the devout.[95]

The vow of celibacy, always the most difficult to enforce, was more honored in the breach than in the observance, and the priestly duties of pastoral counselling and confession often became pretexts for the pursuit of more worldly pastimes. Depicted as gluttonous, avaricious, hypocritical, and relentlessly lecherous, no other figure in medieval literature was the object of such scorn and loathing as the cleric. So deep was this antipathy to the clergy that we find numerous stories which have as their subject the castration of a priest. A hint of this appears in the first part of "Man's Best Friend."

Among the stories we have chosen, the excerpt from the *Petit Jehan de Saintré* shows most fully the corruption and worldliness of the clergy. Having attained his position through the wealth and influence of his father, Lord Abbot gives himself unabashedly to the pursuit of pleasure. He feasts in Lent, makes love to his patroness (under cover of the sacrament of confession), and even aspires to the life of the armed warrior. Likewise the beautiful abbess of "The Spell of the Ring," is depicted as both debauched and avaricious. The painful predicament of the bishop in the second part of this tale underlines the general desire to have a good laugh at the expense of the clergy. Both the carryings-on of the vicar of Brou and those of the "Priest and the Plowmen" show that the general laxity had penetrated to the lowest social orders; but we should not overlook the implication in the former story that the lordly bishop and his retinue were not wont to practice pious asceticism, even though they wished to impose it on the parish priests.

This literature, which derided and castigated those to whom the practice of virility had been forbidden either by nature or by church law, was decidedly masculine in its orientation. If it is true, as Philippe de Vigneulles states, that the tales of the *Cent Nouvelles nouvelles* were told by soldiers in garrison, then perhaps we may assume that the novella was originally destined primarily for a male audience. Such was certainly no longer the case at the time of Marguerite de Navarre, but even her contemporary, Bonaventure Des Périers, felt moved to hint that his *Nouvelles Récréations* might not be suitable for female readers.[96]

A third theme which recurs in nearly all the collections is that of the "bon tour" or trick. This may take the form of a practical joke, of a witty retort, or of a cunning deception practiced on a less wily comrade.[97] Often such tales have as their hero a wise fool like the vicar of Brou or the cantor, whose guileless cunning strips away the pompous hypocrisy of his social betters. The wise fool is of course a common character in folk literature, persisting even today as the "little moron" who purposely misunderstands the literal meanings of words. Behind all the lighthearted playfulness arising from the confusion between the literal and figurative meanings of words, however, lies the problem of semantics and the difficulties involved in human communication. It may be added that such stories as the "Italian Kiss" and others which give a central place to word play show the extent to which the humanists' interest in language and philology had affected the popular imagination.

Such stories celebrate the ingenuity of the individual who manages to get the better of an impersonal system which seeks to exploit him or to impose on him a mindless conformity. They thus make a strong appeal to the common reader, who is himself a victim of the system, as do stories of the "deceiver-deceived" variety, such as the three anecdotes contained in the "Good Judge of Troyes." Although we may admire in his more innocent manifestations the man who triumphs by his wits, his actions may nevertheless imply a ruthless disregard for truth and for the rights of others. The stories of Renart, who outwitted his fellow animals by his superior cleverness, had manifested a certain astuteness. They assigned such roles to animals. In fact, the moral blindness implied by the "bon tour" seems more suited to the jungle than to a Christian society. Thus although the harmless stratagem of the cantor calls forth only amused sympathy, the cynical deceptions practiced by the wives in the *Cent Nouvelles nouvelles*, or by the hero of "The Spell of the Ring," or even by the cruelly wronged Jehan de Saintré raise moral problems of conscience by their flagrant disregard of the Christian ethic. In general then, the prevalence of the "bon tour" in this fiction is one more indication of its cynical view of human nature.

There is good reason to believe that the moral didacticism of the Middle Ages exercised a direct influence on the early Renaissance novella. And in fact, the habit of tacking on a moral at the end of a story was retained in some instances long after the edifying intentions of fiction had been forgotten. It is not, however, in the pious final paragraphs of these stories that we must look to discover the true moral outlook of their authors, for as in most good literature, their message is not explicit but implicit. In these stories are often set forth without editoralizing or comment the infinite varieties of human wickedness and folly. Greed, lust, vanity, dishonesty, and cruelty are all represented in the familiar shapes that they assume in everyday life. The reader has only to identify and condemn them.

What is more, despite the frivolity and cynicism so often present, this body of literature reveals an unspoken but trenchant criticism of contemporary evils: the lack of trust between man and wife, the corruption of the clergy, the decadence of the upper classes, the grasping acquisitiveness of the bourgeoisie, the prevalence of armed bands, the difficulty of obtaining justice in the courts, the dangers of travel, the religious hypocrisy, the impotence of the little man, the tyrannical abuse of male power all are spread before the reader, not in the form of a weighty manifesto, but as part of the vibrant, pulsating panorama of life which emerges from these pages. We must not then be fooled by their weaknesses and limitations into thinking that we are necessarily dealing here with second-rate authors. They were ahead of their times, having long since left behind the dreary didacticsm of the Middle Ages; theirs is already the detached objectivism of modern realism. Even the *Heptaméron*, which at first glance seems to contain a great deal of moralizing, is in reality a presentation of several points of view, offered without interference by the author.

Such then was the prose fiction of the fifteenth and sixteenth centuries—neither profound nor visionary, surely not experimental or symbolic, nevertheless containing much to delight a modern reader. It concentrated first and foremost on entertaining its readers. The joy of the "bonne histoire" supplanted all other considerations. At its best it offers the verve, the gaiety, and the formal satisfactions to be found in the well-told tale, but achieves this goal by depicting with honesty and humor life itself.

Conclusion

In this review of early short fiction in France, we have tried to concentrate on individual strengths and weaknesses and to eschew any implication that the French novella from the fifteenth to the sixteenth century demonstrates a theory of "progress" from a lower to a higher form. The fact is that in many ways so early a work as the *Quinze Joies de mariage* is unsurpassed by later prose fiction in its mastery of certain aspects of storytelling.

In this final section, however, we shall glance briefly at the history of the form up to present times. Though the fifteenth- and sixteenth-century novella really constitutes a whole which should not be divided into arbitrary chronological categories, it is nevertheless possible to discern certain characteristics which predominate during one period, as opposed to the other. As Janet Ferrier has pointed out, the fifteenth-century authors tend to be preoccupied with the formal aspects of storytelling. Plotting variations on a limited number of themes commands the greater part of their attention. Obviously influenced by the *Cent Nouvelles nouvelles* of the fifteenth century, such untrained *novellistes* as Philippe de Vigneulles and Nicolas de Troyes continued with the same approach to fiction as their anonymous predecessor. More sophisticated authors such as

Bonaventure Des Périers, Noël du Fail, and Marguerite de Navarre, however, began to explore other possibilities inherent in prose narrative fiction and to subordinate plot development to characterization, description, wordplay, psychological analysis, or didacticism. In the sixteenth century, the spread of humanism was accompanied by a growing interest in individualism and a tendency to reject the rigorous formalism which had characterized the literature of the late Middle Ages. The two best-known authors of the period, Rabelais and Montaigne, both preferred to invent loose and original forms in which to clothe their ideas, rather than to force their thoughts into the confinement of preestablished genres. In the same way the *novellistes* began to interject conversation and commentary into their narrative.

In the last half of the century, their successors, Jacques Tahureau, Henri Estienne, Guillaume Bouchet, and le Seigneur de Cholières, all became increasingly interested in what Coulet calls the "commentaire dialogué." [98] As a result, they tended more and more to neglect the art of storytelling for its own sake.

This does not mean, however, that the stereotyped structure of the novella vanished entirely from the literary scene at the end of the sixteenth century. Such authors as Jacques Yver (*Le Printemps*, 1572), and Bénigne Poissenot (*Nouvelles Histoires tragiques*, 1586), continued to keep more or less within the traditions of the conventional form. Like Marguerite de Navarre before them, they reintroduced woeful love scenes reminiscent of the medieval courtly romances. It is their work which forms the immediate link between sixteenth- and seventeenth-century prose fiction.[99] For unquestionably, the more refined readers of the new classical period preferred the long-winded, sentimental, pastoral novel, of which the best known example is *L'Astrée*.

They did not, however, altogether lose their taste for the undignified and unrestrained narrative which so amused their ancestors. In one form or another the novella continued to exist. While La Fontaine used the scabrous plots for his verse stories (*Contes et Nouvelles*, 1665), lesser known writers produced popular prose collections filled with the familiar themes of the novella.[100] Even Charles Perrault's so-called fairy tales owed something to this literary heritage.[101] And as for Madame de La Fayette, her novels by their brevity and psychological analyses of passion, show the influence of the *Heptaméron*.[102] In addition, the four digressive episodes of *La Princesse de Clèves* can easily be looked upon as stories within a frame.

In the following century, Voltaire used the *conte* as a vehicle for popularizing his enlightened views on politics and religion.[103] But alongside these didactic narratives, there continued to exist some form of the *conte licencieux* which perpetuated the Gallic traditions of Renaissance fiction.[104]

It was not, however, until the nineteenth century that the short story, as we understand it today, became a legitimate, highly perfected art form.[105] In the hands of the romantics and their heirs, it became a series of sentimental reflections à la Musset, a gothic horror story, à la Barbey d'Aurevilly or Villiers de l'Isle-Adam, or a mystical evocation à la Gérard de Nerval. Only Balzac made a self-conscious attempt to return to the original sources with his *Contes drolatiques*, (1832–37). It was the realists and naturalists, however, who finally brought the form into its own and developed it to its full potential: the *Trois Contes* (1877) of Flaubert, the *Contes du lundi* (1873) and *Lettres de mon moulin* (1869) of Alphonse Daudet. For the first time, we find in Maupassant a modern author who owes an enduring literary reputation almost exclusively to his mastery of the short-story form.

In the twentieth century, most of the great French authors have accorded an important place in their literary production to the short story, reshaping it to fit the changing needs and outlooks of the times. Writers like Colette, Gide, Aymé, Camus, Sartre, and more recently Cesbron, Bazin, and Gascar have all used short fiction for their own literary ends.

Thus the novella or *conte*, which sprang from such humble and obscure origins, has repeatedly demonstrated, throughout five centuries of evolution, tremendous staying power and adaptability to the literary needs and tastes of succeeding generations. Viewed in this light, the selections which follow take on new interest and importance. It is our hope that they will be read and enjoyed both for their own merit and also for their significant contribution to the art of fiction.

Notes for Introduction

1. Any thorough examination of the genre immediately reveals the rich variety which exists within the framework of any definition given. As Fritz Redenbacher remarks: "Nun ist aber die Novellistik der italienischen und französischen Renaissance so ausserordentlich vielgestaltig, dass eine eigentliche Definition den Reichtum nicht mehr umspannen kann." ("Die Novellistik der französischen Hochrenaissance," *Zeitschrift für französischen Sprache und Litteratur* 49 [1926]: 4.)

2. It was not much before the early nineteenth century that a formal distinction was made between the *conte* and the *nouvelle*. (See Albert George, *Short Fiction in France: 1800–1850* [Syracuse: Syracuse University Press, 1964], p. 9.)

3. *Le Roman jusqu'à la révolution* (Paris: Armand Colin, 1967), 1:78.

4. "The merry tale, in other words, is not bound to any definite society but floats freely from country to country." (See Alexander H. Krappe, *The Science of Folk Lore* [New York: Dial Press, 1930], p. 47.)

5. Stith Thompson, *Motif-Index of Folk Literature* (Copenhagen: Rosenkilde and Begger, 1955–58), 6 vols.

6. If Marguerite's *devisants* generally reflect the elegance and refinement of the court, the characters in Noël du Fail, for the most part, are of simple peasant stock.

7. *Contributo allo studio della novella francese del XV e XVI secolo* (Rome: Loescher, 1895).

8. "La Nouvelle française aux XVe et XVIe siècles," in *Mélanges de littérature française du Moyen Age*, ed. by Mario Roques (Paris: Champion, 1912), pp. 627–677.

9. *Novas* is the plural of the Provençal term *novela*. Joseph Anglade remarks: "L'ancienne littérature méridionale a connu ou plutôt a créé la *nouvelle* en vers. . . ." (*Histoire sommaire de la littérature méridionale au Moyen Age* [Paris: E. de Boccard, 1921], p. 156.)

10. "Le talent de Marie de France rappelle beaucoup celui d'un novelliste exercé. . . ." (See Werner Söderhjelm, *La Nouvelle française au XVe siècle* [Paris: Champion, 1910], p. 1.)

11. The influence and popularity of this medieval story is indicated in the number of fourteenth- and fifteenth-century prose adaptations it inspired. In the Renaissance both Bandello (IV, 5) and Marguerite de Navarre (70) used the theme. The most recent analysis of these later reworkings was by Jean Frappier, "*La Chastelaine de Vergi*, Marguerite de Navarre et Bandello," in *Publications de la Faculté des Lettres de l'Université de Strasbourg: Mélanges 1945* (Paris: Les Belles Lettres, 1946), pp. 91–149.

12. Gustave Cohen, *Le Roman courtois au XIIe siècle* (Paris: Centre de Documentation Universitaire, 1946), p. 51.

13. "A new kind of audience in the 15th century enjoyed these stories extracted from their 'courtly' setting." (See Janet Ferrier, *Forerunners of the French Novel: An Essay on the Development of the "Novella" in the Late Middle Ages* [Manchester: Manchester University Press, 1954], p. 15.)

14. At least two of the editors of this work have emphasized the crucial importance of *Aucassin et Nicolette* as a bridge between verse and prose narrative: Louis Moland and Charles d'Héricault, *Nouvelles françaises en prose du XIIIe siècle* (Paris: P. Jannet, 1856) and Hermann Süchier, *Aucassin und Nicolette* (Paderborn: Schöningh, 1921).

15. When the fabliau as a literary form died in the early part of the fourteenth century, it probably left its legacy of social satire and scatalogical humor to the medieval theater. It has been generally conceded that the influences have been from the fabliau to the farce and then to the novella. (See Pietro Toldo, "Etudes sur le théâtre comique français du Moyen Age et sur le rôle de la nouvelle dans les farces et les comédies," *Studi di Filologia Romanza*, 9 [1902]: 181–369.)

16. See J.-Th. Welter, *L'Exemplum dans la littérature religieuse et didactique du Moyen Age* (Paris: E. H. Guitard, 1927).

17. *Le Livre du Chevalier de La Tour Landry*, ed. by Anatole de Montaiglon (Paris: Bibliothèque Elzévirienne, 1854). This work continued to be read throughout the later Middle Ages and on into the Renaissance. Marguerite de Navarre may have used it for some of her thematic material. (See Pierre Jourda, *Marguerite d'Angoulême: duchesse d'Alençon, reine de Navarre* [Paris: Champion, 1930], 2:730.)

18. "C'est dans les *Gesta Romanorum* que les différents types d'*exemplum* moralisé ont reçu leur dernier développement et par là aussi leur forme définitive." (Welter, *L'Exemplum dans la littérature religieuse*, p. 365.)

19. Söderhjelm, *La Nouvelle française*, p. 15.

20. See edition by Moland and d'Héricault, *Nouvelles françaises*, pp. 85–160.

21. "La première nouvelle rédigée directement en prose est peut-être *La Fille du Conte de Ponthieu*." Henri Coulet, *Le Roman jusqu'à la Révolution*, 1:75.

22. George Saintsbury, *A History of the French Novel* (London: Macmillan, 1917), pp. 81–87.

23. The fifteenth century is crucial in our study, for here at last all the important factors come together. It is not really until the fifteenth century that prose is the literary vehicle of expression. "La prose ne commence vraiment à servir de forme littéraire qu'au XVᵉ siècle." (See Jens Rasmussen, *La Prose narrative française du XVᵉ siècle* [Copenhagen: Munksgaard, 1958], p. 5.)

24. Söderhjelm calls it "un mélange de plusieurs genres: roman pédagogique, roman chevaleresque, peinture de moeurs, nouvelle amusante." (*La Nouvelle française*, p. 96.)

25. The influence is more noteworthy in the style and "motifs" as Jean Rychner has most recently pointed out. (See introduction to his edition [Geneva: Droz, 1963].)

26. See Gustave Reynier, *Les Origines du roman réaliste* (Paris: Hachette, 1912), pp. 35–36.

27. Despite Krystyna Kasprzyk's doubts about the exactitude of this earlier translation by Laurent de Premierfait (*Nicolas de Troyes et le genre narratif en France au XVIᵉ siècle* [Paris: Klincksieck, 1963], p. 293), Boccaccio's collection was in fact a tangible factor in the evolution of the French novella.

28. It is, however, more the idea of composing undidactic stories rather than of placing them in a frame which the author of the *Cent Nouvelles nouvelles* "borrows" from his Italian predecessor. There is, to be sure, some grouping of themes in the *Cent Nouvelles nouvelles* (See Coulet, *Le Roman jusqu'à la Révolution* 1:90), but it must be admitted that the frame is

very vague and that the first real French example of the frame story is in the *Comptes amoureux* by Jeanne Flore composed in 1531.

29. At least one other significant author of Italian origins, Poggio Bracciolini, was well known in France before the end of the fifteenth century: "Les facéties du Pogge avaient pénétré en France dès le XVᵉ siècle: répandues par de nombreux manuscrits, souvent imprimées, traduites, en partie, par Julien Macho et, plus tard, par Guillaume Tardif, utilisées par l'auteur des *Cent Nouvelles Nouvelles*, elles avaient connu un succès large et durable." (Lionello Sozzi, *Les Contes de Bonaventure Des Périers: Contribution à l'étude de la nouvelle française de la Renaissance* [Turin: G. Giappichelli, 1965], p. 419.)

30. There are in fact two examples of collections which, for these reasons, are difficult to classify. The first is a curious compilation of "court cases" on love, *Les Arrêts d'Amour*, written by Martial d'Auvergne sometime between 1460 and 1466. Jean Rychner willingly puts it with "la littérature narrative réaliste de cette époque. . . ." (See his edition [Paris: Picard, 1951], p. xl.) Despite a long chapter dedicated to this work, Söderhjelm finds only one "arrêt," however, which could conceivably be considered a novella. (*La Nouvelle française*, pp. 168–71. The second is *Les Nouvelles de Sens*, probably written during the second half of the fifteenth century. As Söderhjelm himself says "C'est une compilation dans le genre des *Exemples* beaucoup plus que dans celui des *Cent Nouvelles nouvelles*. . . ." (*Ibid.*, p. 217.)

31. Notwithstanding his reservations on the question of thematic borrowings, Gaston Paris remarks rather categorically: "La courte narration en prose n'était pas inconnue en France . . . mais elle n'avait pas été cultivée comme genre spécial avant l'imitation de Boccace." ("La Nouvelle française," p. 628, n. 4).

32. Manuscripts circulated quite freely at this time, however. As K. H. Hartley remarks: "It was possible at that period for a poem, a tale, even a didactic essay, to be better known before it went to the printers than when it came from them because afterward its vogue was spent and all of the charm

was gone of passing it from hand to hand beneath the cloak."
Bandello and the "Heptameron" (Melbourne: Melbourne University Press, 1960), p. 1.

33. *Les Contes de Bonaventure Des Périers*, pp. 87–228.

34. *Les XV Joies de mariage*, ed. Jean Rychner (Geneva: Droz, 1963), p. ix.

35. *Ibid.*, pp. xii–xix. Rychner even suggests that Matheolus may have directly inspired parts of the first and fifteenth joys.

36. *Romans français du moyen âge* (Paris: Droz, 1934), p. 375.

37. See the "Meunier d'Aleu" by Enguerrand d'Oisy. (*Recueil général et complet des fabliaux des XIIIᵉ et XIVᵉ siècles*, ed. Anatole de Montaiglon and Gaston Raynaud [Paris: Librairie des Bibliophiles, 1872–90], 2:31.

38. To name a few of the Italian analogues: *Décameron* (IV, 8); Poggio, *Facétie* (238 and 270); Sermini, *Novelle* (26); Sabadino degli Arienti, *Novelle Porretane* (26); Sachetti, *Il Trecentonovelle* (206). A later adaptation appears in Marguerite de Navarre's *Heptaméron* (8).

39. "Qualiter Uxor medicata est oculum mariti" (CII) (*A Selection of Latin Stories* [London: Percy Society, 1842], pp. 91–92.)

40. Walther Küchler finds a parallel in the fabliau "Du Clerc qui fut repus derrière l'escrin." ("Die Cent Nouvelles nouvelles, Ein Beitrag zur Geschichte der französischen Nouvelle." *Zeitschrift für französische Sprache und Litteratur*, 30, p. 289.)

41. The theme does reappear in Nicolas de Troyes, however. (55) (See Kaspryzk, *Nicolas de Troyes*, p. 133.)

42. See Champion edition (Paris, 1928), p. 277.

43. Söderhjelm, *La Nouvelle française*, p. 112.

44. See Gustave Reynier, *Le Roman sentimental avant L'Astrée* (Paris: Armand Colin, 1908), p. 14. For a complete refutation of this theory on the basis of stylistic analysis, see William P. Shepard, "The Syntax of Antoine de La Sale," *PMLA*, 20 (1905): 435–501.

45. In analyzing story 98, Söderhjelm admires the author's dramatic concentration of events (*La Nouvelle française*, p. 137, n. 1). A propos of story 61 which Janet Ferrier compares with a similar fabliau, she concludes that the reworking

of the *Cent Nouvelles nouvelles* is superior in its sophisticated humor. (*Forerunners of the French Novel*, p. 47).

46. *Gedenkbuch des Metzer Burger's Philippe de Vigneulles*, ed. Heinrich Michelant (Stuttgart: Bibliothek des Litterarischen Vereins, 1852), p. 136.

47. See Charles Livingston, "*Decameron*, VIII, 2: Earliest French Imitations," *Modern Philology*, 22 (August 1924): 35–43.

48. See Charles Livingston, "The Fabliau 'Des Deux Anglois et de l'anel,' " *PMLA*, 40 (1925): 217–224.

49. Kasprzyk, *Nicolas de Troyes*, Part II, chapter I.

50. *Ibid.* Consult especially pp. 247–265.

51. *La Vie et l'oeuvre littéraire de Noël du Fail* (Paris: Champion, 1914). See particularly chapter III.

52. *Ibid.*, p. 284.

53. *Sources and Analogues of the "Nouvelles Récréations et Joyeux Devis of Bonaventure Des Périers."* University of North Carolina Studies in Comparative Literature, no. 20 (Chapel Hill: University of North Carolina Press, 1957).

54. Sozzi, *Les Contes de Bonaventure Des Périers*, pp. 95–96.

55. *Ibid.*, p. 118.

56. *La Légende de Pierre Faifeu* (Paris: Willem, 1883). Sozzi in fact considers this work as the probable source for two of the stories in the *Nouvelles Récréations*—23 and 59. (*Les Contes de Bonaventure Des Périers*, p. 217.)

57. In his nineteenth-century edition of the *Nouvelles Récréations* Louis Lacour cites a parallel story in the Chinese collection *Siao li Siao*, but, as Sozzi points out, since no certain date has ever been established for the latter, the conjecture is rather meaningless. (Sozzi, *Les Contes de Bonaventure Des Périers*, p. 120.) As for the third part of the tale, Sozzi cites similar stories in Poggio, Bebel, and Boccaccio (*Ibid.*, pp. 120–21).

58. Toldo had already indicated both the *Cent Nouvelles nouvelles* (45) and the *Decameron* (III, 1) as possible sources. Sozzi's additions are from Barbarino's *Reggimento e Costumi di Donne* and from Sercambi's *Novelle inedite* (4).

59. Number 8 in *Nouvelles françaises inédites du quinzième siècle*, ed. Ernest Langlois (Paris: Champion, 1908).

60. *Facétie* (223).

61. As some evidence of its popularity, Sozzi remarks on a reference to it in a well known play of the late Middle Ages, *La Farce de Jolyet* (*Les Contes de Bonaventure Des Périers*, p. 167, n. 32).

62. *Les Contes de Bonaventure Des Périers*, Volume II, chapter III.

63. It is necessary to mention that Bandello's influence has been questioned because of the dates of publication involved. The first part of his work came out on 1554, four years before the posthumous publication of the *Heptaméron*. The last part was published in 1573. Manuscripts of these works could have been circulated, however. In any event, Jourda decides that it is Bandello who borrowed from the Queen of Navarre (*Marguerite d'Angoulême*, II, pp. 709–723). In his more recent review of the problem, K. H. Hartley concludes the contrary, that is, that Marguerite possessed a manuscript of Bandello's work and ". . . consciously set herself to imitate the greatest entertainer of her time." (*Bandello and the "Heptameron,"* p. 37.)

64. "Nous voici au rouet: identité d'idées veut-il dire plagiat? Parce que deux écrivains développent une même théorie, faut-il nécessairement que l'un d'eux copie l'autre?" (*Marguerite d'Angoulême*, II, p. 757.)

65. Characteristically Marguerite gives to both themes a more serious and even more didactic twist. (See, in this regard, Krystyna Kasprzyk, "La Matière traditionnelle et sa fonction dans *l'Heptaméron*," in *Mélanges de littérature comparée offerts à M. Brahmer* (Warsaw: Editions scientifiques de Pologne, 1967).

66. See Michel François's edition of the *Heptaméron* (Paris: Garnier, 1960), p. 473, n. 490; see also Jourda, *Marguerite d'Angoulême*, II, p. 779.

67. Though Jourda compares the story to a similar plot in Arienti's *Novelle Porretane* (*Marguerite d'Angoulême*, II, p. 700), it is possible to trace the characters back to real persons. (See the note which accompanies our translation.)

68. Jourda rejects Toldo's suggestion that she borrowed from the *Cento Novelle antiche* (135) (*Marguerite d'Angoulême*, II, pp. 686–687), and assumes rather that Brantôme is

correct in identifying the heroine with Marguerite. (*Ibid.*, p. 770.)

69. "When, therefore, the *nouvelle* appears as a literary type in its own right in France, it is not a mere importation from Italy, but the development of a well-established tradition." (*Forerunners of the French Novel*, p. 19.) She also indicates, by way of comparison, that the French writers were less concerned with the sequence of events and more interested in varying juxtapositions of stereotype characters. (*Ibid.*, p. 29.)

70. "L'idée de composer un recueil de contes en prose, dans le dessein explicite d'amuser les lecteurs, et de l'organiser à l'aide d'un cadre plus ou moins développé, vient de l'Italie. . . ." (*Nicolas de Troyes*, p. 288.) Redenbacher arrives at more or less the same conclusion ("Die Novellistik," pp. 14–15).

71. See the old but informative study by Edmond Faral, *Les Jongleurs en France au Moyen Age* (Paris: Champion, 1911).

72. Unless, therefore, one is speaking specifically about thematic borrowing, the traditional Franco-Italian theory of origins, such as Jules Hasslemann outlines it, is not as unreasonable an explanation as it is sometimes made to appear. (*Les Conteurs français du XVI siècle—Extraits* [Paris: Larousse, 1945], pp. 5–6.)

73. See Robert Bossuat, *Le Moyen Age* (Paris: del Duca, 1962), p. 96.

74. See Rasmussen, *La Prose narrative*, p. 32.

75. *Ibid.*, p. 36.

76. In fifteenth- and sixteenth-century France, storytelling remained a favorite pastime. Contemporaneous literature contains numerous references to this fact. The final section of the *Petit Jehan de Saintré* shows a group at court commenting on Jehan's version of Madame's perfidy, told in the form of a tale; the *Propos rustiques* of Noël du Fail describes how the friends and neighbors of Thenot du Coin gathered around the fire to tell stories; and in a famous passage Rabelais gives a picture of Grandgousier engaged in the same activity; the sixty-second tale of the *Heptaméron* likewise depicts a group which used to meet with a certain lady at court, probably Marguerite herself, to exchange tales.

77. Rasmussen, *La Prose narrative*, p. 96.

78. Söderhjelm, *La Nouvelle française*, p. 154.

79. The word "acteur" which can be literally translated "actor" defines the author's active relationship to his work. "L'acteur" seems to be regarded as a kind of bard, reciting to an audience. The word appears before each new idea in the *Petit Jehan de Saintré*, almost like a stage direction.

80. For a thorough analysis of the differences in orientation between the *Heptaméron* and the *Decameron*, see Yves Delègue, "*L'Heptaméron*, est-il un anti-Boccace?" *Travaux de linguistique et de littérature*, 4, 2 (1966): 23–37.

81. Delègue writes: "On est allé souvent chercher bien loin l'origine du genre de l'"essai' tel qu'on le retrouve ensuite chez Montaigne: Marguerite, à notre sens, en donne les premiers exemples." (*Ibid.*, p. 27, n. 19.)

82. In some cases the author will add a brief moral, doubtless a vestige of telling stories for didactic purposes, as in the *exempla*.

83. This tendency is, in the eyes of Ferrier, basic to the style of the French novella. (*Forerunners of the French Novel*, pp. 1–5.)

84. Sozzi actually considers only twenty-four out of the total number to fall into this category (*Les Contes de Bonaventure Des Périers*, p. 247), but, despite the variety of beginnings, they all seem like artificial pretexts to get on with the business of telling the story.

85. In the sixteenth century this antifeminism culminated in the celebrated *Querelle des Femmes*. For more thorough discussions of the *Querelle* and its influence on literature of the French Renaissance, see Abel Lefranc, "Le Tiers Livre du Pantagruel et La Querelle des Femmes," in *Grands Ecrivains, les lettres et les idées depuis la Renaissance* (Paris: Champion, 1914), pp. 251–303. See also Emile Telle, *L'Oeuvre de Marguerite d'Angoulême, reine de Navarre et la Querelle des Femmes* (Toulouse: Lion et fils, 1937).

86. Champion would like to have us believe, however, that dishonesty and infidelity were not just fictional clichés, but an accurate reflection of life as it really was. (See preface of his edition.)

87. The *Quinze Joies* make no pretense of factual veracity since they are concerned exclusively with generalized truths

which apply equally to all those who find themselves caught in the marriage trap. They claim only to be true to life, therefore, rather than actually true.

88. Kaspryzk, for example, considers the emphasis on veracity as one of three constants in all French novellas (*Nicolas de Troyes*, p. 328).

89. Although their names were altered, both the Lord of Avannes and the Count Jossebelin actually existed. Jossebelin, who was Jean II vicomte de Rohan, committed the murder occurring in "A Love Match" in 1478. He was imprisoned in November of that year and not released until February 1484. The Lord of Avannes was Gabriel d'Albret, Lord of Avesnes, a member of the Albret family to which Marguerite was related by her second marriage. Gabriel died unmarried. Brantôme alludes to the wise lady whom he loved but does not identify her by name.

90. Hatzfeld finds marked similarities between these passages and certain painted miniatures of the time. Helmut Hatzfeld, "The Discovery of Realistic Art in Antoine de La Sale," *Modern Language Quarterly*, 15 [1954]: 168–181.

91. This subject deserves further exploration. The article by Maurice Lacombe, "La Vie Conjugale au XVᵉ siècle," *Correspondance historique et archéologique* (1911): 35–42; 100–119, is not only limited in its scope (dealing only with the *Quinze Joies de mariage*), but superficial.

92. In this regard, the most famous example occurs in Rabelais's *Tiers Livre*, in which Panurge's fear of cuckoldry makes it impossible for him to decide to take a wife. This fear continues as a comic theme well into the seventeenth century and we find numerous examples of it in Molière's theater.

93. This was the nature of the relationship between Jehan and Belles Cousines and also between the lady and her lover in the seventieth novella of the *Heptaméron*, an adaptation of the older *Châtelaine de Vergi*. In the earlier version the relationship was not chaste, however. (See Frappier, *"La Chastelaine de Vergi."*) This attitude towards love also pervades the fourth and twenty-sixth novellas of the *Heptaméron*. The whole question of the *practice* of courtly love is exceedingly complex. Other aspects include the vow of secrecy and the testing of the lover. For more comprehensive studies of

courtly love in the Middle Ages, see Moshé Lazar, *Amour courtois et 'Fin'Amors' dans la littérature du XIIe siècle* (Paris: Klinksieck, 1964), Maurice Valency, *In Praise of Love* (New York: Macmillan, 1958), Francis X. Newman, ed. *The Meaning of Courtly Love* (Albany: State University of New York Press, 1968).

94. Since in the courtly tradition love and marriage were unrelated, the question of unfaithfulness was most important between a woman and her lover. In his twelfth-century *De Arte honeste amandi*, Andreas Capellanus devotes a whole chapter to this subject. (See the translation by John Parry, *The Art of Courtly Love* [New York: Frederick Ungar, 1957], pp. 31–32.)

95. The humanists and reformers criticized the theological basis for the intercession of the priesthood and the moral corruption of the clergy in general, but the church itself was harshly suspicious of the mendicant friars who wandered from place to place disrupting parochial affiliations. (See Jacques Le Goff, *Les Intellectuels au Moyen Age* [Paris: Edition du Seuil, 1962], pp. 108–113.)

96. See *Nouvelles Récréations*, ed. Lacour (Paris: Librairie des Bibliophiles, 1874), I, 11. "Première Nouvelle en forme de préambule." Des Périers suggests that if any of his female readers are too "tendrettes" they should ask their brothers or their cousins to place a cross beside stories which they might find too "appetizing." He goes on to warn them, however, that their male relatives may deceive them with a "quid" for a "quod" and advises them to go ahead and read everything after all!

97. Whereas Kaspryzk implies that the "bon tour" theme might be either German or Italian in origin (*Nicolas de Troyes*, p. 299), Redenbacher seems to think the story revolving around a clever word play is more probably Italian ("Die Novellistik," p. 12).

98. *Le Roman*, I: 132.

99. Though the *Vies des dames galantes* by Brantôme rightfully belongs with the tradition of "petite histoire," its style definitely reflects the narrative techniques of the novella. Brantôme, in fact, not only knew the works of these writers of fiction, but was himself an excellent raconteur. (See *Vie*

des dames galantes, ed. Maurice Rat [Paris: Garnier, 1960], pp. ix–x.)

100. See Charles Louandre, *Chefs-d'oeuvre des conteurs français contemporains de La Fontaine* (Paris: Charpentier, 1906).

101. "C'est une erreur de ne voir dans ces récits que des histoires pour enfants. . . ." (Jean Sareil and Jacqueline Sareil, *Contes classiques* [Englewood Cliffs, N.J.: Prentice-Hall, 1967], p. 61.)

102. In *La Princesse de Clèves,* the Dauphine speaks specifically about ". . . Marguerite, soeur du roi, Duchesse d'Alençon et depuis reine de Navarre, dont vous avez vu les contes. . . ." (*Romans et nouvelles,* ed. Emile Magne [Paris: Garnier, 1961], p. 299.)

103. Alfred Engstrom singles out Diderot as the most important eighteenth-century contributor to the form: "Diderot alone among the significant French writers of the eighteenth century wrote brief fiction that can be formally related to the short story." (*The Formal Short Story in France and its Development Before 1850* in *Studies in Language and Literature* [Chapel Hill: University of North Carolina Press, 1945], p. 633.)

104. Sareil remarks: "D'autre part, l'esprit gaulois des fabliaux, qui s'était si heureusement conservé aux siècles suivants, ne va plus connaître de limites avec le relâchement des moeurs qui suit la mort de Louis XIV. Les contes licencieux deviennent à la mode et constituent toute une littérature, quelquefois spirituelle et divertissante, mais qui reste malgré tout secondaire." (*Contes classiques,* p. 3.)

105. Beginning with Mérimée, considered the first legitimate writer of *modern* short stories (see Engstrom, *The Formal Short Story in France,* p. 634), the numbers of writers who composed short fiction increased very rapidly: "Between 1829 and 1832 so many *contes* and *nouvelles* appeared that the critics groaned in complaint." (George, *Short Fiction in France,* p. 7.) It should be noted that neither George nor Engstrom give much weight to the role of the early stories we have described here. Their interest has not been to trace the development of short fiction from earliest times, but to search for prototypes of the *modern* short story.

Selected General Bibliography

AUERBACH, ERICH. *Zur Technik der Frührenaissancenovelle in Italien und Frankreich.* Heidelberg: Winter, 1921.

COULET, HENRI. *Le Roman jusqu'à la Révolution.* 2 vols. Paris: Armand Colin, 1967.

DEJONGH, WILLIAM FREDERICK JEKEL. *A Bibliography of the Novel and Short Stories in French From the Beginning of Printing Till 1600.* Albuquerque, N. M.: University of New Mexico Press, 1944.

DELÈGUE, YVES. "*L'Heptaméron* est-il un anti-Boccace?" *Travaux de linguistique et de littérature* 4 (1966): 23–37.

ENGSTROM, ALFRED. "The Formal Short Story in France and its Development Before 1850." In *Studies in Language and Literature.* Chapel Hill: University of North Carolina Press, 1945, pp. 249–261.

FERRIER, JANET. *Forerunners of the French Novel: An Essay on the Development of the Novella in the Late Middle Ages.* Manchester: Manchester University Press, 1954.

FRAPPIER, JEAN. "*La Chastelaine de Vergi*, Marguerite de Navarre et Bandello." In *Publications de la Faculté des Lettres de l'Université de Strasbourg: Mélanges 1945,* pp. 91–149. Paris: Les Belles Lettres, 1946.

GEORGE, ALBERT. *Short Fiction in France: 1800–1850.* Syracuse: Syracuse University Press, 1964.

HARTLEY, K. H. *Bandello and the "Heptameron."* Melbourne: Melbourne University Press, 1960.

JEFFELS, RONALD R. "The *Conte* as a Genre in the French Renaissance," *Revue de l'Université de Ottawa,* October-December 1956: 435–450.

JOURDA, PIERRE. *Marguerite d'Angoulême: duchesse d'Alençon, reine de Navarre.* 2 vols. Paris: Champion, 1930.

KASPRZYK, KRYSTYNA. *Nicolas de Troyes et le Genre narratif en France au XVIᵉ siècle.* Paris: Klincksieck, 1963.

MOLAND, LOUIS, and D'HÉRICAULT, CHARLES. *Nouvelles françaises en prose du XIIIᵉ siècle.* Paris: P. Jannet, 1856.

PABST, WALTER. *Novellentheorie und Novellendichtung zur Geschichte ihrer Antinomie in den romanischen Literaturen.* Hamburg: Cram, De Gruyter and Co., 1953.

PARIS, GASTON. "La Nouvelle française aux XVe et XVIe siècles." In *Mélanges de Littérature française du Moyen Age,* ed. by Mario Roques. Paris: Champion, 1912.

RASMUSSEN, JENS. *La Prose narrative française du XVe siècle.* Copenhagen: Munksgaard, 1958.

REDENBACHER, FRITZ. "Die Novellistik der französischen Hochrenaissance," *Zeitschrift für französische Sprache und Litteratur.* 49 (1926): 1–72.

REYNIER, GUSTAVE. *Les Origines du roman réaliste.* Paris: Hachette, 1913.

RYCHNER, JEAN, ed. *Les XV Joies de mariage.* Geneva: Droz, 1963.

SAREIL, JEAN, AND SAREIL, JACQUELINE. *Contes classiques.* Englewood Cliffs, N. J.: Prentice-Hall, 1967.

SÖDERHJELM, WERNER. *La Nouvelle française au XVe siècle.* Paris: Champion, 1910.

SOZZI, LIONELLO. *Les Contes de Bonaventure Des Périers: Contribution à l'étude de la nouvelle française de la Renaissance.* Turin: G. Giappichelli, 1965.

THOMPSON, STITH. *Motif-Index of Folk Literature.* 6 vols. Copenhagen: Rosenkilde and Begger, 1955–58.

TOLDO, PIETRO. *Contributo allo studio della novella francese del XV e XVI secolo.* Rome, Loescher, 1895.

WELTER, J.-TH. *L'exemplum dans la littérature religieuse et didactique du Moyen Age.* Paris: E. H. Guitard, 1927.

Les Quinze Joies de Mariage

Introduction

Les Quinze Joies de Mariage is a curious work about which very little is known. Despite a riddle on the last page, no one has solved the mystery of the author's true identity. Nor are scholars in agreement as to the date of composition, guesses ranging from 1380 to 1430. Internal references to certain articles of dress and to incidents in the Hundred Years' War have only served to confuse rather than to enlighten the researchers. All that can be said with certainty is that the work was written near the beginning of the fifteenth century by an anonymous author who belonged to the provincial bourgeoisie. A few words in the text have been traced to the dialect originating north of Poitiers, and perhaps the author was born or lived in that region. The strong antifeminist tenor of the work and the author's admission that he had never married because he was in another form of "servitude" would indicate that he was a secular cleric.

The work seems to have been originally intended as a didactic satire—thus the author's habit of generalizing to prove a point and the characteristic locutions "it may happen that . . ." or "sometimes it happens that. . ." Similarly, he seems to make the situations purposely as vague and all-inclusive as possible. For instance, in the second selection the wife goes "to her mother's, to her sister's, or to her cousin's; but preferably to her mother's." And the mother's friends "sit around a good fire, if it is winter, or if it is summer, they sit on rushes." In addition, none of the characters is ever identified or personalized, they exist only as types: the husband, the wife, the mother-in-law, the chambermaid, the women friends.

Despite the obvious desire to prove a thesis, however, the work displays an incisive knowledge of feminine psychology, a wealth of realistic detail, and a strong sense of narrative flow that make it impossible not to classify it as a work of fiction.

The structure of the book is simple: in parody of "The

Fifteen Joys of Our Lady," a devotional exercise, the author enumerates the fifteen "joys" of marriage—which of course are not joys at all. The work is unified by means of a repeated image—that of the *nasse*, or literally bow-net, which is developed in the prologue and is carried from episode to episode to symbolize the unhappy state of matrimony. In like manner, each section comes to a close with the same ominous prediction that the husband will end his days in misery. Each chapter presents one or more aspects of marital life: the bride who teases her husband into buying her new dresses until he eventually goes bankrupt, the wife who becomes a gadabout, the expectant mother who drives her husband to distraction with her unreasonable whims and demands, while her women friends, the omnipresent "commères," eat him out of house and home, the nagging shrew who slaps the children to make them cry when her husband comes home after a hard day; and so on, to the fifteenth joy, which tells of a wife caught in *flagrant délit* who manages to convince her husband that *he* is in the wrong.

The technique is likewise simple but efficacious. The adroit repetition of epithets sharpens the irony of the situation. Hence the husband is always the "poor man" or the "good man" with more than a hint of simple-mindedness implied. The humor often relies on one of the classic techniques of the Gallic tale, the euphemistic understatement.

The work is most remarkable, however, for its realistic tableaux: the gay, young bachelor catching sight of a young woman dressed to kill, the wife turning away in the bed, arising grumpily in the morning, and laughing under the sheets when she gets her way; the husband running after his rival, the wife blushing as she admits the true state of affairs to her mother, the women friends eating and drinking around the fire, the husband choking on his food and driving his knife into the table, and the lover hovering near the fountain in the hope of having a word with the conniving chambermaid.

The overall tone is one of pitiless satirical exaggeration. Heaping one outrageous detail upon another, the author takes gleeful delight in damning the weaker sex. It is not enough that the wife nags her husband until he buys her a new gown, she must put on a martyred air, pretend she doesn't want it, and refuse to take any of the blame for the end result of her extravagance. Similarly, from the moment when the women invite the lover to come into the house, until the final apotheosis of hypocrisy, when they assure the husband that they would never tolerate a fallen woman in their midst, the author spares no detail which will reveal their incredible shamelessness. It has been suggested, however, that the real object of his scorn is not the woman but the man, who allows himself to be so duped and henpecked.

In addition to being a brilliant example of mordant wit, the following extracts display a sure sense of rhythm and tempo which build flawlessly to their denouements. The author had an amazing ear and captured unerringly the pungent, familiar conversation of his contemporaries. We have tried to translate this down-to-earth style into equivalent English idioms and at the same time to avoid slang or modernisms which would destroy the period flavor of the work.

Text Used

RYCHNER, JEAN, ed. *Les XV Joies de mariage.* Geneva and Paris: Droz, 1963. We also examined the more recent edition by Joan Crow, Oxford: Blackwell, 1969, which bases its text on the little-known manuscript: London: Robinson Trust. Phillipps 8338.

Selected Critical Bibliography

COVILLE, ALFRED. *Recherches sur quelques écrivains du XIVᵉ et du XVᵉ siècles.* Paris: Droz, 1935, pp. 129–74.

CRESSOT, MARCEL. *Vocabulaire des quinze joyes de mariage d'après le texte de la seconde édition de la Bibliothèque elzévirienne* de 1857. Paris: Droz, 1939.

LACOMBE, MAURICE. "La Vie conjugale au XVᵉ siècle (D'après *Les XV joies de mariage*)." *Correspondance historique et archéologique* (1911): 35–52; 100–119.

Les Quinze Joies de Mariage
'THE FIRST JOY'

The first joy of marriage comes when a young man is at the height of his youth, innocent, pure, and good-humored; and when his only interests are preening himself, composing ballads and singing them, eyeing the prettiest girls, and figuring out how he can find money to enjoy pleasures and good times in keeping with his condition. Nor is he a bit worried about where it comes from, for perhaps he still has his mother and father, or some relative, who gives him whatever he needs. And though he has his delights and pleasure in full, he cannot bear them, but looks upon those who are married and firmly trapped in the net, and who it seems to him are enjoying themselves, because they have the bait right there in the net with them, namely the woman, who is beautiful, stylishly arrayed, and well dressed in fine clothes, which perhaps her husband has not paid for; since, he is made to believe, either her mother or father gave them to her as part of her trousseau. And the young man turns round and round the net until he finds his way in and gets married. And so eager is he to taste the bait that it often happens he thinks little of the consequences and throws himself in, regardless of the cost.

Now he is in the net, poor man, he who used to think only of singing, buying ribbons, silken purses, and niceties for pretty girls. For a while he amuses himself and takes delight in his state and gives no thought to escaping, till one day he takes stock a bit, but it is too late. He must provide for his wife in the style to which she is accustomed. And being perhaps happy and merry-tempered, she may have perceived at a party the other day young ladies, townswomen, and others of her class, who were dressed in the latest style. Thus it seems to her that she should be dressed like the others. She looks for the place, time, and hour to bring up the matter with her husband. Women would most likely prefer to discuss their intimate problems where their husbands are most docile and most inclined to give in, that is, in bed, where our friend about whom I have spoken wishes to surrender himself to his delights and pleasures. To him it appears there is nothing else to do.

Les Quinze Joies de mariage "The First Joy"
". . . his only interests are . . . eyeing the prettiest girls. . . ."
[From a sixteenth-century English edition, reproduced by permission of the Pierpont Morgan Library, New York.
Quinze Joies de mariage, PML 21589.]

Then his wife begins to speak in this manner, "My love, leave me alone, for I am very unhappy."

"My sweet," he says, "and why?"

"Most assuredly," she says, "I have good reason to be, but I shall never tell you any more about it, for you pay no attention to what I say."

"My sweet," he says, "tell me why you say such things to me."

"God help me," she says, "sir, there is no need to tell you, for it's something which if I told, you wouldn't think very important, and it would seem to you that I had brought it up for some other reason."

"Indeed, you shall tell me," he says.

Then she says, "Since it is your wish, I'll tell you. My love, you know I went to a certain party the other day, where you sent me, but which I did not enjoy. While I was there, I believe there was no woman, however lowly her station, who was as badly dressed as I. Although I do not say it to brag, thank God, I come from as good a background as any lady, maiden, or townswoman who was there. Ask anyone who knows anything about families! I don't say this for my own sake, since I don't care about myself, but I am ashamed for your reputation and that of my friends."

"Now really, my dear," he says, "What kind of people were at this gathering?"

"Faith," she answers, "there wasn't the lowliest among those I would consider my equals who didn't have a gown of scarlet wool or of Malines or of finely woven green, fur-trimmed in fine gray or miniver, with large sleeves and matching shell-shaped hood, with a ribbon of red or green silk trailing down to the floor, all made in the newest style.* And I still had my wedding gown, which is threadbare and short, because I've grown since it was made. For I was still a young girl when I was given to you; and I am already so worn out and have put up with so many hardships that I could pass for the mother of

* These details are valuable documentation for both the student of medieval dress and for the scholar, who hopes to date the work. Malines is a city in the Netherlands famous for its cloth. As for the shape of the hood, scholars are undecided about the exact meaning of this passage. (See Rychner's edition, pp. xl–xli.)

those whose daughter I might be. Indeed, when I was with them, I was so ashamed I did not dare look at them nor know how to keep my composure. And it hurt me even more when the lady of such and such a place or the wife of so and so remarked to me in front of the others that it was disgraceful that I was not better dressed. And in fact, they needn't worry about seeing me there for a long time to come."

"Come, come, my dear," said the good man, "Listen. You know perfectly well, my sweet, that when we set up house, we had no furniture and had to buy beds, mattresses, wall-hangings and lots of other things, and at the moment we do not have a great deal of money. And you know we have to purchase two oxen for our tenant farmer of such and such a place, and that the other day the gable of our barn fell because of faulty roofing and must be repaired first thing. And if I must attend the court session at . . . because of the case pending concerning your property there, from which I get little or no profit, I shall have to spend a lot of money."

"Ah, sir, I might have known the one thing you'd reproach me for would be my land." Thereupon, she turns to the other side saying, "In God's name, leave me alone. I'll never bring the subject up again."

"Lord's sake," says the good man, "you're angry for no good reason."

"On the contrary, sir," says she, "if you've made little or no profit from my land, there's nothing I can do about it. As you well know, I was asked for in marriage by so and so, and more than twenty others who were interested only in me personally. And you know very well that you came and went so often that I wanted you alone, which my father held against me and still does, for which I ought to hate myself, as I believe I must be the most miserable woman that ever was. And I ask you, sir," she says, "if the wives of this man and that, who wanted to marry me, are in the same state as I am? And yet they are not from the same background as I. By Saint John, the dresses they pass down to their servants are better than the ones I wear on Sundays. I don't know why they say it's awful that so many people die. God willing, I shall not live long! At least you'd be rid of me and wouldn't be bothered by me any more."

"Good heavens, my sweet," he says, "you oughtn't to say such things, for there is nothing I wouldn't do for you. But you must face the facts. Turn around, and I shall do what you wish."

"For God's sake," she says, "leave me alone. I'm not in the mood for it, and I pray to God you never will be any more than I am, for then goodness knows, you'd never touch me."

"No?" says he.

"Certainly not," says she.

Then to put her to the test, or so it seems to him, he says to her, "If I were to die, you'd marry someone else soon enough."

"Oh," says she, "for all the pleasure I've gotten out of it! I swear to God that never again will the lips of a man touch mine, and if I thought I had to outlive you, I'd see to it that I went first." And with this she starts to cry.

And thus the lady restrains herself, even though she feels quite differently, and the good man is happy and sad—happy because he thinks she is cold and chaste at the thought of such distasteful things and because she loves him; sad, because he sees her crying, which makes him heavy-hearted and full of pity. He will not be consoled until she is comforted, and he tries in many ways to please her. But she, set upon winning the battle she's waged to get her dress, will have none of it, but gets up early in the morning at a God-forsaken hour and sulks all day so that he does not hear a single nice word from her. The next night, after she has gone to bed, the good man listens to hear if she is sleeping and checks to see if her arms are uncovered and if necessary covers her. Then she pretends to be sleeping and the good man says to her, "Are you sleeping, my dear?"

"Not at all," says she.

"Have you calmed down?"

"Calmed down?" she says. "My anger is of little importance, thank God," she says with a sigh. "Since that is the way God wants it, I have enough."

"By God, my dear," he says, "if it pleases Him, we shall have enough. And I have given thought to one thing, that I shall dress you in such a manner that I swear you will be the best-dressed woman at my cousin's wedding."

"For sure," she says, "I shall attend no party this year."

"By faith, my love," he says, "yes you will, and you'll have what you ask for."

"What I ask for?" says she, "but I ask for nothing. So help me God, I don't ask through any desire to make myself pretty, for I would rather not leave the house except to go to church. I only mention it because of what the others said, since I learned about it through one of my close friends who heard these remarks and reported them to me."

Thereupon the poor fellow, a new householder, thinks about all the things he has to buy, and that maybe he hasn't much furniture, and that maybe the dress will cost fifty or sixty gold pieces. And mulling it over, he finds no way to get the money. And yet he must have it, for he has such an opinion of his wife that he thanks God in his heart for having given him such a precious jewel as she.

Thus he tosses and turns from side to side and doesn't get enough sleep the entire night to do him any good. And sometimes it happens that the wife is so cunning that she sees what she's done and laughs to herself under the sheets.

When morning comes, the good fellow, who is worn out by the terrible anxieties of the night, gets up and goes out. Perhaps he fetches the cloth and fur, indebting himself to the merchant, either borrowing or pledging twenty or forty pounds of his income, or pawning the old piece of gold or silver jewelry, which had belonged to his grandfather and had been left to him by his father. And at last he returns home, armed with all the things his wife had asked for. But the latter acts as if she doesn't care and curses those who were the first to introduce such ostentations. And when she sees that the deed is done and that he has brought the cloth and fur, she says to him, "My dear, do not reproach me one day that I forced you to spend your money, for I swear that there's no dress in the world I'd give a penny for, so long as I am warmly clothed." In short, the dress is made, the belt and hood to match, and they are displayed in many a church and at many a ball.

But the day arrives when it is time to pay his creditors and the poor man cannot pay, and they will not wait any longer and press charges of seizure or excommunication against him.

The wife hears the news and witnesses the seizure and perhaps they take the lovely things which caused the debts. Now it may happen that after excommunication, he will be declared anathema,* for which reason his wife is obliged to stay at home. And God knows the pleasure and joy in which our poor man lives and passes his days, for his wife goes shouting throughout the house, saying, "Cursed be the day that ever I was born and did not die in my swaddling clothes. Alas," she says, "I work so hard to run the household and everything I can do to save is lost. If I had wanted to, I could have made twenty matches where I might have enjoyed great honors and riches, for I know how their wives are doing now. Poor neglected soul, why doesn't Death come and take you?"

And so the woman complains and never thinks of her own responsibility in the matter, of the dresses and jewels she wanted, of the feasts and wedding parties she attended when she ought to have been home tending to her housework, but puts all the blame on the poor man, who as it happens is blameable only to the extent to which she is the true cause. What is more, according to the rules of the marriage game, he is so henpecked that he does not realize she is at fault. Do not ask about the anguished thoughts of the poor man, who neither sleeps nor rests, but thinks only of how he may appease his wife and settle his debts. But he is even more vexed because his wife is as miserable as can be.

So he languishes and falls into penury, which he will hardly ever be able to relieve, since he is so far behind. But he's just as happy as he can be.

Thus he is caught in the net and maybe never repents. And if he weren't there already, he would soon put himself into it. There he will waste his life away, pining all the while, and he will end his days in misery.

* In canon law, after spiritual excommunication, the victim may be subject as well to a kind of civil excommunication cutting him off from all financial intercourse.

Les Quinze Joies de Mariage
'THE FIFTEENTH JOY'

The fifteenth joy of marriage, which I consider to be the greatest and worst torment this side of death, comes when, by misfortune, a man has circled around the net until he has found the way in and perchance fallen upon a wife who makes merry and amuses herself and indulges in worldly pleasures whenever she pleases. So repeatedly does she do so that the husband grows suspicious and sees what is going on. Then quarrels and tormentings commence, as is always the case. But you can be sure that where her pleasure is concerned, the wife will not desist for all his nagging, should it be the death of her, but will do exactly as she pleases, once she has begun.

Thus it comes to pass that the husband, either by accident, or because he has been on the watch, sees going into his house the companion who has been helping do his chores when he is away, at which he grows heartsick and livid with rage. In a frenzy he rushes into the bedroom where they are and finds them together or very close. His first thought is to kill the poor foolhardy companion, whom he has already judged and so taken by surprise that he hasn't the power to speak or to defend himself. But as the husband is about to strike him, the lady, for pity of the poor man, and also out of a sense of duty, for it is always a duty to prevent murder, throws her arms around her husband and says to him, "Oh, by all that's holy, my lord, beware of doing something you'll regret!" Hereupon, the suitor, profiting from the delay, takes to his heels, with the other after him. He cannot take time to kill his wife, and the poor companion, who is running as fast as he can, escapes him, and small wonder, for there is no man so quick to be gone, whatever the necessity, as a rascal escaping from the hands of those who are after him.

Then not knowing what has become of him, the husband returns promptly to the bedroom, in the hope of finding his wife, so as to punish or kill her, which would be a very sinful deed on his part, since he is not certain that anything wrong has happened between the two of them.

Now we must find out what has become of the poor wife,

helpless as she is. She has gone to her mother's, or to her sister's, or to her cousin's, but it is better for her to be at her mother's. The poor thing tells her mother all that has happened to her, but she tells her that the suitor came in quite by chance, that he had never been there before, and that her husband had discovered him, by accident, talking to her quite innocently.

"What? In the devil's name!" she says. "Was there anything between you?"

"I swear to God, it's true that he had made me two or three propositions, but I had flatly refused. All he did was come in and talk to me about it, and I was just telling him to leave."

Then she swears up and down that she would rather see him hanged. Or perhaps she confesses the whole matter to her, for the mother tells her that she knows all the old games well enough.

"Indeed, I have a suspicion there's more to it than that. I'll never believe that he would have dared to enter your bedroom if he hadn't known you fairly well. Don't be afraid to tell me the truth," she says, "so that I can think of the best remedy."

The girl lowers her head and blushes.

"Aha!" says the mother, "I know very well what the situation is. Tell me how it happened."

"Believe me, the wicked man was after me for over two years, and I had always defended myself quite well, until one day when my husband was away. Then he entered our house, I don't know how, since I am sure I had locked the door, and he took advantage of me. Upon my soul, I defended myself more than half the night, until I was out of breath, but you know there is nothing a poor woman can do when she is all alone."

"Aha! By all the devils in hell," says the mother, "I knew it! Well, in the future, show better sense than to let the fellow do it again. And don't let him into your house!"

"Oh madam, the best thing would be to tell him not to come, for I know very well that he is terribly worried right now, because he thinks my husband has killed me, and he is just mad enough to come and see for himself whether I'm dead or alive."

"What I marvel at," says the mother, "is that he didn't kill the both of you."

"Blessed Mary, madam, I swear to God, if I hadn't thrown

my arms around my husband, he would be dead, the poor thing!"

"You were wise to prevent that. When a poor man exposes himself to danger for the sake of a woman and suffers sleepless nights because of it, she should die rather than let anything happen to him."

"Alas, madam, if you only knew the kind of man he is. I give you my word, I've seen the poor thing come on foot through sleet and rain, when it was pitch dark outside so that he wouldn't be seen. And he would wait in our garden more than half the night, when I couldn't find a way of going to him. And when I arrived, I would find him half-frozen, but he didn't even notice it."

"I was always amazed at the way he used to treat me with such respect," says the mother. "When I go to church, he comes up to me with the holy water, and wherever he meets me, he showers me with attention."

"Truly, madam, he's fond of you."

"Well, let's not waste time," says the mother. "We must do the best we can to remedy the situation. Come here," she says to the chambermaid. "Go tell such and such of my women friends that I want the pleasure of their company, and that I need them for something."

The chambermaid goes out and tells the women friends that the mother is sending for them. The women friends arrive at the mother's house and sit down around a good fire, if it is winter, or if it is summer, they seat themselves on the rushes,* and to begin with, all have a good drink of the best the house has to offer, while waiting for the rest to improve.

Then one of the women friends says to the girl's mother, "My dear, how has your daughter been getting along?"

"By our Lord, my dear, she's had a terrible misfortune, and that's the reason I asked you all to come here."

Then she tells them the whole story. (Sometimes she doesn't tell them about the real state of affairs, but it is also possible that she tells them the whole truth, because several of them

---

* In the Middle Ages, it was the custom to strew rushes and sweet-smelling herbs on the floors to make them cool and pleasant in summer.

have been in the same difficulty and would know how to give the best advice, and the others are very sensitive to the problem, but they have conducted themselves so well and so secretly that there hasn't been the least breath of scandal, thank goodness!) Then they offer their counsel and everyone gives her opinion or tells what she did in a similar case, for the best argument is always based on what has been seen in the past, and the best strategy is always based on experience. Some agree, others debate the pros and cons to see how they can salvage the unhappy state of affairs, and afterwards they draw their conclusions with great care. And God willing, they will get together often in the future, to their mutual satisfaction, but the good man, who is the victim of the whole business, will pay the bill.

After they have decided what course to take, they enjoy themselves and joke with each other.

One says to the daughter, "I wouldn't want to have as bad a night as your husband will have tonight."

Another says, "I would really like to know what he's doing now and see his face."

"Lord," says another, "When you heard talk about such a one and me, and as you know, my husband accused me, from which I defended myself very well, thank heaven, he couldn't eat or sleep for more than three months. And when he was in bed, he did nothing but toss and turn and sigh. Upon my soul, I laughed to myself so hard under the covers that I had to put the sheet in my mouth."

"Alas," another puts in, "what the poor man who ran away must be going through now!"

"Ah dear friend," says the mother, "the guilty party couldn't keep from coming twice to the front of the house, but I ordered him not to come again."

Then the chambermaid says, "Upon my word, I came on him just now near the fountain. He gave me a huge pâté to bring to you and told me that he will send you a pie tomorrow morning, and he sent his best wishes to you and the company. Truly, it's a marvel."

"Alas," says one of them, "what a pitiful thing!"

"Indeed," says another, "We'll eat the pâté for his sake before we leave."

"By Holy Mary," says another, "I wish he could be here."

"Ah Lord," says the maid, "how happy that would make him! He's so nervous he's as pale as death."

"In faith, my dear, let's send for him."

"It's all right with me," answers the mother, "But be sure that he comes in by the back door."

Then perhaps he comes in and they joke and enjoy themselves and shower him with pity and take him into their midst.

Later they send for the good man's chambermaid, who knows all about the matter, was part of it from the beginning, and probably has received a fine dress for her pains.

The maid arrives and one of the women friends asks her, "Tell the truth, Jane, how is your master getting on?"

"Getting on!" she replies, "that's not the right question, for heaven help me, never once since yesterday morning when this dreadful thing happened has he eaten or drunk or rested. In faith, he sat down to table this morning, but he couldn't get anything down, for when he had put a piece of meat into his mouth, he couldn't swallow it and spat it out. And then he fell to thinking at table and was so downcast that he grew as pale and disfigured as a dead man. Next he took his carving knife and drove it into the table and went out into the garden. Then he came back, and he couldn't sit still or control himself, and all day and all night he's been sobbing. It's impossible not to pity him."

"Pity him!" says another. "He'll get over it, God willing. Goodness, dear friend, you've seen others just as sick who are cured, thank the Lord. But truly," she says to the chambermaid, "you're really to blame. You knew what was going on, and your mistress trusted you to keep watch."

"Ah by the Blessed Sacrament, I never thought he'd come back at that time of day, for I'd never seen him play that trick before, curse him!"

"Amen!" they cry.

And so it goes. They joke and make fun of the good man.

Then they decide who shall go first to speak to the good man, who is in his house like a person condemned to be hanged. First come in gaily one or two of his especial women friends and neighbors.

And one, the minute she reaches the threshold cries to him, "What are you doing, my friend?"

He doesn't answer a word, but lets them cross over to him. They come and sit down as close as possible to him and one of them says to him, "How have you been amusing yourself, my friend?"

"Not at all," he replies.

"What do you mean by that? Really." she says, "I'm going to scold you, for my dear friend, your wife's mother, has been telling me I don't know what foolishness, and on my oath, you aren't intelligent if you believe such gossip, for by my soul and body, I'm as certain as I am of dying, and I would swear by all that's holy that she has never done you any wrong or ever intended to."

And another says to him, "By our lady of Puy,* to whom I made a pilgrimage, may it please God, I've known her since she was a baby, and she is the best girl for miles around. Indeed it's a great pity she was ever given to you, for you've defamed her without cause, and you'll never be able to make it up to her."

"I swear it," says the chambermaid, "my dear ladies and friends, I don't know what my lord thought he discovered, but never in my life have I seen anything to reproach in Madam, and I've served her very loyally. It would really have been something if I hadn't known about it."

"In the name of God," says the good man, "I saw her with my own eyes!"

"In faith," retorts one of the women friends, "you did not, whatever you may say. Just because two people are close to each other is no reason to think that they're doing something wrong."

"I know very well," says the maid "that the rascal wanted to go in that direction, but there is no man in the world to whom Madam wishes more evil than to him, and I don't know how he got into the house, for by my share of paradise, he had never been here before, and Madam would like to see him hanged and burned at the stake. I've served you loyally for four years, poor creature that I am, but I would swear on all the holy relics in this town that Madam has behaved toward you as well as the most respectable woman who ever lived.

* Le Puy in southern Auvergne, an important shrine and the object of many pilgrimages.

Ah, woe is me! How could anything have taken place," she says, "without my knowing, if there had been anything bad in it? By my soul, I was as close by as possible. Please to God that I should be as innocent of all my sins as she is of that one, even though no man ever touched my lips save the one I married, who has gone to his reward, may it please God, and I don't fear any man living."

Then the other women friends come in, one after another, and there isn't one who doesn't offer a good argument.

One says, "By the Blessed Sacraments, my friend, I believe I'm one of the women who loves you the most in the world next to your wife, and I swear to you on my honor that if I had seen any wrong in her I would have told you so."

"Upon my honor," says another, "it was the devil who did it to put dissension between them, because he couldn't have harmed them in any other way."

"Alas," says a third, "The poor woman does nothing but cry!"

"By our Lord," says another, "she'll die if she keeps it up."

"And do you think," says another, "that we're so foolish that if she were what you say she is, we'd let her associate with us? By my faith," she says, "not for a moment! We're not so foolish that we would stoop to speak to her or even let her live on our street or anywhere near us."

Next the mother arrives in tears and pounces on him and acts as if she wants to scratch his eyes out and says, "Aha! I curse the hour that she was ever given to you. You've ruined her honor and mine. Alas," she says, "we did you a great favor in giving her to you. If she had wanted to, she could have been married to a fine gentleman and would have had all sorts of honors now, but she wouldn't have anyone but you. Well, it serves her right, the wicked girl, she had it coming to her."

"Ah, my friend," says one of the other women, "don't upset yourself so."

"My friends," she answers, "if my daughter had done any-thing wrong, even though she was my daughter I wouldn't have hesitated to strangle her myself, but do you think it makes me happy to see my daughter shamed without reason and to such an extent that she'll never get over it?"

Then they all begin to scold and to blame him, and the poor man begins to have second thoughts and doesn't know what to do. But in fact, he begins to feel better and to calm down. The mother leaves and the women friends try to soothe him and say that it is no wonder that the mother is angry, and they take it upon themselves to bring back the daughter and take their leave.

Finally there arrives on the scene an old friar who is his confessor and his wife's also. He knows all about what has happened and receives a pension every year for absolving them from everything. He comes to the good man and says, "I was absolutely amazed at what I heard. Indeed, I think you're the one to blame, for I swear by Holy Saint Dominic (or Holy Saint Augustine) I have known your wife for over ten years, but I take it on the peril of my soul that she is one of the most respectable women in all the countryside, and I know it very well, for she is my daughter in confession and I have probed her thoroughly, but I have found nothing but all the virtue a woman can have. Nor has her body ever been tainted by sin, and I offer my own soul as a pledge."

And at last the husband gives in. He repents having gone so far and believes that nothing ever happened. Now let it be known how he'll be repaid for having raised such a fuss. In the future, he will be even more henpecked than before and perhaps will become an object of scorn, for his wife whom he has defamed will be without shame from now on, because she knows very well that what she has done is no longer a secret and nothing will hold her back.

Probably the mother, the women friends, the cousins, and the neighbors, some of whom knew nothing of the problem, will all be on her side from now on, and will help her with the arrangements in the same way that they helped her to pull the wool over her husband's eyes because he had been so headstrong. The suitor will do them many a good turn and bring them many a pie, which they will eat together. But the good man will be the loser, nor will he ever hear a word of what is going on, thanks to the cunning of the womenfolk, for since he will never believe that they would consent to such acts, he will not suspect anything.

He will waste his fortune to maintain them in this manner.

The maid, who knows the whole business perfectly and has worked hard to restore peace, will be as grand a lady as her mistress. She will receive visitors on her own too, and her mistress will be her accomplice, for one good turn deserves another.

Thus he is caught in the net, and whatever he may do, or however his wife may treat him, she will never love him. He will grow old and poor according to the rules of the game. He will waste his life away in pain, suffering, and groaning, in the state where he is and will be always, and will end his days in misery.

Antoine de La Sale (1385?–1460?)

Le Petit Jehan de Saintré

Introduction

Antoine de La Sale was born in the south of France in either 1385 or 1386, the son of a mercenary soldier who had allied himself with the house of Anjou, at that time one of the greatest in Provence. The young Antoine continued in the same service for almost fifty years, making himself useful in a number of military and administrative capacities, chief among which was that of preceptor to Jean de Calabre, eldest son of the illustrious roi René. Then, when he was past sixty, he entered the service of the comte de Saint-Pol, in the province of Burgundy, as tutor to the comte's three sons. It was during these later years that the aging courtier began to supplement his pedagogical activities with literary production. In 1445 there appeared *La Salade*, followed in 1451 by *La Salle*, both collections of edifying anecdotes. In 1456 he completed his *Petit Jehan de Saintré*. His *Réconfort à Madame de Fresne* was sent out the following year, and his *Lettre sur les Tournois* was written in 1459.[1] The last mention of him appears in 1460, when he would have been about seventy-four.

A self-taught author, La Sale seems to have wielded his pen chiefly for didactic purposes, compiling, as had so many medieval scholars before him, strings of learned quotations and homilies, interspersed with narrative, in the hope of effecting some practical or moral improvement in his reader. As a tutor of young princes, he was particularly interested in instilling the virtues of chivalry and courtliness into the young. He had a real gift, however, for narrative prose, and occasionally he broke off his pedantic soliloquies to recount the voyages of his youth or retell the legends and tales he had picked up along the way. In *La Salade*, for instance, he gives one of the first versions of the Tannhäuser myth.

Unlike his other works, which are largely potpourris of

pedagogical wisdom, the *Petit Jehan* represents an attempt at unified narrative fiction. It traces the career and development of a young page in the court of Jean le Bon through the various phases of his career: squire, knight, and courtly lover. The focal point is Jehan's relationship with "La Dame des Belles Cousines" or "Madame," a close relative of the queen, Bonne de Bohême. This young widow singles out the page when he is still a child and places him under her protection. Becoming at once his patroness and preceptor, she instructs him in the art of courtly love and gives him practical lessons in currying court favor, attiring himself as a gentleman, and equipping his horses and men.

The first part of the book is thus chiefly didactic in intent. Jehan is the idealized prototype of all young courtiers, to whom La Sale would like to offer good advice on growing up and taking their place in the world. The work is dedicated in fact to his former pupil, Jean d'Anjou, duc de Calabre. Having traced the education of his young paragon, La Sale then proceeds to describe his illustrious career as a knight, thereby displaying a great knowledge of tourneying, blasonry, and ceremonial etiquette. In these sections, the work is almost devoid of the marks of narrative fiction as we know it today. There is little attempt to delineate character or to create action through conflict, and what realistic description exists tends to be static and overly specific, aimed more at inculcating good taste in the reader than in recreating reality by means of fiction.

At the point where the hero has achieved renown as a crusader, however, the plot suddenly veers unexpectedly away from this dry chronicle. Jehan informs Madame that he has decided to undertake a series of tournaments at the court of Germany and finds, to his astonishment, that his mistress, with whom for the past fifteen years he has maintained the most ideal of relationships, lashes out at him with indignation. Madame thus stands revealed for the first time, not as a selfless ministering angel, but as a willful, domineering female, determined to have her own way at all costs. Jehan remains firm in his resolution to go to Germany, nevertheless, and they part with some bitterness.

At this point our excerpt begins. It shows the great verve and narrative flair La Sale imparted to the second half of his novel. The characters of the Lord of Saintré and Madame take on new dimensions. She becomes wily, hypocritical, sensual, and inexcusably vulgar; he, stern, dignified, unfailingly courteous, but coldly vengeful. In addition, a new character takes his place between them: Lord Abbot, surely the most memorable of shamelessly lecherous monks, who represents not only the debauchery of the dissolute clergy, but the frank, luxury-loving sensualism of the emerging bourgeoisie. Passing from crisis to crisis, the action skilfully alternates suspense and resolution, culminating in the dramatic confrontation between the abbot and the knight. It is a tale of treachery and revenge, but it is also a story of social conflict between the dying ideals of chivalry and the materialism of the middle class. This can be seen most clearly in Lord Abbot's denunciation of the "knights and squires." Although it is obvious that La Sale's deepest sympathies lie with Jehan, he puts his finger unerringly on one of the great problems of his time, the increasing decadence and hypocrisy of the leisured class.

All of this transpires against a vivid background in which the modes of hospitality, means of transportation, churchgoing customs, domestic service, diet, and interior decoration of the period are described in rich detail. The characters of the inconstant lady and the worldly abbot belong to the traditional matter of the novella, but La Sale's treatment of the stock situation is singularly subtle and delicate. Never does he allude to the grosser aspects of the relationship; rather he presents it with the coy discretion of the well-bred gentleman and achieves thereby a higher and more refined brand of humor than that usually called forth in the novella.

The length of the *Petit Jehan de Saintré* made considerable cuts and deletions necessary, in order to include the portion found here. There is good critical and historical precedent for this, however. In the sixteenth century, this section of the novel was included in the *Comptes du monde adventureux*.[2] Moreover, in his classic work on fifteenth-century fiction, Söderhjelm classifies this episode as a "nouvelle" complete in itself. Thus although technically the *Petit Jehan* is a novel rather than a novella, this excerpt belongs by theme and literary method to the tradition studied here and its omission would have left a serious gap in this anthology.

Since La Sale spent his life among the artistocracy, his style is courtly and pedantic rather than colloquial, and his characters speak with none of the fluent abandon which pours so delightfully through the pages of a work like the *Quinze Joies*. We have tried therefore to reproduce the aristocratic flavor of the work and its slightly stilted tone. We hope that we have managed to maintain one of La Sale's unique contributions to narrative technique, however, the individualized speech patterns of each of the three protagonists.

Notes for Introduction

1. The theory that he was also the author of the *Quinze Joies* and the *Cent Nouvelles nouvelles* is generally discounted by modern scholars. See especially William P. Shepard "The Syntax of Antoine de La Sale." *PMLA*, 20 (1905): 435–501, and edition by Jean Rychner, *Les Quinze Joies de mariage* (Geneva: Droz, 1963), pp. l–liii.

2. It is interesting to note, however, that this later adaptation underscores the change in tastes by divesting itself of most of the didacticism of the original. (See Gabriel Pérouse, "*Les Comptes du monde adventureux* et le roman de *Jehan de Saintré*," *Bibliothèque d'Humanisme et Renaissance*, 30 (1968): 461–462.

Text Used

ANTOINE DE LA SALE. *Jehan de Saintré*. Edited by Jean Misrahi and Charles Knudson. Geneva and Paris: Droz, 1965.

Selected Critical Bibliography

CHOLAKIAN, PATRICIA F. "The Two Narrative Styles of A. de La Sale." *Romance Notes*. 10, 2 (1969): 1–11.

COVILLE, ALFRED. *Le Petit Jehan de Saintré; recherches complémentaires*. Paris: Droz, 1937.

DESONAY, FERNAND. *"Le Petit Jehan de Saintré." Revue du XVIᵉ siècle.* 14 (1927): 1–48 and 213–280.

NÈVE, JOSEPH. *Antoine de La Salle; sa vie et ses ouvrages.* Paris: Champion, 1903.

PÉROUSE, GABRIEL A. *"Les Comptes du monde adventureux* et le roman de *Jehan de Saintré." Bibliothèque d'Humanisme et Renaissance.* 30 (1968): 457–469.

SHEPARD, WILLIAM P. "The Syntax of Antoine de La Sale." *PMLA* 20 (1905): 435–501.

Le Petit Jehan de Saintré
'THE KNIGHT, THE LADY, AND THE ABBOT'

Madame, who remained alone, without her lover, could take no pleasure in tourneying, jousting, dancing, hunting, or any other form of amusement. And when she saw lovers conversing and diverting themselves together, two by two, all her suffering was renewed in her heart until she fell into a languor. She gave up eating, drinking, and sleeping, until from fasting and sleeplessness, little by little, her high coloring gave way to pallor, which caused much amazement.

Seeing her thus indisposed, pale, and pensive, the queen asked her repeatedly what was the matter.

"My lady, it's nothing," she said. "You know that we women are ill when it suits our fancy."

"Indeed," replied the queen, "and many times when it does not. But truthfuly now, dear cousin, tell us what is the matter and what sort of illness is troubling you and whether we can help you, for you can be sure that we will do all we can wholeheartedly."

"Ah, my sweet, gentle lady, I thank you most humbly."

And that was the end of the conversation.

But the queen, who loved her dearly, did not omit to summon her physician, Master Hugh de Fisol, a very competent doctor and a learned man, who, through the queen learned of her condition and ordered the queen to look to her health, saying that he would visit her in the morning. And so he did.

When Master Hugh had examined her in the morning, he found her body healthy, clear of any sign of illness of the head or fevers or any other sickness, except in the heart, in which there was some sorrow, which if a remedy were not soon found, would put her in danger of death, for this sorrow was impeding all the natural functions connected with her heart, and already they were almost all blocked.

Nevertheless, he comforted her as well as he could and then said to her, "My lady, as regards your body, I find it in good condition with the exception of your heart, and there, if some great secret sorrow is not quickly tended to, you will fall into a deep languor which will be very difficult to cure. Therefore, my lady, rid yourself of this sorrow and I shall take care of the rest."

When Madame heard Master Hugh come so close to the cause of her trouble, she said to him, "Master Hugh, woe is me, I have only one sorrow in my heart, with which by your word alone you can surely help me. And I swear that if it pleased you to do so, I should be forever in your debt and what is more, I would give you a fine coat of the best cloth that is made."

When Master Hugh heard her mention a fine coat, he said with obvious joy, "My lady, I am at your command, for there is nothing in my power that I would not do for you."

"Indeed, Master Hugh," said Madame, "we thank you for that. Doctors are father confessors. What I want to tell you will not bring you dishonor nor harm, therefore I beg you to keep it secret."

"My lady, speak freely, for I give you my oath that no word of it shall ever be revealed."

"Very well, Master Hugh, we tell you that the displeasure and suffering in our heart is nothing but the longing we have to go to see our estates for two or three months. And the need is great, for more than sixteen years have gone by since last we were there, and as a result our affairs have worsened. And we know for certain that if Madame knew that this wish came from us, she would not be happy about it."

"Oho, my lady!" said Master Hugh, "I shall take charge of it, and be of good cheer, for you shall go there and I know exactly the way to do it, but you must keep to your room for three or four days and leave the rest to me."

Master Hugh then went to the queen and said to her, "My lady, I have just been to see Madame your cousin."

"Alas," said the queen, "How is she, Master Hugh?"

"Madame, to tell you the truth, very poorly, and I see only one remedy."

"Alas, what do you say? What remedy?"

"By our Lord, my lady, she must go refresh herself in her native air for two or three months."

"Alas! if she were there, would she be cured?"

"My lady," said Master Hugh, "I hope to God, yes. And I

am going to prescribe food and medicine to make her comfortable."

Without delay the queen went to see Madame, whom she found in bed. Then she comforted her as well as she could, saying especially that she would soon be cured if she were in her native air, as Master Hugh had said, and that for the Lord's sake, she should be cheerful and prepare herself to go wherever she wished for the recovery of her health and cure.

Madame, who did not seek any other medicine but to flee the displeasure her heart felt when she saw the other lovers dancing, singing, playing, and conversing, when she could not do the same until the return of her own perfect love, took comfort from her departure and, in brief, took leave as soon as possible of the king, the queen, and the lords of the court, bade farewell to all, and left. But when she took leave of the queen, the queen only gave her permission to stay away for two months, if she was in good health by then. Thus promising to return, she took leave and started out.

. . . .

. . . [An] abbey, which shall be nameless, had been founded by Madame's forebears, and endowed so richly that at that time it was one of the ten greatest in France. The Lord Abbot at that time was the son of a very rich townsman who by gifts and by the influence of noblemen and through friends at the court of Rome had given so much that his son had been made abbot. He was twenty-five years of age, of large build, strong and adept at wrestling, jumping, javelin throwing, stone throwing and tennis. There was not a monk, knight, squire, or townsman who could measure up to him, when he was in private. What more can I say? So as not to seem lazy, he busied himself with merrymaking, and in addition, he was generous and openhanded with all his possessions, for which he was much loved and admired by all good companions.

When the Lord Abbot heard of Madame's arrival, he was delighted, and at once had one of his wagons loaded with fat saddles of venison, boar's heads and sides, hares, rabbits, pheasants, partridges, fat capons, chickens, pigeons, and a cask of Beaune wine, all of which he sent to be presented to the said lady, begging her to accept them. When Madame saw this fine present, you needn't ask if she was overjoyed and ordered that the man who brought it be entertained and that Lord Abbot be thanked.

At that season Lent was near and at the abbey there were great indulgences on Mondays, Wednesdays, and Fridays during Lent. Seized with great piety, Madame decided to go there, but after the press and crowds of people had passed during the first fifteen days. Then she informed the Lord Abbot that she would be at Mass in his abbey on the morrow to earn the indulgences.

The Lord Abbot, who had never seen her, was overjoyed, and gave orders to adorn the high altar with relics and also the oratory and the chapel where her forebears lay buried. Furthermore, he sent to the town for lamprey, salmon and others of the best fresh and salt water fish which could be found. Then he ordered the stables to be made ready, and likewise had food prepared in various ways, and ordered fires laid in several chambers, for it was still the cold season. And when Madame arrived and stepped down at the gate of the monastery, there were the officials, the most notable monks of the church, who on their knees with the Lord Abbot offered her all the goods of the establishment along with their services, for which Madame thanked them nobly, and when she had made her offering at the high altar, she was led into his chapel to hear Mass.

As they went out at the end of the devotions, there was the Lord Abbot, accompanied by the priors and the convent, who on their knees said to her: "Our most revered lady, you are most welcome in your own house, and we are most joyous and happy that God has given us the grace to see you here. We offer you, as our patroness and foundress, the abbey, its goods and its wealth."

Then Madame said to him, "Abbot, we thank you with all our heart. Indeed, if there were anything which we could do for you and for the entire convent, we should do it most willingly."

Then Madame asked to see the relics. The Lord Abbot arose, having been on his knees, took the heads, arms, and other bones of the holy remains which were there in great plenty, and said:

"My lady, here lies the most valiant prince our founder, who from the first conquests in the Holy Land brought back this head, this hand, and these bones of my lords Saints so and so and so, and my lord his brother gave this finger, these jawbones, and these armbones of my lord Saint so and so and of Saint such and such, thus to be brief, all your ancestors have donated this great number of relics and built this church and a great part of the rest which you see here. And the remainder was built by my predecessors, the abbots, and by the lords and ladies, our neighbors, who lie here."

When Madame had kissed the relics and given a cope and two tunics along with hangings for the high altar, all of fine, soft red velvet and richly brocaded with gold, she decided to go home, and while the carriage horses and the others were eating and they were getting ready to harness up, the Lord Abbot led Madame into his chamber to warm herself. The chamber was neat, well carpeted, hung with tapestries, and glassed with fine windows, as if its owner enjoyed comfort and a good time.

And the latter, a very good host, said to everyone, "Let us go out and leave Madame to warm herself and rest a little in privacy." And so they did.

And when Madame and the women and girls of her company were well warmed and rested, Madame sent to ask if her carriages were ready. Then the Lord Abbot, who had already told his steward that Madame would dine within and that all the food was to be made ready, and asked him to put his hand to it, at these words came towards Madame, and led her into a very nice little dining room, almost like a vestry, well hung with tapestries, strewn with rushes, its windows glassed, and a fine fire burning. And there were three tables covered with marvellously fine linen and a sideboard displaying beautiful, costly plate.

And when Madame saw the tables set up here, she said to the Lord Abbot, "Abbot, do you want me to eat dinner?"

"Dinner?" said he. "And isn't it time, my lady? Look at the clock!" (which he had set forward an hour and a half and which was about to strike noon.)

When Madame heard noon strike, she wanted to depart in haste, and when the Lord Abbot saw that she wanted to depart, he said to her, "My lady, by my oath of fealty, you shall not leave until you have dined."

"Dined?" said Madame. "Certainly I couldn't think of staying, for I have a great deal to do."

"Ho, steward, and you my ladies, will you allow me to be refused this request?"

Then the women and girls and especially the steward, all those who had been fasting and were hungry, thinking that they would dine much better than they usually did at the manor, began to wink and nudge each other, all begging that the Lord Abbot's first request be granted, until finally Madame consented. Then the Lord Abbot, full of joy, gracious, and amiable, quickly fell to his knees and thanked Madame and also the other women and girls. The horses were led back to the stable, at which all the rest of the company, even though they had already broken their fast, were very delighted.

"Now," said Lord Abbot, "My lady, you are in a holy penitential season and in a house ordered to do penance, and therefore do not be surprised if you are received and served very humbly. And what is more, until late yesterday evening, I knew nothing of your coming."

"Abbot," said Madame, "we can only be well taken care of."

Then the Lord Abbot called for water to wash their hands, which was warm rose water, at which Madame and the others were thrilled. Madame wanted Lord Abbot to wash himself first, since he was a prelate, but he really did not want to do so. To end Madame's entreaties, however, he went to wash at the sideboard.

Then the table was set in place and Madame asked Lord Abbot to sit down, to which he replied, "My lady, you are mistress and abbess here, sit down and leave everything to me."

When Madame was seated . . . Lord Abbot, with a napkin tucked under his chin, went to the wine cupboard and had Madame served with sops soaked in white hippocras * and then with Lenten figs roasted in sugar.

Madame begged him repeatedly to sit down, but could not make him do so, for he said, "My lady, don't be angry, I shall

---

* A sweet white wine. The custom of soaking sops in wine may be found in the Bible.

keep the steward company and for this once show him the way."

And when Lord Abbot and the steward arrived and the first dish was served, Madame said to Lord Abbot, "Really, Abbot, if you don't sit down, we shall all get up."

"Very well, my lady, I must and shall obey you."

Madame wanted to push the table back to let him sit down, but Lord Abbot said, "God willing, the table shall never be moved on my account."

Then he had a stool brought and sat facing Madame, a bit lower down. Then he had some white Beaune served, and then three or four kinds of red, which were served to all.

What shall I tell you? Each urged the other to enjoy himself heartily and to drink, so much so that Madame had a better time than she had in ages and while they drank, their eyes, the heart's archers, began, little by little, to shoot from one heart to the other, until their feet, covered by the large tablecloth that hung to the floor, began little by little to touch each other and then to tread on each other. Then Cupid's enflamed dart pierced the heart of first one and then the other until they lost their appetites. Lord Abbot, however, who was the gayest of all, drank first to one and then to the other. What do you want me to tell you? Never was there so jolly an abbot. First he gets up and has his stool carried in front of the ladies and sits there a little while. Then he goes over to the young girls and urges them to eat and to enjoy themselves, then he goes to the chambermaids and drinks to them, and at last returns to Madame and sits down gaily across from her.

Then the archers of love begin to shoot even harder and their feet tread upon each other's even more than before. As for the good cheer of wines, victuals, lampreys, salmon, and many other fish of the sea and of fresh water, which were served, to be brief, I shall pass over them for the moment, in order to go forward and come to the point of the story, which is pleasing.

When the tables were cleared away and the steward and the others had gone to dine, Madame thanked the Lord Abbot for the good cheer he had provided, and walking and talking, they stood at the other end of the room where they conversed gaily until everyone had dined. And while the others were eating, the Lord Abbot had his bed made up with the finest linen so that Madame might rest.

When the steward had dined, Madame sent for the carriages.

"What, my lady!" said Lord Abbot, "Do you want to break the good customs of this place?"

"And what are they?"

"My lady, they are that if any women or girls of rank have dined here, they and their company must go to bed here also, sleeping or waking, be it winter or summer, and if they have supped, for that night I give them my bed chamber and go to lodge elsewhere, and therefore, Madame, you must not refuse to keep the custom of your abbey."

So forceful were the entreaties of Lord Abbot and of the ladies, that Madame graciously decided to maintain this custom. Then Madame went into his bed chamber, where wine and spices were set in readiness.* The door was closed, and Madame rested herself until vespers.

When the ladies and girls were by themselves, Isabel began to speak, saying, "You aren't saying anything, my lady, nor are you other sillies, about Lord Abbot's hospitality and how he has regaled us and feasted us with good wines, fine foods, and good fish aplenty."

"He certainly seems to be a fine man," said Madame.

"What do you mean fine?" says Madame Jeanne, "I've never seen such a charming monk."

"And you, my lady," said Lady Katherine, "You had to be persuaded to stay."

"Ah," said Isabel, "I knew very well by his entreaties it promised to be a good thing, and that he was doing it with his whole heart."

Then as women usually do, the girls all praised together the generosity, the gaiety, and the handsome person of Lord Abbot, so much that they didn't know how to stop themselves. Madame, who had already been smitten by these qualities, and who had forgotten her sorrows said briefly, "He is a *very* fine man."

---

* It was the custom to eat spices, such as candied ginger, with wine in order to increase the sense of thirst.

And while they were still talking so much about Lord Abbot, vespers began to chime and in order to be present, they had to arise without having slept. After vespers had been said and Madame was readying herself to get into her carriage, Lord Abbot took her by the hand and she said, "Abbot, where are you taking us?" "Please, my lady," said Lord Abbot, "allow me to lead you to a trifling snack, for it is time to eat." And so saying, Lord Abbot takes her arm and pressing her hand, leads her down to the lower hall, which was hung with tapestries and heated by a good fire. There a buffet and tables had been spread with salads, cress, vinegar, platters of roasted lampreys, in pies and in their sauce, great soles, boiled, fried, and roasted in orange juice, mullets, barbels, roasted salmons, boiled and in pies, huge plaice, fat carps, platters of crayfish, great, plump eels in jelly with fish sauce, platefuls of various grapes, covered with red, white, and golden jellies, Bourbon tarts, sweet pastries, flans of almond cream, very thickly sugared, apples and pears, both cooked and raw, almonds, sugared and blanched, walnuts in rose water, figs from Morocco, Algiers, and Marseilles, raisins from Corinth and Orthes, and many other things, which for the sake of brevity I do not mention, all set out and arranged as if for a banquet.

Madame, who was fasting and planned to take nothing but some spices and some wine, found the tables decked out in this manner. And since at dinner the treacherous god of love had assaulted her so fiercely that his amorous darts had replaced her desire to eat, now nature's demands must be met, and this gave her such an appetite that she did not need much persuading. When the other ladies in the company saw Madame seated and Lord Abbot opposite her, halfway down the table, they all, or the greater part of them, let themselves be overcome and convinced by the entreaties of Lord Abbot, and also out of duty to Madame and to keep her company, they all sat down at both ends of the table and on either side. To increase their joy, four or five gracious monks sat in their midst. Then you should have seen them eating and drinking in equal measure.

What can I say? No group of people had ever had more joy and merrymaking. But for today, they must finally leave

Lord Abbot, with great regret and many sighs on the part of Madame. As they got into the carriage, Lord Abbot and the priors were there to thank Madame most humbly and to commend to her the church and the convent.

Then Madame said, "We shall see you quite frequently, for we intend to earn our share of your indulgences even more in the future than now," (at which all were quite content) "but as for you Abbot, we ask you to stop your generous gifts of food, for truly you have exaggerated and we can accept no more."

"Very well, my lady, a bit of cinnamon toast soaked in white wine and hippocras, or in Muscatel, in Grenache, in Malvoisie, or in Greek wine, just as you please, after Mass, to keep out the chill, you won't refuse that?"

"Yes I do," said Madame, "for these days, we intend to fast."

"Fast? My lady, for that you won't be giving up fasting, and besides, I shall give you absolution."

And at these words, Lord Abbot mounted his horse and escorted Madam some of the way, after which he took leave of her.

When Lord Abbot had left them and returned to his abbey, all began to vie with each other to see who could praise him the most.

Isabel, who was the merriest, was the first to speak and said laughing, "Oh, my lady, my lady, how I hate you for refusing those good dinners. No one should refuse a good thing when it comes his way."

Then Lady Jeanne said, "What Isabel! you are truly wrong. Madame intends to go there often. Do you expect her to dine there every time?"

Madame Katherine said, "You are both wrong. There is no reason why Madame should dine there every time. On the other hand, I should not blame her if from time to time she should accept his offer, for by my faith, he makes it with an open heart and willingly, if I am not mistaken, and what is more important, I think he is well able to do so. What do you say, my lady, am I not right?"

Madame, who had heard them all out, replied, "It is sufficient to take the wool from the lamb. Therefore I shall confine myself to the cinnamon toast in hippocras and other strange and delicious wines, which ought to be enough for us, for truly we intend to earn all these indulgences, or most of them, for we don't know if we shall have the opportunity again or return here another time."

And in this way, they arrived at the manor.

Madame, whose heart was enflamed with the fire of this new love, did not stop moaning, groaning, and sighing all night, so much did she desire to see Lord Abbot again and to be able to converse with him to her fill. And Lord Abbot, attacked by this same love, due to the sweet and amorous glances they had given to each other, had no rest that night, for the sighing and desires of ardent love kept him from sleeping all night.

And when the much longed-for daylight came, Madame said to her women that in order to earn the indulgences more worthily, she truly wished to confess herself to Lord Abbot, who was a prelate and a man of great devotion it seemed to her.

Then Lady Jeanne said to her, "My lady, that would be a good thing, and for my part, I already did so yesterday." Then Madame had her little page Perrin mount his horse and take word to Lord Abbot that he should come to her at once.

Lord Abbot was quick to obey Madame with all speed. Therefore, when he had made his bow to Madame before all her women, Madame said to him publicly, "Abbot, in order to earn your indulgences more worthily, we are determined to make our confession to a priest."

"Ah, my lady," said Lord Abbot, "now God is with you and, my lady, who is your confessor, so that I may give him some spiritual strength, if need be?"

Then Madame said, "There is no one here more worthy or more capable than you."

"Ah, my lady, that is only because of the crozier, for of all else, I am the most ignorant of anyone."

After these words, Madame went into her dressing room, which was carpeted and well hung with tapestries, and had a good fire, and Lord Abbot followed her devoutly. Then the door was shut and for two hours, in all goodness and honor, she was most repentant and contrite over her good deeds and loyal love.* And without villainy on his part, Lord Abbot confessed her with great gentleness.

And as they went out, Madame went to her chest and took out a very beautiful and large rose-colored ruby, set in gold, and placed it on his middle finger, saying, "My heart, my only thought, my true desire, I accept you as my only love and wed you with this ring."

Then Lord Abbot thanked her as humbly as he could and remembered a folksaying which says, "He who serves and does not serve to the end loses his wages."

Then he gave absolution to Madame and kissed her gently in charity and took leave.

And as he passed through the outer chamber, he said very virtuously to the women and girls, "Don't go inside until she calls you. My sisters and friends, I commend you to God until my return."

For some time Madame remained alone to recover her color, which she had lost in the fervor of her penitence. Her ladies and girls and all her household were waiting to hear Mass so long that the clock struck eleven before Madame called Jeannette and put on her simplest clothes, and, to hide her face better, put on her largest wimple, and in this simple, comely state came out of her room. Her head lowered, her eyes downcast, she went devoutly to Mass and afterward to dinner. And so passed that day.

On the next day, Wednesday, when the indulgences were offered again, Madame returned to the abbey to receive them. Full of joy, Lord Abbot had soaked bread made ready and brought out hippocras and a great variety of strange and exotic wines, white and red herrings, and other foods for the company, and what is more he took special care of the horses.

When Madame had heard Mass, Lord Abbot took her by the arm and led her to his well-heated room, where breakfast was laid out, and when Madame had breakfasted well, Lord Abbot took her saying, "My lady, you must understand that your company will bring us great joy, and therefore I want to show you through my new building."

* An allusion to her love for Jehan.

Then the two of them went from room to room until the ladies did not know where to find them. And when at last they emerged from a secret chamber, Lord Abbot gave Madame a piece of very fine, smooth black velvet, which she sent for secretly later.

And then Madame returned to the great hall of state where they all were and when her women came up to her, she scolded them, pretending to be angry, and saying, "And where have you come from? I told you to follow me and I thought you were doing so, but you prefer to stay by the fireside and eat wine sops than to accompany me!"

"Oh, my lady, by my faith, we could not keep up with you and then we couldn't find you."

"Ah, my lady," said Lord Abbot, "let them be forgiven this time."

Then Madame began to praise highly the building belonging to the Lord Abbot, which she had seen. Then she went out to get into her carriage and there Lord Abbot took leave of her.

What more need I say? Not a week of Lent went by that she did not go devoutly to earn the indulgences, and many times she went to dine privately without much company, also to banquet or to sup, and after her nap she often went to hunt foxes and badgers in the woods or to hunt other forms of amusement, and in this manner she passed her time joyously all through Lent.

Thus it happened that the two months after which she had promised to return to the queen went by without any news of her by letter, or otherwise, whereupon the queen, greatly puzzled, wrote to her in this wise:

[The queen writes that she misses her cousin and is surprised to have had no word from her, and she sends the letter by her secretary, Julien de Broy.]

.   .   .   .

While Madame was at the abbey receiving indulgences, the said Master Julien de Broy, secretary to the queen, arrived and found her seated at table where she was dining, whereupon openly and joyfully, as one of her special friends at court, and expecting to be warmly received, he presented to her the letters from the queen. Madame, who felt nothing but displeasure at his arrival, took the queen's letters with very few words and read them. Then to get rid of him the sooner, she made haste to eat and have the tables cleared.

After which, she left immediately for her manor to write a reply, saying to Master Julien, "Eat and come to me at once."

. . . .

And as he was conversing with the Lord Abbot, [Master Julien] saw on the latter's finger, the large and beautiful rose-colored ruby which he had often seen Madame wearing before. And though he said nothing, nevertheless, he did not think it unimportant. And when he had dined and retained from Lord Abbot's words what he wanted to, he thanked him very heartily, mounted his horse and went to Madame as she had asked him to.

[Madame writes that she is detained by business, and Master Julien delivers a full report of his reception to the queen, who asks him to tell no one of what he has seen.]

. . . .

That month and the next went by and still Madame neither returned to the queen nor wrote to her. Then astonished at this, the queen had other letters similar to the first sent to her. The postrider who was carrying the letters was in haste to return quickly and sought so diligently that he found her in the fields with the Lord Abbot and handed her the letters. Madame, who was to sup there in the fields with Lord Abbot, made a reply in writing, stating that she would be with her shortly. Then the postrider took leave without eating or drinking and almost without saying anything else to her, and made great haste to return.

When the queen had received the letters and read them, and also when he had told her that he had found her in the fields with Lord Abbot, she was saddened and thought what well she might and decided that she would not write to her again, and that she might come when she wished or remain absent as long as she wanted.

Madame, for whom it would have been mortal anguish to leave her good father, said to him, "My only love, as long as I am able to escape and delay, you may be sure that I shall not forsake your most beloved company."

What shall I tell you? A part of the summer passed by in hunting, hawking, fowling, and many other delightful pastimes.

[After a successful sojourn spent tourneying at the court of the German emperor, Saintré returns to France.]

.   .   .   .

When they [Saintré and his company] came before the king, he received them with great merrymaking, as did the queen, the other lords, ladies and girls, as well as the rest of the court. Thus, to be brief, when all had greeted them, and they had rested a bit, the Lord of Saintré, quite astonished and amazed that he did not see Madame, since she was the one he most desired to see in all the world, wondered if she were ill. Therefore he went to Madame de Sainte More, his cousin, and letting one thing lead to another, as if he had no particular plan, he said, "Oh, by the way, cousin, now that I think of it, is Madame sick, since she isn't here?"

"Madame?" said she. "She is certainly ill in the queen's heart, for she has pissed in her silken vest. About three weeks or a month after you left, she took sick and wasted away before our eyes, so badly that according to the queen's physician, she was about to fall into a consumption or die if she were not restored by her native air. Then the queen granted her leave for two months and at the end of two and a half months, since she hadn't returned, the queen sent letters by Julien de Broy to remind her of her promise, and after another two months, she wrote to her again, and always she replied, 'I am coming, I am coming,' and she has yet to come."

When Milord of Saintré heard that she was sick in this way, he thought of the things she had told him, that her heart could know no joy until he returned, and he thought, as indeed was the case, that she had gone away to forget the sorrows of love. Then he was somewhat more lighthearted than he had been, for he supposed that she did not yet know of his arrival and that as soon as she learned of it she would return. But it really would be more suitable if he went to see her, before her return, so that he could converse with her more at leisure.

So he thought this over for ten or twelve days and then said to the king, "Sir, if it were your good pleasure to give me leave to go and see my mother for eight or ten days, I should like to beg it of you most humbly, for she has sent for me."

The king said to him, "How is this, Saintré? Can't you stay? But since your mother has sent for you, we give you leave for a month."

And when the Lord of Saintré had thanked him, he worked night and day to clothe his servants, himself, and his horses, in order that he might seem more romantic and pleasing to her who had all his heart. Then he took leave of the king, the queen, and my lords, and did not stop until he had arrived in the good town a league from Madame's manor. There he dined, then . . . accompanied by two knights and twelve of his household squires, all very well turned out in matching robes bearing Madame's emblem, he came to see her at her manor. And when he was at the door, he told the porter that he should inform Madame that Milord of Saintré had come.

"Indeed," said the porter, "Madame went to the abbey this morning, to hear Mass and dine there."

Then he went on to the abbey and found that Madame and Lord Abbot, after eating and sleeping, had gone hunting with the hawks.

Then he asked to be shown where he could find them and, when he had gone a little distance, he called four or five of his men and said to them, "Spur your horse in that direction, and you go that way, and you the other way, and if you see any ladies on horseback, come and tell me."

Then each went into the fields and it was not long before one of them came running and said, "My lord, I saw about twenty horses and there are six or eight well-dressed ladies and girls."

Then the good knight, who still knew or imagined nothing of Madame's false love, went as fast as his horse could gallop, thinking the moment would never come when he could see his most beautiful and desired lady. And when he saw her, his heart burst with joy. Therefore, handsome as were he and all his men, he spurred on his fine-spirited charger straight towards her. There one of Lord Abbot's monks saw them and he went to Lord Abbot and told him of it.

When Lord Abbot, who was riding alongside Madame, saw

the horses galloping towards him, if any man felt self-assured, it was not he, for he thought that they were some relatives of Madame's, who had been informed of their love and wanted to do violence to his habit. Therefore he kicked his mule and turned quickly to one side, and with his hawk on his arm and three monks who were bearing some huge bottles and the basket containing the refreshments, he kept himself out of the way, as if he did not dare to approach Madame. And the fact is, he abandoned her.

Mounted on her high hackney with her hawk on her fist, Madame waited quietly with her attendants to see who these people might be, and when her servants recognized the Lord of Saintré, she said, "May God send bad luck to every one of you! Must you make such a fuss for one man?"

And as she was speaking these words, the Lord of Saintré, his heart bursting with joy, dismounted quickly.

When Madame saw him on the ground, she said to him so loudly that several heard her, "Ha sir, you are most unwelcome!"

The Lord of Saintré, who had not heard these words, knelt down joyfully and touched her hand saying, "Oh, my most revered lady, how are you?"

"How am I?" she said, "Is it necessary to ask about what can be seen? Don't you see that I am on my hackney and holding my hawk?"

Then she turned her hackney and called to her hounds to begin hunting as if she took no account of him and scorned him.

Hearing Madame's cruel reply, the Lord of Saintré did not know what to think, but as the ladies and girls passed by, he touched each of their hands and embraced and kissed them. Then he mounted his horse and went after Madame. And then each one came to bow to him and to greet him.

And when he had come up to Madame, he said to her sorrowfully, "Alas, my lady, are you in earnest or are you testing me, that you have given such a lukewarm welcome to me, who has loved you so and who has never disobeyed you. My lady, has anyone told you the contrary? If anyone has, you shall see the truth."

Madame, who found his presence and all he said displeasing, said to him, "Don't you know how to sing any other tune? If not, be still."

And while these words were passing between them, Lord Abbot was reassured and had one of his monks ask the steward who this lord was, and when Lord Abbot heard that it was the Lord of Saintré, he came forward to greet him and said, "Most honored lord, you and your handsome company are most welcome, for upon my faith, I had a greater desire to see you than any other lord on this earth."

The Lord of Saintré, who understood by these words and by the monks who were standing behind him that this was the abbot, said to him, "Lord Abbot, I am happy to meet you and your company."

"My lord," said Lord Abbot, who was now completely reassured, "and what have you to say about my most revered lady, who has stooped so low as to show patience with her poor monk and to come hunting with him?"

"Madame," replied the Lord of Saintré, "acts as an honorable and respected lady, and it is an honorable occupation to pass one's time enjoyably, and what is more she has always loved the holy church."

At these words, Lord Abbot drew away step by step and left Madame and the Lord of Saintré together, and since vespers had already been rung, he started toward the manor and sent one of his monks to the steward asking whether he knew if Madame would invite the Lord of Saintré to supper. The steward went up to Madame and told her what Lord Abbot had asked. Madame, who did not hear well the first time, asked him what he was saying.

Then he repeated it so loudly that the Lord of Saintré heard him, and when Madame had understood, she thought for a moment and then said to him, "Tell him to do as he wishes, but not to twist his arm with too much begging."

The Lord of Saintré, who had heard all this and understood the matter very well, decided privately that they would not have to twist his arm, but that to play them one better, he would accept their very first invitation. Madame, who was annoyed by her first love, said that she was tired and that they should head back to the manor. Lord Abbot, who was a gracious host, was there before them and had everything in readiness.

Having dismounted, the Lord of Saintré wished to help Madame to dismount, but she called for one of her servants.

When they were all on foot, the Lord of Saintré wanted to take leave of Madame, but while she was giving him her hand, Lord Abbot said to Madame, to show his good manners, "Are you letting him leave?"

"That is up to you and him," she said.

Then the Lord Abbot said to him, "Really, my Lord of Saintré, can't you tarry awhile with Madame? I beg you to stay."

Then the Lord of Saintré said to Lord Abbot, "My Lord Abbot, I do not wish to disobey or to refuse your very first request."

Then the Lord of Saintré retained two squires, a valet, and a page, no more, and sent the rest of his company back to the town for supper and told his steward to return to him soon at Madame's manor. After the tables were set and the supper made ready, Madame washed her hands alone and Lord Abbot and the Lord of Saintré afterward. Then by order of rank, Lord Abbot was seated at the high end of the table, facing Madame with his back against the bench, then Madame, then the Lord of Saintré, Lady Jeanne, and finally Lady Katherine.

. . . And when their bellies were somewhat filled, at the moment when tongues begin to loosen, Lord Abbot began to rouse himself and said, "Ho, my Lord of Saintré, wake up! wake up! I drink to your thoughts and what are they? All you do is think."

Then the Lord of Saintré said to him, "My Lord Abbot, I am doing combat with so much good food and wine, which I see before me, that I don't have the leisure to do anything else."

"My Lord of Saintré," said Lord Abbot, "Don't you know, I have often wondered if it is so that among you noblemen, knights and squires, who so often do feats of arms, and when you return, you say you have won. . . ." Then he turned to address Madame and said to her, "My lady, isn't it so?"

"Truly, Abbot, you are speaking the truth and how could it be otherwise? Fine sir, tell us your thoughts."

"My lady, said Lord Abbot, "do you really want me to speak out? It shall be with your leave and by your command. I don't know whether my Lord of Saintré won't be offended, but since you wish it, my lady, my thoughts are these:

"There are many knights and squires in the courts of the king, the queen, and also of the other lords and ladies and such like, who say they are the loyal servants of the ladies, and in order to win your favors, if they don't have them, they weep before you, sighing and moaning and making themselves so sorrowful that out of pity, you poor ladies, who have tender and sympathetic hearts, are necessarily deceived and fall prey to their desires and into their nets. Then they go from one to the other taking as a token a garter, a bracelet, a ring, or a trinket, what do I know, my lady? And then one of them tells ten or twelve of you, 'Ah, my lady, I am carrying this token for love of you.' Oh! Poor ladies, how you are abused by your lovers, many of whom do not in this case have any loyalty towards their ladies. Then the king and the queen and all the lords praise them and fuss over them and give them generous gifts, which they use very well for their own benefit. Now isn't this true? My lady, what do you think?"

Madame, who was delighted to hear this, said to him with a smile, "And who told you so, abbot? For my part, I think it is that way." And while she was speaking, she put her foot on Lord Abbot's.

"Again, my lady, I shall tell you more. When these knights and squires go to their deeds of arms and have taken leave of the king, if it is cold, they go to the stoves of Germany, where they amuse themselves with the girls all winter long, and if it is hot, they go to the delightful kingdoms of Sicily and Aragon, to those good wines and good foods, to those fountains and good fruits, and to those beautiful gardens, and all summer long they feast their eyes on those beautiful ladies and also the gentlemen, who entertain them well and honor them. Then they have an old musician or trumpeter, wearing an old tunic [with their coat of arms] and they give him one of their old robes and cry to the court, 'My lord has won! My lord has won! He has earned the prize of arms!' And you poor ladies, aren't you taken advantage of? Upon my faith, I pity you."

Madame, who was as delighted as could be by these words, turned her head a little and said to the Lord of Saintré, "What have you to say, Lord of Saintré?"

The Lord of Saintré, very displeased with the attacks and insults which Lord Abbot had made on the gentlemen, said to Madame, "If it pleased you to take the side of the gentlemen, you know just the opposite very well, my lady."

Then Madame said, "We have certainly seen some who didn't act this way, but what do we know of the others? For our part, we share the abbot's opinion." And as she spoke, she put her foot on the abbot's, smiling and winking at him.

"Aha, my lady," said the Lord of Saintré, "now you speak as you wish, therefore I pray that God may give you perfect knowledge."

Lord Abbot said, "And what knowledge do you want Madame to have, besides the truth of the case?"

"The truth?" said the Lord of Saintré, "My lord Abbot, to the words of Madame I say nothing. She may say what she pleases. But I reply to you, who have accused the knights and squires, that if you were a man whom I could answer, you would find out who you are talking to, but on account of your dignity and Him to whom you belong, I shall say nothing more, and perhaps sometime you will remember this."

Lord Abbot, who was alight with love's fire, said jokingly to Madame, "My lady, it's because of you that I am being threatened in your home."

And while he spoke, the war of the feet went on without stopping, and when he saw Madame smiling and winking, he knew that Madame was well pleased with the game, so he said, "Ha, my lord of Saintré, I am not a fighter or a man of arms to combat you. I am a poor, simple monk, who lives on what I have, for God's love. But if there were a man, whoever he might be, who would contradict me on this point, I would fight with him on that account."

"Would you?" said Madame immediately, "would you be so daring?"

"Daring, my lady? I only know how to wrestle, but I trust in God and my good and just grievance that I would get the upper hand. Now! Is there any man here, among all these warriors who will take up my challenge?"

Hearing the outrageous words of Lord Abbot, which seemed to stab him straight through the heart, and even more so because of the favor Madame showed him, the Lord of Saintré wished he were dead.

Madame, who saw that he said nothing, said to him, "Ha, Lord of Saintré, you who are so valiant and have done so many fine deeds of arms, it is said, wouldn't you dare to wrestle with the abbot? Truly, if you don't, I shall say that he is right."

"Alas, my lady," he replied, "you know that I have never been a wrestler, and these lordly monks are masters of the art, as well as of tennis, throwing javelins, stones, iron weights, and all sorts of tests, in private, and for this reason, my lady, I know very well that I should be powerless against him."

"And I ask you to do it," said Madame. "Now I shall see if you will go against me, and by faith, if you refuse, I shall hold you up to reproof everywhere as a very fainthearted knight."

"Oh, what are you saying, my lady? I have done a good deal more for a certain lady, but since this is how it is, I shall do your bidding."

"What did he say?" said Lord Abbot.

"He said," replied Madame, "that he will not fail you and that he has accomplished greater feats."

"Did he really, my lady? Well, we shall see."

Then without waiting longer or clearing anything from the tables, Lord Abbot gleefully sallied forth from the table, then Madame and the Lord of Saintré, at which the others were amazed.

Then Lord Abbot took Madame aside and led her into a fine courtyard, from which the sun had passed, and said to her, "My lady, sit here under this fine, flowering hawthorne and be our judge."

And Madame seated herself, as happy as could be, and made her women sit near her. But although they tried not to show it, there was little of what they saw that pleased them.

Then Lord Abbot did what neither Saint Benedict, Saint Robert, Saint Augustine, nor Saint Bernard, all prelates of the holy church, would ever have done in their lives. In public, he stripped down to his doublet, detached his hose, which in those days were not all in one piece, and rolled them down below his knees. After which he came first to stand before Madame, and having made his bow, he ran around laughing, jumping into the air, showing off his great thighs, as rough and hairy as a bear's.

Next came the Lord of Saintré, who had undressed at one end of the courtyard, his hose being richly embroidered with large pearls, and he made his bow to Madame, concealing the very bitter sorrow in his heart.

Then they were face to face, but before the match had begun, Lord Abbot turned to Madame and knelt on one knee in mockery, saying, "My lady, with clasped hands I beg you to recommend me to my Lord of Saintré."

Madame, who knew very well the strength of the abbot, smiled and said to the Lord of Saintré, "Ah, Sire of Saintré, I recommend to you your abbot and beg you to spare him somewhat."

The Lord of Saintré, who knew perfectly well that they were mocking him said, "Ah, my lady, I shall have greater need to be recommended to him."

After these words, Lord Abbot and the Lord of Saintré laid hold on each other and circled around once or twice. Then Lord Abbot stretched out his leg and crooked it around the Lord of Saintré's, then suddenly let go and picked him up so that the Lord of Saintré's feet were quite a bit higher than his head, then threw him down on the green grass and holding him under him, Lord Abbot cried out to Madame, "My lady, my lady, intercede for me with the Lord of Saintré!"

Then laughing heartily, Madame said to him, "Ah, Sire of Saintré, have pity on the abbot." But she was so full of joy and laughing so hard that she could hardly speak.

When Lord Abbot got once more to his feet and came laughing to Madame, she said to him, "Again, do it again!"

Then Lord Abbot said to Madame so loudly that the Lord of Saintré and everyone else could hear, "My lady, I did this to prove my point as God and Love have been my witnesses, but if the Lord of Saintré wanted to maintain that he loved his lady more loyally than I do mine, here I am, a simple and feeble monk who would combat him in such a contest."

"Would you?" said Madame.

"Would I? Yes, by our Lord, against all those who approach me."

Then laughing, Madame said to the Lord of Saintré, "What do you say to this, fine sir? Wouldn't any gentleman of heart answer this?"

"My lady," answered the Lord of Saintré, "any gentleman of heart would reply to his equal, and in a manner befitting the circumstances."

"These are excuses," said Madame. "That is how you tried to get out of the other match. He has been right to reproach the heart of a gentleman who does not dare to uphold his loyalty in a wrestling match. Truly, I think that whoever searched you thoroughly would not find much loyalty there."

"Alas, my lady," said the Lord of Saintré, "and why do you say that?"

"I say it because you feel you are wrong, and you are."

Then the Lord of Saintré said, "Now I see very well, my lady, that we must recommence the contest and that there is no excuse, no matter how reasonable, which can dissuade you, and since it is your pleasure, I am happy for it."

Lord Abbot, who heard all these things, said by way of a joke, "Oh, my lady, I wouldn't dare to, for without the just cause that I had, he would have overwhelmed me and thrown me down, for I found such strength in him that it is no wonder that he has vanquished so many men. Since I have taken on the quarrel, however, I want to sustain it. And now stand back! Stand back!"

And everyone withdrew and Lord Abbot, who was unleashed and had lost all self-control and good sense, began to cry, "Aha, loyalty, defend your rights!"

And at these words, he came at the Lord of Saintré with a trick turn and almost tripped him, but they turned and swayed until with another throw, even stronger than the first, he knocked down the Lord of Saintré and then said, "My lady, our judge, have I done my duty well? Who is the more loyal?"

"Who is it?" said Madame, "It is you who have won."

The poor Lord of Saintré could not say a single word, because of the wrestling match and the great pleasure Madame had taken not only in it, but in seeing him the weaker and less skillful in wrestling. Then each went to get dressed. The two squires who had stayed to serve him thought they would die of grief when they saw that Lord Abbot and Madame were joking and making fun of the Lord of Saintré, who was such an honorable and valiant knight that his equal could not be found in the kingdom of France, and they said to him, "You won't be a man if you do not avenge yourself for this great insult."

But he replied, "Don't worry yourselves. Be patient like me, and let me take care of it."

The Lord of Saintré, who had lost entirely, and in such a false way, the love of his lady by her own dishonesty, the one whom he had served so long and faithfully, was of a well-disciplined nature and bore himself as if nothing had happened.

Then with a great show of joy, he redoubled the gaiety of Madame and Lord Abbot and said to them, "Alas, my lady, what a pity it is that such a fine and powerfully built man as my lord the Abbot has never been put in arms and sent to guard the frontier against the enemies of this kingdom, for I do not know two or three men, no matter how strong, whom he could not put to shame."

Hearing such praise, Lord Abbot jumped into the air and made a great circling leap in front of Madame and her company. Then he ordered wine and cherries to be brought for refreshment.

[The priors and older monks send a delegation to reprimand Lord Abbot for his undignified and discourteous behavior. To make amends Lord Abbot offers gifts to the Lord of Saintré, who refuses everything, asking only that the abbot and Madame come to dine with him on the morrow. Saintré then orders two sets of armor to be brought to his lodgings.]

.   .   .   .

And when the night had passed and the day come, the Lord of Saintré heard Mass. All his baggage and all his servants departed except the twelve that he retained. The food for the dinner was readied and the tables laid. Then he mounted his horse, with all his company, and went ahead to Madame, and when he had traveled about half the distance, he found Madame and Lord Abbot in the fields.

Then they greeted each other courteously and Lord Abbot

began by saying, "Ho there! If you speak of the wolf, you will see his tail. Aren't your ears burning, my Lord of Saintré?"

"I can't say," replied the Lord of Saintré, "for I was thinking of how your patience must be tried. Have you had any breakfast, my lady, or have you, my Lord the Abbot?"

"Yes," answered Madame, "being in doubt about your broths, we breakfasted on toast soaked in hippocras and Duke's Powder." *

"May it do you much good, my lady, and you too, my Lord the Abbot."

As all three conversed together, the words of Madame were always addressed to the abbot. Seeing that his words were wasted, the Lord of Saintré drew in his bridle and tried to speak to Lady Jeanne, but she told him to ride behind her. Next he went to Lady Katherine, then to Lady Isabel, but they all told him the same thing, for all had been forbidden to speak to him. Then the Lord of Saintré turned back to Madame and in a short while they arrived at his lodgings.

Then the Lord of Saintré took Madame's arm and led her with her women to a room and led Lord Abbot to another, and while they were resting in their rooms, he told his steward that as soon as they were at table, the horses should be saddled and bridled in the stable and made ready to mount. Then, to be brief, all was ready for the dinner.

And when Madame and Lord Abbot had washed their hands, and Lord Abbot was seated at the head of the table, as befitted a prelate, and a little farther down was Madame, who could not bear to be very far from him, and then the other ladies at the lower end, Saintré, despite entreaties, refused to be seated, but put a napkin on his shoulder and went up and down serving the good wines and the plentiful dishes of all sorts. What more can I say? One could hardly describe the pleasure that Lord Abbot derived from the Lord of Saintré.

And when all the bellies had been well filled and stuffed and the gullets well sprinkled and the thirst quenched, the

---

* A fine dish prepared with cinnamon and sugar. It was purported to have aphrodisiac qualities, thus making Madame's reply doubly insolent.

Lord of Saintré asked Lord Abbot if he had ever been armed.

"Armed?" said Lord Abbot. "No, indeed."

"Oh, Lord," said the Lord of Saintré, "What a fine thing it would be to see you armed. And what do you say, my lady, isnt that true?"

"Truly," said Madame, "I do believe and in fact I am certain that if he were armed, there are some who mock him now who would be the worse for it."

"Madame, I don't know anyone who mocks him, but I vow that I have never seen a man who would look better in armor."

Thereupon he told Perrenet, his manservant, to do as he had told him. Then Perrenet set up a table at the end of the room and placed upon it a very large suit of armour without either an axe or a sword.

And when Lord Abbot saw this beautiful, shiny armour, which gave him great pleasure, and heard himself praised so lavishly, he thought that the Lord of Saintré meant to give him the armour out of generosity, and that for that reason, he had ordered it brought in. Therefore he decided that if he were asked to arm himself, he would certainly not refuse. Then to show how much he liked the armour, he began to praise it greatly.

"Since it is to your liking," said the Lord of Saintré, "you shall surely have it, if it is your size."

"Really, my lord?"

"Yes, Lord Abbot, and something even better if you request it from me."

"By my faith! And for the love of Madame, I shall neither eat nor drink until I am armed." Then he cried, "Take away these tables, take them away! We have eaten too much already."

Lord Abbot, overcome with joy, stripped to his doublet, and thereupon the Lord of Saintré took a bodkin and plenty of laces and completely armed the body and legs of Lord Abbot and clamped the bassinet tightly to his head and put the gauntlets on his hands.

And when Lord Abbot was thus completely armed, he turned first one way and then the other, strutting around, saying to Madame and her ladies, "What do you think to see this monk armed? Does he look good?"

"Monk?" said Madame, "Such monks are few and far between."

"Ha, by God, if only I had an axe and someone to fight with me!" Then jokingly, "Ho, my lady, this armour really weighs more than my own, but it will do for me since I have won it."

But as he spoke these words, the Lord of Saintré said, "You have not won it yet, but you shall win it soon." Then he had the other harness brought in and was soon armed in it.

When Madame heard these words and saw the Lord of Saintré quickly arming himself, she suspected what was coming. She said to him, "Sire of Saintré, what do you intend to do?"

"My lady," said he, when he was ready, "you shall soon see."

"I shall see?" said Madame, "Sir cuckold, do you intend to fight an abbot?"

The Lord of Saintré, being completely armed, commanded his servants to guard the door and to prevent anyone from entering or leaving the room and said to the women, girls, monks, and all the others present, "Stay over there by that door, and if any man or woman makes a move or says a word, I'll cleave his skull down to his teeth!" Then the women and monks could be seen trembling with terror and cursing the hour that they had assembled there.

Then he came to Madame and said to her, "You graciously consented to be the judge of the wrestling match between Lord Abbot and me. Now I humbly beg you to be the judge of the fighting for which I have been trained and to join me in fulfilling Lord Abbot's request."

"I don't know what request you mean," said Madame. "If you harm him in any way, I shall consider it an injury to myself and you'll have to answer to me."

The Lord of Saintré came to Lord Abbot and said to him, "Lord Abbot, at your request and Madame's I wrestled twice with you, two trips and falls which I can still feel, and no excuse helped me against her request and yours that I go through with it. Now I ask and beg you, for the love of the woman whom you love so loyally, to fight with me in the manner in which I have learned to fight."

"But my Lord of Saintré," said Lord Abbot, "I wouldn't know how to fight armed."

Then the Lord of Saintré said, "You shall go through with it or go through the window."

Madame, who saw that in all events, the Lord of Saintré was resolved and determined to fight, said to him treacherously, "Sire of Saintré, we wish and command you, upon pain of falling into our disfavor, to disarm both of you immediately, and if you do not, we shall make your body and soul suffer punishment and anger as a fool and as a cuckold."

When the Lord of Saintré saw himself thus reviled and threatened for the sake of Lord Abbot and his love, he said to her, "Now false, faithless, so and so that you are, I served you very loyally for a great length of time, as well as any man could ever serve and please a woman, and now for a ribald monk, whom you happened to meet, you have thus falsely and faithlessly dishonored yourself and abandoned me. And so that you may remember that you have no right to revile or threaten me for him or anyone else, I shall give you . . . nothing less than you deserve, to make you an example for other faithless women."

With that he took her by the top of her headdress and raised his hand to strike her, but suddenly remembering the kind deeds that she had done for him and knowing that he could be blamed for it, he restrained himself. Then he made her, weeping and nearly fainting with grief, sit down on the bench, from which she did not dare to move.

Then he had brought two axes, two swords, and two daggers which he girded on Lord Abbot and put into his hands so that he could take his choice. Then he said to him, "Lord Abbot, Lord Abbot! Remember how you insulted the knights and squires who go doing battle throughout the world to add to their honor, for you shall atone for it! Now, Lord Abbot, defend youself!" Then he lowered his visor and had Lord Abbot's lowered and set upon him.

When Lord Abbot saw that he was obliged to fight and to counterattack, he raised his axe with such force that, if he had struck the Lord of Saintré, considering his strength and power

Le Petit Jehan de Saintré

"Then he pierced his tongue and his two cheeks with his dagger. . . ."

[From ms. Cotto Nero DIX, folio 103 (r°), miniature number 6, reproduced by permission of the British Museum, London.]

and also his advantage in height, he would have knocked him to the ground or wounded him, which would have well pleased Madame; but by the will of God and by the skill he had learned in such feats of arms, he covered himself and received the blow with his axe. And thereupon the Lord of Saintré struck at him with the point of his axe and forced him to draw back to a bench opposite Madame, where he tumbled over backwards, falling with such force that everything seemed to come clattering down, and cried "Mercy, mercy, mercy, my lady! Oh, my lord of Saintré, for the love of God, mercy!"

[Calling to mind the words of the Bible, Saintré restrains himself from killing Lord Abbot.]

. . . .

Nevertheless, in order to avenge himself and by the divine will, which would have permitted him to punish him in this way because of such an obvious and manifest sin, he threw away his axe, took his dagger in his hand, and then raising his visor, he said to him, "Now, Lord Abbot, know that God is a true judge, for your strength and your false, evil, and insulting speech have not had the power to keep you from being punished in the presence of the lady before whom you vaunted yourself and before whom you have lied so dishonestly and maligned the knights and squires. And for that, this very false tongue shall pay." Then he pierced his tongue and his two cheeks with his dagger and left him in that condition, saying to him, "Lord Abbot, now you have justly won the armour."

Then he had himself disarmed, and when he was completely out of his armour, he saw Madame with her hair undone and her clothes all in disarray and he said to her, "Farewell, lady, the most false who ever lived." And as he was speaking, he saw that she was wearing a blue belt shot through with gold. This he unfastened saying, "And how, my lady, have you the heart to wear this blue belt? The color blue stands for loyalty, and truly you are the most disloyal woman I know. You shall wear it no more."

Thus he unfastened and took off the belt, folded it and put it into his bosom. Then he went to the women and girls, the monks and other people who stood in the corners of the room, wailing like sheep, and said to them, "You were witnesses of what was said and done, which to my great sorrow is the cause of my having done what I did, and as to the unpleasantness which you have experienced and are experiencing, forgive me for it, I beg of you, and may God be with you."

Then the door was opened and he went downstairs and said to the landlord, "If Lord Abbot wants the large suit of armour, you are to give it to him, but the smaller one and the two axes are to be returned to Jacquet, and tell him to come to me soon. Fair host, are you well satisfied?" And so saying, he mounted his horse and commended the landlord to God.

.   .   .   .

Les Cent Nouvelles Nouvelles (1456–1462)

Introduction

Two of the most important prose fiction pieces of the fifteenth century are anonymous, *Les Quinze Joies de mariage* and *Les Cent Nouvelles nouvelles*. In the case of this latter work, the question of authorship is further complicated because the unique Glasgow manuscript and the early Vérard editions seem to attribute the collected stories to some thirty-five different authors, most of whom have been identified as real persons belonging to the court of Philippe le Bon, Duke of Burgundy. Only five tales (61, 91, 92, 98, 100) bear the designation of "acteur.' Certainly, it is not within the scope of this brief essay to prove or disprove whether he was, as many have believed, Antoine de La Sale.[1] Suffice it to say that the unified style of the entire collection would suggest that the "acteur" did more than simply add his own contributions to the other ninety-five stories.

In summary, we can assert quite safely that sometime between 1456 and 1462 (dates based essentially on internal evidence), an educated courtier, probably in the hire of Philippe le Bon, produced for his "très redoubté Seigneur" (highly respected Lord) a collection of stories which he entitled *Les Cent Nouvelles nouvelles* in imitation of the famous Italian counterpart, and that he justified the use of his qualifying adjective by asserting that "the material, the form and manner thereof, is of rather recent recollection and of a very new style."

Just how "new" these stories really are, however, is subject to some question. Our first story, "The Self-Made Cuckold" (9), is, to be sure, one of the countless variations on the theme of adultery. Nonetheless there is something new and interesting here, even in the context of the typical *Cent Nouvelles nouvelles* tales. As a rule, the *Cent Nouvelles nouvelles* is neither pedagogical like the *Petit Jehan de Saintré* nor mockingly didactic like the *Quinze Joies de mariage*. Although writing for the aristocracy, the author implies a criticism of that class in his denouement. It is perhaps psychologically understandable that the lord of the castle should blame the young girl in order to free himself of guilt, but the ungrateful attitude of her ladyship seems unjustifiably cruel.

In "The Miracle of the Snow Child" (19), fantasy and bourgeois commercialism blend in a tale which offers the reader a rare opportunity to witness that the scheming wife does not always have the last word. Once again, the dialogue gives evidence of an author who can manipulate the subtle nuances of ironic understatement and dramatic tension, as when, for example, the husband takes such obvious delight in prolonging his story of revenge.

As for the third story, "The Voice from on High" (34), we have a stock situation, for the main characters are time-worn figures: the cuckolded husband, the deceiving wife, and the lovers. And yet the author does manage to add a new dimension to the old story with his remarkable use of dialogue in the passage where the guilty wife and the wrathful husband exchange insults, while the two lovers cower in their separate hiding places.

As we have seen already, the characteristic narrative technique here is to take an old theme and try to give it a new twist. The "Prisoner of Love" (61) is a particularly successful example of this method, for the author's whole aim is to lead us up to the dramatic exit of the braying jackass.

It would be dishonest not to include from the *Cent Nouvelles nouvelles* some example of that coarser brand of farce so much a part of the Gallic traditions of humor. "Holy Pilgrimage" (93) brings together once again that unholy alliance between sensual churchman and deceitful wife. In this particular version, however, the abundance of realistic details saves an otherwise banal siutation from melting into the indistinguishable mass of this type story. The humorous and convincing exchanges between husband and wife, the latter's trip to the cobbler, and the description of the wine-bibbing husband and his intemperate friends afford the contemporary reader a valuable documentation on fifteenth-century bourgeois mores.

And all these well-chosen details culminate in a final confrontation where the author achieves an element of novelty through the husband's comic but ironic resignation to a relationship which students of modern socio-psychology will recognize as the "separate-track marriage."

Altogether uncharacteristic of the collection is the relatively longer story, "Lovers' Tragedy" (98). There is no coarse humor or irony here, and indeed the entire tone suggests a different sort of audience. Such a romantic tale of chivalric heroism proves that the courtly tradition had by no means vanished.

It is little wonder that scholars have sought to attribute *Les Cent Nouvelles nouvelles* to so impressive a parent as Antoine de La Sale, for this collection gives abundant indication of a writer who is keenly aware of the stylistic exigencies of this relatively recent art form. His sensitivity to the dramatic effects achieved by realistic detail and dialogue make him a real contributor to the development of the short story.

Notes for Introduction

1. Antoine de La Sale's name is affixed to only one story, the fiftieth, yet for generations, scholars have argued for and against his authorship. Among those who have considered him the "acteur" are Le Roux de Lincy, M. Stern, Thomas Wright, Ernest Gossart, Gaston Paris, and Oscar Grosjean. Those opposed to the proposition are L. E. Kastner, Joseph Nève, Carl Haag, William P. Shepard, and Pierre Champion.

Text Used

Les Cent Nouvelles nouvelles. Edited by Pierre Champion. 2 vols. Paris: Champion, 1928. (We also consulted the more recent edition by Franklin P. Sweetser. Geneva: Droz, 1966.)

Selected Critical Bibliography

KÜCHLER, WALTER. "Die *Cent Nouvelles nouvelles*." *Zeitschrift für französische Sprache und Litteratur*. 30 (1906): 264–331; 31 (1907): 39–101.
(See also the introduction and notes to the Champion edition.)

Les Cent Nouvelles Nouvelles (9)

'THE SELF-MADE CUCKOLD'

In order to continue telling new stories about how adventures happen in different places in different ways, we must not forget how one time a gallant knight of Burgandy, who resided in one of his beautiful and strong castles, equipped with men and arms as becomes a man of his condition, fell in love with a young lady of his household, or more precisely, the principal lady-in-waiting after Madame his wife. And love held him so firmly that he did not know what to do without her. He spoke to her continually, always sought her out, in short, was unable to enjoy anything without her, so much was he smitten by his love for her. The lady, good and wise, wishing to protect her honor, which she held as dear to her as her very soul, and wishing also to protect the loyalty she owed to her mistress, paid no attention to her lord, however much he may have wished her to. And if, on occasion, she was obliged to listen to him, God knows the harsh answer she gave him. She scolded him for his foolish undertaking and for the great cowardice of his heart. And what is more, she told him that if this chase continued, her mistress would be apprised of it. But in whatever manner or however much she threatened him, he did not give up his scheme, but pursued her more and more until the poor girl was finally forced to inform her mistress. Warned of the new loves of her lord, the said mistress was very discontent without showing it. Nonetheless, rather than say anything to him, she thought out a plan, which went like this: she told her lady-in-waiting that the next time her lord approached with amorous entreaties, she should stop refusing him and give him leave the following day to come to her in her bedroom and into her bed.

"And if he accepts the day," said the lady, "I shall come and take your place. Leave all the rest to me."

In order to obey her mistress as she should, she was happy to do as she was told. Whereupon, it was not long before his lordship returned to the task and, if he had lied well before, now he forced himself even more to convince her. And you should have heard him at that moment telling her that he would prefer death to living in this world without immediate remedy. To make a long story short, the lady of the wife was as well schooled and instructed by her mistress as anyone could be. She proposed to the good master an hour on the next day for performing the task, at which he was so happy that his heart jumped for joy, and he repeated to himself that he must not miss his rendezvous.

On the chosen day of battle, there arrived in the evening a noble knight, neighbor to his lord and lady, and his very great friend, who had come to see him. He offered him his warmest hospitality, as he knew very well how to do. And Madame did likewise; and the rest of the household made a great effort to please him, knowing that such was the wish of the master and mistress. After feasting at a great banquet supper, it came time to retire and, wishing good night to her ladyship and to her women, the two good knights began talking about one thing and another. And among other things, the visiting knight asked the lord if there were any young girls in town worth running after, for the spirit was upon him, after all the feasting, and the weather was pleasant at this hour. My lord, who wished to hide nothing from him because of his fondness for him, told how he had a rendezvous with his chambermaid,* and to make him happy, after he himself had been with her for a while, he would get up and fetch him so that he might finish off the rest. The visiting knight thanked his companion and God knows how the time dragged for him until the hour arrived. The host took leave of him and as was his custom, retired to his dressing room to take off his clothes.

Now you must know that while the two men were talking, my lady got into the bed where my lord was supposed to find his chambermaid and waited in that very place for whatever God had in store for her. My lord conveniently took a long time undressing, thinking his wife would already be asleep, as she often was, because she went to bed before him. He sent his valet away, and in his long gown went to the bed where Madame was waiting for him, expecting to find someone else

---

* The storyteller's reference to "sa chambrière" is of course inconsistent here. Previously, she is his wife's "damoiselle . . . voire et la première après madame sa femme." This is either negligence on the part of the author or an expression of the husband's scruples about duping a high-born lady.

there. Very quietly he removed his nightshirt and hopped into the bed. Since the light was out and his wife did not utter a word, he thought he had his chambermaid. Hardly had he arrived, but he put himself to the task and so well did he perform that the third and fourth times around were no strain on him. She was quite willing and soon afterwards, seeing that that was all, fell asleep. My lord, far lighter than before, seeing that Madame was sleeping and remembering his promise, rose quietly and went to his companion who was only waiting to take up his arms. He told him to take his station but to say nothing and to return when he had completed his task and had his fill. The latter, more alert than a rat and faster than a greyhound, got up and left in excitement and took shelter next to Madame, without her knowing. And when he felt safe, if my lord had done his job well, he in fact did it better and faster, which surprised Madame no end. Following the happy pastime, which cost her a little effort, she fell back to sleep again. And like a good knight, didn't he depart from her, return to his lord, who as before, took up his place once more next to Madame and more enthusiastically than ever prepared for battle, so much did this new maneuver give him pleasure.

So many hours passed in sleeping as in doing other things, that the day broke. And as my lord turned over, expecting to lay eyes on the chambermaid, he saw and recognized that it was my lady, who at that moment said to him, "Aren't you a deceitful, worthless, and despicable whoremonger for expecting to possess my chambermaid, and for having kissed me so much and so excessively to fufill your unbridled passion? For which, thank God, you are deceived, since no one but me will have what is mine this time."

If the good knight was amazed and angry at seeing himself in this fix, it is little wonder. And when he spoke, he said, "My sweet, I cannot hide my foolish deed and it bothers me greatly that I ever did it. So I beg you to be calm and not to think about it any more, for never in my life will it happen to me again. That I promise you, on my faith. And so that you never have reason to think about it, I shall send away the chambermaid who made me desire to do you this wrong."

Happy to have experienced the night's adventures rather than her chambermaid, and hearing the sincere repentance of my lord, my lady was quite easily satisfied, but not without many words and remonstrances.

In the end, everything went well and my lord who had extra tow on his spindle,* arose and went to his friend, to whom he recounted the whole episode, asking of him two things: first, that he keep this unpleasant experience secret, and second that he never appear anywhere where his wife might be present. Very unhappy about this unfortunate occurrence, the other comforted the knight as best he could and promised to fulfill his very reasonable request.

Thereupon he mounted his horse and departed. The chambermaid, who was in no way guilty in the said mishap, bore the brunt of the punishment by being sent away. Thus, my lord and lady lived happily together for a long while, without her ever knowing that she had had an affair with a strange knight.

Les Cent Nouvelles Nouvelles (19)
'THE MIRACLE OF THE SNOW CHILD'

There once lived in England a good and wealthy London merchant, whose firm courage and virtuous heart were so consumed with a burning desire to travel and to experience the many adventures which daily occur throughout the world, that he left his beautiful and good wife, his household of children, relatives, and friends, his estate and the better part of his wealth, and well supplied with cash and a great many of those goods which England exports to foreign lands, such as tin, rice, and a multitude of other things, which for the sake of brevity I will not mention, set out from his homeland.

On this his first voyage, the good merchant was gone for five years, during which time his wife preserved her virtue, made a profit on many goods, and did so well that her husband, at the end of the said five years, praised her greatly and loved her more than ever.

* Tow refers to the shorter and less desirable fibers of the flax. Champion interprets this to mean that he found himself in difficulty. (See Les Cent Nouvelles nouvelles, p. 293.)

Still unsatisfied with all the many marvelous and strange things he had seen and learned, or with the fortune he had made, four or five months after his return, the merchant's heart made him again set sail. And dreaming of adventures in foreign lands both Christian and Saracen, he stayed away so long that ten years passed before his wife saw him again. He wrote her well and often, so that she knew he was still alive. She, still young and healthy, and lacking naught else of the Lord's goods, save her husband's presence, was forced by her long wait to take on a lieutenant who, in short order, gave her a handsome son.

This son was brought up, fed, and educated alongside his other brothers and, at the return of the woman's merchant-husband, was about seven years old. Upon his return, the rejoicing between husband and wife was great, and while they were engaged in pleasant and happy chatter, the good woman, at the request of her husband, brought before them all their children, including the one who was added during the absence of him whose name he bore. The good merchant, seeing his fine group of children and remembering full well the number of them at the time of his departure, saw that he had one more, which much startled and amazed him.

And so he went to his wife and asked who this handsome boy was, the youngest among their children.

"Who is he?" she said. "By my faith, sire, he is our son. Who else's should he be?"

"I don't know," he said, "but since I've never seen him before, are you surprised I should ask?"

"By Saint John, not in the least," she said, "but he is my son."

"And how can that be?" said her husband, "you weren't pregnant when I left."

"True enough," she said, "as far as I know, but in truth I dare say, the child is yours, and no other than you has touched me."

"I never said otherwise," he said, "but the fact is I left ten years ago and this child appears to be seven. How then could he be mine? Is it possible you carried him longer than any of the others?"

"I swear," she said, "I don't know. But what I am telling you is true. If I did carry him more than any other, I know nothing about it, and if you did not give him to me before you left, I can't think where he might have come from, unless it was one day, shortly after your departure, when I was in our garden one morning and was seized with a sudden desire to eat a sorrel leaf, which at that time was covered over and buried under the snow. I picked a wide and beautiful leaf which I thought to eat, but it was only a bit of hard, white snow. No sooner had I swallowed it than all over I felt just as I did when I was pregnant with my other children. Indeed, at the end of my pregnancy, I bore you this very fine son."

The merchant realized immediately that he was a member of the fellowship,* but did not wish to let on; rather, he replied with words which confirmed the tall tale his wife was giving him.

"My love, you are not telling me anything which is impossible and which couldn't have happened to others. God be praised for what he has sent to us! If he has given us a child, by miracle or by some secret process we do not comprehend, he has not forgotten to send us the riches to take care of him."

When the good wife saw that her husband was willing and ready to believe what she told him, she was not a little pleased. The merchant, wise and prudent, during the ten years he stayed home without undertaking any of his long voyages, never spoke to his wife in any way which might lead her to suspect he knew aught of these matters, so virtuous and patient was he.

He had not as yet had his fill of traveling and wanted to begin again, and he said to his wife, who pretended to be very distressed and unhappy, "Calm yourself, if it is the will of the Lord and of Saint George, I'll be back very soon. And because our son, born during my last voyage, is already grown up and fit and ready to see and learn, if it so pleases you, I shall take him along with me."

"By my faith," she said, "that's a good idea and I hope you will do it."

"It shall be done," he said.

And with that he left, taking along with him the son of whom he was not the father and who for some time had been

* Of cuckolds. *Fr. nos amis.*

in his thoughts. The wind was so good that they arrived in the port of Alexandria, where the merchant got rid of most of his goods. And so that he would not be burdened with the child of his wife and another, who might after his death inherit his property like his other children, he was not so foolish as not to sell him into slavery for a good price. And because the boy was young and strong, he received nearly two hundred ducats for him.

Finally, thanks be to God, he returned safe and sound to England. There is no need to describe the joy of his wife when she saw him in good health. She did not see her son, however, and did not know what to think. She could not keep from asking her husband what he had done with their son.

"Ah, my love," he said, "I must no longer conceal it from you. A terrible thing has befallen him."

"Alas, what?" she said. "Did he drown?"

"In truth no," he said, "but the fact is that the fortunes of sea led us by chance to a country where it was so hot we thought we would all die from the great heat of the sun which cast its rays upon us. And one day when we had disembarked in order that we might each dig a hole in which to protect ourselves from the sun, our dear son, who as you know was made of snow, was before our very eyes suddenly dissolved and on the shore melted into water by the heat of the sun. Before you could recite seven psalms, there was nothing left of him. As quickly as he had come into the world so suddenly did he leave it. Believe me that I was and still am very upset, for never among all the wonders I've seen, have I witnessed anything so amazing."

"Well now," she said, "since it has pleased God to take him from us as he had given him to us, praised be His Name."

Now as to whether she suspected that it had happened otherwise, the story is silent and makes no mention of it, save that her husband gave her tit for tat, even though for all that he always remained a cuckold.

'THE VOICE FROM ON HIGH'

I knew in my time an excellent and worthy woman deserving of notice and recommendation; for her virtues ought neither to be hidden nor kept secret, but publicly heralded before all. With your permission, in brief, you will hear the telling of this tale, by which I expect to increase and augment her very high reputation.

I swear by Saint Denis, this worthy and honest woman, who was married to another member of the society,* had several suitors who pursued and desired her favor, which was not very difficult to win, so sweet and full of compassion was she, willing and able to distribute it whenever and wherever she pleased. It happened one day that her two lovers, each unbeknownst to the other, came to see her, as they often did, to ask for their baking day † and right to an audience. She, who neither flinched nor faltered for two or for three, assigned them the day and hour at which to appear at her house, namely the next day, one at eight in the morning, the other following at nine. And she instructed each emphatically and expressly not to miss his assigned hour. They promised on their faith and honor that barring some unavoidable delay, they would arrive at the designated time and place.

When the following day arrived, at four in the morning the husband of this worthy woman rose, dressed, and got ready. He called and bade her to get up. He was not obeyed, however, but rather was refused outright.

"Oh dear," she says, "I have such an awful headache that I couldn't possibly stand on my feet; I couldn't even get up to die, I'm so weak and weary. And to tell you the truth, I didn't sleep last night. So I beg you, please leave me here. Hopefully, when I'm alone, I'll get a little rest."

Though skeptical, he did not dare contradict nor reply; but as he had errands, he left to do his business in town, while his wife was not idle at home. It had barely struck eight when at

* Of cuckolds.
† A euphemistic allusion, based on the fact that people reserved in advance their day for using the baker's oven.

the assigned hour, along came the good fellow of yesterday knocking at the door. She pushed him in. He soon dispensed with his long outer garment and the rest of his clothes and then came to keep Mademoiselle company, lest she be frightened. They were so much intertwined in each other's arms and otherwise that time slipped away and passed and they didn't take notice when they heard someone knocking rudely at the door.

"Oh my goodness," she said, "Here comes my husband! Hurry up and get your clothes."

"Your husband!" he says. "Do you recognize his knock?"

"Yes," she says, "I am sure it's him. Hide yourself so he won't find you here."

"If it's him, he's bound to see me. I don't see any way of escaping."

"See you!" she says, "God willing, he will not, because you would be dead and me too. He's unbelievably mean. Climb up into this little attic and keep still and don't move, so that he doesn't see you."

The other climbed up as she told him to and found himself in this tiny attic which was very old, with broken boards and laths and holes in several places. And Mademoiselle, feeling that he was safely put away upstairs, bounded to the door, knowing perfectly well it was not her husband, and let in the one who had promised to come to her at nine. They came into the bedroom, where they did not remain standing for long, but stretched out, embraced, and kissed in the same or similar manner as had the one in the attic, who through a crack, saw those assembled below, which did not make him any too happy. And he questioned for a long while in his heart whether it was better to speak out or better to keep still. But he finally decided to keep quiet and say nothing until he could figure out where he stood. And think what patience he had! So long did he wait and watch the lady and the latest arrival that the good husband came home to check on his very good wife's condition and health, which he was well advised to do. When she heard him, she had only enough time to break up the meeting suddenly. And because she didn't know where to hide him, since she would never have sent him to the attic, she stuck him in the space between the bed and the wall and covered him with her clothes saying, "I don't know where else to put you. Just be patient!"

She had hardly finished speaking when her husband who, it seemed to him, had overheard some noise, came in and found the bed all jumbled and messed up, the bedcovers disarranged and strangely helter-skelter. It looked more like the bed of a young bride than that of a sick woman. Now with the look of things, his former suspicions made him call his wife by name and say, "Whore, despicable creature that you are, I suspected as much this morning when you were playing sick! Where is the good-for-nothing? I swear to God, if I find him, things will end badly for him and for you too!"

Wherupon he put his hand on the bedcover saying, "Isn't this a pretty picture! It looks as if pigs had slept here."

"And what's the matter with you, you ugly drunkard?" said she. "And must I pay for the excess wine which has put your throat to singing? Is that your idea of a friendly greeting, calling me a whore? I want you to know that I am no such thing, but too good and loyal for a scoundrel like you. I only regret having been so good to you, because you don't deserve it. And I don't know what keeps me from getting up and scratching your face so that you'll forever have a reminder of having accused me unjustly."

If anyone should ask me how she dared at this point to answer and speak like this to her husband, I would offer two explanations: the first, that she had justice on her side, and the other, that she felt that she had the upper hand in the matter, for one is inclined to think that if they had come to blows, the one in the attic and the one beside the bed would have assisted and helped her.

The poor husband didn't know what to say, hearing his devil of a wife shriek like that, and because he saw that neither shouting nor scolding would do any good, he placed the entire case in the hands of God, who is just and impartial. Ending his reflections, he said among other things, "You're too quick to excuse yourself from what I know I see clearly. In the end, I don't care what people say. I never pick quarrels. He who is above will pay for everything." And by "He above" he meant God, as if he were trying to say, "God, who gives each what he deserves, will pay you your just deserts."

But the gallant in the attic heard the words and seriously believed that the other man was talking about him and that he risked being hauled over the coals for someone else's wrongdoings. So he answered out loud, "What, sir? It's enough that I pay for my half, the fellow next to the bed can certainly pay for the other. He's as guilty as I am!"

Imagine the amazement of our host! For he believed that God was speaking to him. And the man beside the bed did not know what to think, for he knew nothing about the other one. He stood up, however, and the other came down and recognized him.

Thus they departed together and left the company terribly distressed and unhappy, which did not bother them in the least, and for good reason!

Les Cent Nouvelles Nouvelles (61)
'PRISONER OF LOVE'

At one time there lived in a good town of Hainaut a fine merchant married to a worthy woman. He was often away on business, in search of wares, which, it so happened, gave his wife an opportunity to love another, something she continued to do for a rather long while.

The secret, however, was discovered by a neighbor, who was a relative of the husband and who lived across the street from the tradesman, from whence at night, he observed and saw the lover go in and out of the house of the merchant. When the victim of these happenings learned from his neighbor what was going on, he was greatly distressed. Thanking his relative and neighbor, he said he would look into the matter shortly and that some evening he would hide in his neighbor's house so as to see better who was coming and going into his own house.

So finally he pretended to leave and told his wife and servants that he didn't know when he would be back. He set off very early one morning only to return at vespers. He left his horse off somewhere and secretly made his way back to his

Les Cent Nouvelles nouvelles (34) "The Voice from on High"
"It's enough that I pay for my half, the fellow next to
the bed can certainly pay for the other."
[From ms. Hunter 252, miniature number 34, reproduced by
permission of the Glasgow University Library, Glasgow.]

cousin's house and from there watched through a small lattice, waiting to see what could hardly please him. Thus he waited until about nine o'clock at night when the lover, whom the young lady had informed of her husband's absence, walked two or three times past his mistress's house, examined the door to see if he could get in, but found it still closed. He thought to himself that it was not yet time because of these precautions.

And while he wandered about, the good merchant, who thought surely this was his man, came down, went to the door, and said, "My friend, our mistress has heard you and since there is still time enough and she is afraid that the master will be back, she asked me to bring you in, if it pleases you."

The friend, thinking this was the servant, took a chance and followed him in. He opened the door quietly and led him to a back room where there was a very large chest, which he opened and which he made him get into, so that, if the merchant returned, he would not find him and so that in a short while his mistress might come to let him out and speak with him. All this the good lover endured in anticipation of something better and also because he thought that the other was telling the truth.

The merchant immediately departed as stealthily as possible and went to his cousin and his wife and said to them, "I promise you that the rat has been caught, but we must decide what to do with him."

And then his cousin, and especially his wife, who had no use for the other woman, were delighted with the news and said it would be a good idea to show him to the woman's relatives so they might see how she had been carrying on. When this was decided, the merchant went to the home of his wife's parents and told them that if ever they wished to see their daughter alive, they must come immediately to his house. They quickly jumped up and while they made ready, he also sought out two of her brothers and sisters and repeated to them what he had said to the mother and father. Then he led them all to his cousin's house and there told them the whole story, just as it was, and how he had caught the rat.

It seems appropriate now to know how the gentle lover, in the meantime, was faring in this chest, from which he was deftly delivered, considering the circumstances. The lady, who wondered why her lover did not arrive, paced back and forth hoping she might hear something. It wasn't long before the friend, catching the sound of footsteps nearby and wondering if he was going to be left there, began banging with his fist against the chest until the lady heard it and was greatly alarmed.

She nonetheless asked who was there and the lover answered, "Alas, my dearest love, I am here, dying of heat and fear, and wondering why you have had me shut in here, and if you are coming or going."

Then wasn't she greatly surprised and said, "Oh Virgin Mary, do you believe, my love, that it was I who had you put in there?"

"By my faith," he said, "I don't know, but the fact is that your servant came to me and said you had asked me in, and I got into this chest so that if your husband should return tonight, he would not find me."

"Aha," said she, "by my life, that must have been my husband. This time I am a lost woman, and our whole secret is discovered and known."

"Do you know what this means?" he said. "You have got to get me out or I'll break everything, for I can't stand it any longer."

"In faith," said the young lady. "I have no key and if you break it I am done for. My husband will say I did it to save you."

Finally the young lady looked until she found some old keys, among which there was one which freed the poor prisoner. And when he was released he harangued his lady and showed her how angry he was with her, all of which she bore patiently. And with that, the gentle lover wished to leave, but she held him, threw her arms around him and said that if he were to leave thus, she would be just as dishonored as if he had broken the chest.

"What else is there to do?" said the lover.

"If we do not put something inside for my husband to find, I'll not be able to say I did not let you out."

"And what shall we put there?" said the lover, "so I can leave, for it is time."

"We have in our stable," she said, "an ass which, if you help me we will put there."

"Yes, upon my word," he said.

Thereupon, the ass was pushed into the chest, which they then closed back up again. And with a sweet kiss, the lover took leave and went out by a back entrance, while the young lady got quickly into bed.

It was not long thereafter that the husband, while these things were taking place, gathered her relatives together and led them, as has already been told, to his cousin's house, where he related all that he had been told about his situation and also how he had locked up the lover.

"And," he said, "so that you will not accuse me of blaming your daughter without due cause, I shall let you see and touch the scoundrel who has dishonored us thus, and I pray you to kill him before he escapes." And each said it should be so.

"And what is more," said the merchant, "such as she is, I shall give your daughter back to you."

And with that the others, greatly saddened by this news, accompanied him, and they carried torches and flambeaux so as to search everywhere more easily and so that nothing could escape their attention. And they banged so hard on the door that the young lady came before anyone else could be aroused and let them in. When they had entered, she lit into her husband, her father, her mother, and the others to show that she was surprised at whatever could have brought them there at that hour of the night.

And at these words, her husband raised his fist and gave her a good swat and said, "You'll know soon enough, deceitful so and so that you are."

"Ah be careful what you say. Is that why you brought my mother and father here?"

"Yes," said the mother, "dishonest wench that you are. We'll show you your lover-boy in just a minute."

And then her sisters said, "In God's name, sister, you didn't learn to act like this at home."

"My sisters," she said, "by all the saints in Rome, I have done nothing but what a righteous woman should and could do, nor do I believe you can prove the contrary."

"You're a liar," said her husband, "I shall prove it at once, and the scoundrel will be killed before your eyes. Get up and open that chest."

"Me?" she said, "I do believe you're dreaming or out of your mind. You know perfectly well I've never had the key, and that ever since you stored your letters in there, the key has been hanging from your belt along with all your others. And if you want it opened, open it. But I pray to God that as truly as I have never had anything to do with whoever is in there, that he may deliver me with honor and joy, and that the ugly jealousy that you have against me will be exposed and shown for what it is; and thus, as I have every reason to hope, it shall be."

"I think," said the husband, who saw her on bended knee, sobbing and trembling, "she knows how to play on your sympathies, and whoever believed her would soon be taken in, but don't doubt for a moment that I saw through her treachery long ago. I shall open the chest and I beg you, gentlemen, to lay hold of the scoundrel lest he escape, for he is strong and quick."

"Don't worry," they all said. "We know what to do." Thereupon they drew their swords and seized their clubs in order to bludgeon the poor lover, and said to him, "Make your confession now, or you'll never have a priest any closer."

The mother and sisters, who did not want to witness the murder, drew away; and when the poor fool had opened the chest and the ass saw the light, it began to bray so wildly that no one there was collected enough to keep his wits about him. And when they saw it was an ass, and that the merchant was mocking them in this way, they wanted to seize him and hurl upon him as much abuse as Saint Peter had honors. Even the women wanted to jump on him. In fact, if he had not fled, the woman's brothers would have killed him on the spot, because of the enormous blame and disgrace he had brought and wanted to bring upon her. And in the end, so much was made of this affair that the town fathers had to restore peace and harmony, and the accusers never ceased to bear a grudge against the merchant.

And the story goes that peace was not made without great difficulty, many complaints on the part of the young lady's friends, and in addition, several exacting promises from the merchant. And ever since, the latter has conducted himself

Les Cent Nouvelles nouvelles (61) "Prisoner of Love"
". . . and when the poor fool had opened the chest and the ass
saw the light, it began to bray so wildly. . . ."
[From ms. Hunter 252, miniature number 61, reproduced by
permission of the Glasgow University Library, Glasgow.]

most graciously. Never was there a man better to his wife than was he all of his life. And thus they passed their days together.

Les Cent Nouvelles Nouvelles (80)
'GREAT EXPECTATIONS'

In the country of Germany, I once heard it related as true by two trustworthy, reliable gentlemen that a young girl of about fifteen or sixteen happened to be given in marriage to a virtuous gentleman who fulfilled his duty by doing that which women earnestly and quietly desire when they have reached that certain state and age. But, though the poor fellow did his job well and perhaps applied himself more than he needed to, his efforts were not well received. He managed only to make his wife sulk incessantly and often weep piteously as if all her friends had died.

Her husband, watching her lament in this way, was totally dumbfounded as to what could be bothering her and sweetly asked, "Alas, my love, what is the matter? Are you not properly clothed, housed, and waited upon? Do you not have everything which people of our condition can reasonably expect?"

"It is not that which troubles me," she said.

"Then what is it, tell me?" he said, "And if I can help you, believe me that I shall give all my worldly goods to do it."

Most of the time she never said a word, but was forever gloomy and presented more and more of a cheerless, downcast countenance, which her husband, since he could not learn the cause of this sorrow, bore with little patience. He inquired so much that he learned the cause in part, for she told him it was terribly annoying that he was so inadequately equipped with you may guess what, that is to say, the rod used to plant men, as Boccaccio calls it.

"Indeed," he said, "is that the reason you're so unhappy? Upon my word, you have reason to be. Yet, there's nothing to be done and you must resign yourself to it, such as it is, unless of course you'd like to make an exchange."

This situation continued for a long time until one day the

husband, seeing her obstinacy, invited a great many of her friends to dinner and related the facts as they have been thus far recorded and said that it seemed to him she had no reason to complain of him on this account, for he believed himself to be as amply supplied with this natural instrument as any of his neighbors.

"And in order that I may be better believed and that you see how wrong she is, I shall show you everything."

With that, he placed his merchandise on the table for all to see, men and women alike and said, "Here is the crux of the matter," And his wife wept more than ever.

"And by Saint John," said her mother, her sister, her aunt, her cousin, and her neighbor, "You are mistaken, my dear. What do you want? What more do you expect? And who is she who wouldn't be pleased to have a husband thus equipped. God willing, I should consider myself very happy with as much, indeed with far less. Calm yourself, calm yourself, and enjoy yourself in the future. My God, I believe you are the most fortunate of us all."

And the young wife, hearing the academy of wives speak in this manner, said to them, all the while weeping profusely, "Look at the small donkey we have. He is hardly one-and-a-half years old and has an instrument as big and thick as the length of your arm." And so saying, she held her right arm by the elbow and shook it vigorously, "while my husband, who is twenty-four years old, has no more than the little he has shown. Do you really think I should rejoice?"

Everyone began to laugh so much and she to weep even more that for a long while not a word was spoken. Then the mother began to speak and taking her daughter to one side, said this thing and the other until she was somewhat placated, though not without great difficulty. And so it is with the girls of Germany, and so it will soon be in France, God willing.

Les Cent Nouvelles Nouvelles (93)
'HOLY PILGRIMAGE'

While I have a good audience, I should like to tell a charming story which took place in the pretty country of Hainaut. In a large town of the above-mentioned region, there lived a fine married women who loved the sacristan of her parish church more than she loved her husband. And in order to find a way to be with her sacristan, she pretended to her husband that she owed a pilgrimage to a certain saint not far from there, at a distance of about one league, and that she had made a vow to him when she had been in labor, begging him to be satisfied if she were to go on a day chosen by her, along with one of her neighbors, who was going at the same time.

The good, simple husband, who suspected nothing, consented to the pilgrimage, but wanted her to return the same day that she left.

"Perhaps," she said, "I shall return by dinner, as time will tell, but first of all," she said, "I must have a pair of good shoes."

She was willingly granted everything and, because the husband was to stay alone, he asked her to prepare both his dinner and his supper before leaving, or else he would eat at the tavern.

She did what he asked, for on the day of her departure, she got up very early to go to the butcher's and ordered a tasty chicken and a piece of mutton and then left her order with the cobbler who made her shoes. When all these preparations were completed, she told her husband that all was ready and that she was going to fetch holy water in order to leave afterwards.

She entered the church and the first man she found was the very one she was looking for, namely the sacristan, to whom she related all her news, how she was excused to go on a pilgrimage for the whole day, etc. "But there is one complication," she said, "I am sure that as soon as he feels I am out of the house he will head for the tavern. And, if I know him, he will not return until vespers. And still I'd rather stay home while he's away than go out. So watch around our house for about half an hour, so that if by chance my husband is away, I can let you in by the back door, and if he is there, we will set out on our pilgrimage."

She returned to the house, where she found her husband still, which didn't please her any. He said to her, "What, are you still here?"

"I am going to get my shoes," she said, "then it won't be long before I leave."

She went to the cobbler's and while she was trying on her shoes, her husband passed in front of the cobbler's shop in the company of a neighbor who often went to the tavern. And although she supposed that, because he was with the said neighbor, he was headed for the tavern, this was not in fact his intention. Instead, he was going to the marketplace to find two or three friends to share his dinner with him, on the pretext that there was too much for him alone, that is to say this chicken and piece of mutton.

We will now leave our husband to seek out his friends and return to the wife who was putting on her shoes. As soon as this was done, she returned home as quickly as she could, where she found the good sacristan processing around the house.

"My love, we are the happiest people on earth, for I saw my husband going toward the tavern, I am sure, for he's leading one of his associates by the arm and this fellow will not let him come back whenever he pleases. Therefore, let's enjoy ourselves until tonight. I prepared a good chicken and a lovely piece of mutton of which we'll make a feast." And without saying another word, she led him in and left the door ajar so that the neighbors would suspect nothing.

And now let us return to our husband who found two good companions besides the first one I've mentioned, whom he led home to finish off this chicken along with a good bottle of Beaune or some better wine if such could be had.

Upon arriving home, he was the first to go in and the moment he entered, he found our two lovers doing a little work. And when he saw his wife with her legs up in the air, he told her she didn't have to worry about wearing out her shoes and that she had given the cobbler a lot of work for nothing, since she planned to go on a pilgrimage in this manner.

He called his friends and said, "Gentlemen, look at how my wife tries to save me money. Fearing that she might wear out her fine, new shoes, she travels on her back. You won't find her equal."

And taking a small morsel of leftover chicken, he told her to complete her pilgrimage. Then he closed the door and left her with her sacristan. And without saying another word, he went off to the tavern. And inasmuch as he had said little or nothing about this pilgrimage his wife had made at home, he was not scolded upon his return this time, or any of the other times he went drinking.

Les Cent Nouvelles Nouvelles (98)
'THE LOVERS' TRAGEDY'

At the outer limits and frontiers of France, there lived a rich and powerful knight, distinguished not only because of the ancient nobility of his ancestors, but because of his own illustrious and virtuous deeds. By his wife he had an only daughter, a very beautiful and well-educated maiden about fifteen or sixteen years of age. This good and noble knight, seeing that the said daughter had reached an age fit and proper for being joined in marriage, wished heartily to give her to a neighboring knight, rich and noble not so much in birth as in great material goods and temporal power; what is more, he was aged somewhere between sixty and eighty.

This desire so filled the thoughts of the father of whom I have spoken, that he never rested until the pledges and promises were agreed to between him and his wife, mother of the said maiden, and the said knight, concerning marriage with his daughter, who knew nothing about and cared not at all for these meetings, promises, and arrangements.

Rather close to the manor of this knight, father of the maiden, there lived another young knight, valiant and moderately wealthy, though not so much as the older one of whom I have spoken, who was consumed with a burning love for this maiden. And because of his virtuous and princely renown, she too was greatly taken with him. Although it was dangerous for them to speak to each other, since the father was suspicious and forbade and eliminated all manner and means for them to do so, nonetheless, he was unable to blot out the all-powerful and pure love which bound together and consumed their two hearts. And when good fortune did bring them together, they thought about and discussed nothing but how, through legal marriage, they might realize their deepest desire.

Now the time grew closer when this maiden was to be given to the old gentleman, and her father revealed his discussions and plans to her and settled upon the day when she was to be married, which distressed her no small amount. She thought, however, of finding a way out and sent for her beloved, the young knight, asking that he come to her secretly as soon as possible. And when he had come, she told him about the engagement contracted between herself and the old knight and asked how it might be broken, for she wished to be wife to no man but him. The knight answered her, "My sweet love, since in your kindness, you wish to humiliate yourself in offering me what I would never dare ask for without shame, I thank you; and if you wish to persevere in your good intentions, I know what we must do. We shall name and choose a day when I shall be in this city accompanied by my friends and servants, and at a certain hour, you will come alone to some place which you will indicate to me now. You will mount my horse and I shall take you to my castle; and then, if we can mollify my lord your father and my lady your mother, we shall proceed to consummate our vows." The maiden said she found this a good plan and knew how best to make it work. And thus she told him to come on a certain day at a certain hour and in a certain place, where he would find her and could then do as he had devised.

The appointed day arrived and thus, this fine, young knight appeared at the place where he had been told to come and where he found his lady. She mounted behind him on his horse and they rode hastily until they were far away. When they were at some distance, the good knight, fearing he might tire his sweet love, slackened his pace. He sent out his men in all directions to see if someone was following them and then set out across the fields in as leisurely and casual a manner as possible, without regard to roads or paths. He charged his men to meet at a large town which he named and where he intended to stop and rest. This town was set away from the main road for travelers on horseback or on foot.

The said lovers traveled until they arrived alone at the above-mentioned village, where they were celebrating the local feast day, to which had come crowds of people of all sorts. They entered the best tavern in the place and promptly asked for food and drink, for it was well past dinner and the maiden was exhausted. A warm fire was built and good food prepared for the knight's retinue which had not as yet arrived.

They had hardly gotten settled in the inn when there came in four of the coarsest plowmen or worse still cowherds, who burst boisterously into the inn, demanding in a loud voice where the slut was whom a ruffian had only a short while ago brought in behind him on the back of his horse, and with whom they wanted to drink and sleep. The innkeeper, who knew the said knight well and realized that these rowdies were making a mistake, told them graciously that she was not what they had supposed.

"That's neither here nor there," they said, "and if you don't bring her to us at once, we'll break down the doors and take her by force despite you both."

When the good innkeeper heard and recognized their hard-headedness and saw that his softspoken words were of no avail, he gave the knight's name, which was well known in those parts, but little known to the commoners, since he had always been out of the country gaining honor and great glory in battles in far distant lands. He told them too that the woman, born of a great house and of noble parentage, was a young maiden related to the said knight.

"Alas, sirs," he said, "without harm to you or to anyone else, you can subdue and satisfy your strong passions with others, who on the occasion of the village feast-day have come for no other reason than for you and your likes. For God's sake leave this noble girl in peace and imagine the dangers you would be bringing upon yourselves. Do not be so presump-tuous as to think that the knight will let you take her without trying to stop you. Consider, consider your unreasonable de-mands and the great harm you wish to do for so little gain."

"Stop preaching," the scoundrels said, all aflame with the fire of carnal lust, "and step aside so we can get to her or we'll bring shame and disgrace upon you, for we'll lead her here in public view and each of us four will have our sport with her."

The conversation ended, the good innkeeper went up to the room where the knight and the gentle maiden were, then called the knight to one side and told him about the intentions of the four crazed peasants; and he, when he had carefully heard the whole story, with hardly any show of emotion, went downstairs armed with his sword, to speak to the four bullies and asked them in a very polite manner what it was they wanted. And they, rude and foul-mouthed as they were, answered that they wanted the slut he had locked in his room, and that if he didn't surrender her to them quietly, they would take her by force and ravish her.

"Good sirs," said the knight, "if you really knew who I am, you couldn't take me for the kind of man who leads a woman such as you think this one to be across the fields. I have never, thank God, done such a thing, and if ever the desire should take hold of me, may God never allow it, I would never do it on my land or on the land of my people. My high birth and integrity would never permit me to act in such a way. This woman is a young maiden, my cousin, born of a noble family. I have brought her along and intend to pass the time pleasantly and pleasurably, accompanied by my servants who, though they are not here, will join us soon, however, as I am expecting them. Do not be deceived into thinking that I hold myself so low as to allow her to be insulted or molested in any way, for I shall defend her as long as the strength of my body endures, even until death."

But before the knight could finish speaking, the villainous culprits stopped him, refusing first of all to believe that he was the person he said he was, inasmuch as he was alone and the said knight never traveled except in the company of his many servants. Therefore, they advised him that if he were wise, he would surrender the said woman or they would take her by force, whatever the consequences. Alas, when the valiant and courageous knight saw that his gentle answers were of no avail and that only force and arrogance would work, he braced himself and resolved that the peasants would never have the maiden or he would die in her defense.

Finally, one of the four men, the others following, moved forward to strike down the door with his staff, and they were valiantly beaten back by the knight. Thus began the battle which lasted for a long time. Although the two sides were not equal, this fine knight defeated and repulsed the four scoundrels. And while he was chasing them, one of them, who had a sword, suddenly veered round and plunged it into the knight's stomach and pierced him through and through so that the knight immediately fell dead, at which they were all very happy. This done, in order to avoid an outcry, they forced the innkeeper, by threatening to kill him, to bury the knight without scandal in the garden of the inn. When the knight was dead, they came and hurled themselves against the maiden's door and pushed it open.

She was very upset that her lover had delayed so long, and as soon as she saw the peasants, she at once surmised that the knight was dead and said, "Alas, where is my champion? Where is my only protection? What has become of him? How is it that he has left me alone in this way?"

Seeing how troubled she was, the ruffians sought to deceive her falsely with sweet words, telling her that the knight had gone to a house and that he had asked her to go there with them and that he would be able to protect her there better. But she would not believe any of it, for her heart continued to tell her that they had killed and murdered him. She then began to lose her head and cried out more bitterly than before.

"What's all this?" they said, "why are you carrying on with us in this strange manner? Do you think we don't know who you are? If you suspect that your ruffian is dead, you're right. We've rid the country of him. So make up your mind that each one of us four will bear you company." And with these words, one of them stepped forward, grabbing her in the rudest way possible and saying he would have her before she could get away, like it or not.

When the poor maiden saw that she was trapped and that the gentleness of her speech was having no effect, she said to them, "Alas, my lords, since you have thus made up your minds, since my humble entreaties can neither soften nor dissuade you and since I must surrender myself to you, at least have the common decency to leave me first with one of you without the presence of the others."

Though very reluctantly, they granted her what she asked, and then made her choose which of them should remain with her. She picked that one among them whom she deemed to be the most kindly and docile of them all, but he turned out to be the worst.

The door was closed, and immediately thereafter the gentle

maiden threw herself at the feet of the scoundrel and with heartrending petitions, begged him to take pity upon her. Relentlessly persevering in his designs, however, he said he would have his will of her.

When she saw how hard and unyielding he was and how ineffectual was her humble pleading, she said to him, "All right then, since it must be so, I shall resign myself, but I beg you to close the windows so that we may have more privacy."

He did her bidding, and while he was closing them, the maiden drew a small knife from where it was hanging on her belt, cut her throat, and gave up the ghost.

When the ruffian saw her dead on the floor, he fled with his companions. It is to be supposed that they were punished according to the demands of so piteous a crime.

And so, one after the other, the two lovers finished their days without ever experiencing the joys and pleasures with which they hoped to live and hoped to enjoy together all the days of their lives.

Philippe de Vigneulles (1471–1527?)
Les Cent Nouvelles Nouvelles

Introduction

Thanks to Philippe de Vigneulles' *Mémoires*, we have not only a chronological summary of the major events of his life, but a fascinating commentary on the times in which he lived. Born in 1471 in the small town of Vigneulles, not far from Metz, Philippe de Vigneulles was the fourth son of Magui Poinsay and Jehan Gérard. He described his mother as a small, gentle woman who had a good singing voice. His father, we learn, was for some time the local mayor. When still a young man, Philippe learned about the hardships of war, as the Duke of Lorraine laid siege to Metz and attacked the environs. One of the more poignant passages in the autobiography describes Philippe's distress upon discovering that his father, like himself, had been captured. Philippe gives a most realistic picture of the flea-ridden cell where he and others suffered the hardships of captivity until their release in 1491. A year later, he married, against his will, Mariette d'Angondange. When, however, after only one year of marriage, his wife died, Philippe took as his bride, his first love, Zabellin, daughter of the mayor of Le Sairte. Philippe chose as his life work the *métier* of draper and hosier and settled with his new wife in Metz where his business flourished and where he soon became one of the wealthiest citizens of the city.

Philippe described himself as a pious, diligent man. In the Jubilee Year of 1500, he decided to make a pilgrimage to Rome. When he finally returned, he seemed, if not more holy, at least more conversant in Italian, for he boasted of bringing back a number of books.

Hard times set in, however, and in 1507 an epidemic killed three of his children. Philippe himself was ill and the family decided to move temporarily to Lessey to live with Zabellin's brother. Partly as a distraction from his sadnesses and from his own sickness, Philippe began to compose the stories of his *Cent Nouvelles nouvelles*. His journal ends in 1522, but we assume that he returned to Metz, where he died either in 1527 or 1528.

Philippe's colorful, anecdotal autobiography probably gives the contemporary reader a fairly accurate portrait of the moneyed middle class, which in its leisure turned to the arts. Philippe speaks of his performances in local play productions, his dabblings in poetry and music and most especially his work as a painter of miniatures. He mentions his prose adaptation of the *Roman de Garin Le Lorain*, which today is still unedited in the library of Metz. In that same library are the three original manuscript volumes of his *Chroniques de la Ville de Metz*. But these were not the only examples of Philippe's intellectual enterprises, for in his *Mémoires*, he also refers to "ung livre contenant cent nouvelles ou contes joieulx. . . ." (p. 283.)

The story of how one distinguished American scholar, Professor Charles Livingston, tracked down the unique manuscript of this second *Cent Nouvelles nouvelles* counts among the more intriguing episodes in the annals of contemporary scholarship.[1] Suffice it to say here that the mutilated manuscript gives evidence of a collection of 110 stories, the first 100 probably composed beween 1505 and 1515 and the additional 10 dating from some later period. Of these, however, there are only 50 more or less intact. Over the past forty years the late Professor Livingston published 16 of these tales in various journals.[2]

The first story we have translated here, "Modicum et Bonum," (14) is in the tradition of the verbal joke, based essentially on a stupid misunderstanding. Philippe tells his story well, but mars the total effect, unfortunately, by adding another incident, which also draws its humor from the wordplay based on dialect. The second selection, which we have entitled "The Peddler" (71), is especially noteworthy because of its remarkable compactness.

Philippe de Vigneulles did not himself consider his fictional writing the most significant of his literary occupations; the fact that his manuscript was left unpublished is in some measure his own judgment upon it. Yet this second *Cent Nouvelles*

nouvelles, written by a literary hosier from Metz deserves a place in any anthology devoted to the fifteenth- and sixteenth-century French novella.

Notes for Introduction

1. See Charles Livingston, *Les Cent Nouvelles nouvelles de Philippe de Vigneulles* (Paris: Champion, 1924).
2. We are indebted to Mrs. Livingston for her encouragement in the present project.

Texts Used

At the time of translation, the complete edition was not yet ready. We were therefore obliged to use the texts found in articles published by Professor Livingston over a number of years:

LIVINGSTON, CHARLES. "*Decameron*, VIII, 2: Earliest French Imitations." *Modern Philology* 22 (August 1924): 35–43.

———. "The Fabliau 'Des Deux Anglois et de l'anel'." *PMLA* 40 (1925): 217–224.

VIGNEULLES, PHILIPPE DE. *Cent Nouvelles nouvelles*. Edited by Charles H. Livingston, Françoise R. Livingston, and Robert H. Ivy, Jr. Geneva: Droz, forthcoming.

Selected Critical Bibliography

LIVINGSTON, CHARLES. *Les Cent Nouvelles nouvelles de Philippe de Vigneulles*. Paris: Champion, 1924. (Republished from the *Revue du XVIᵉ siècle*, 10, 1923.)

Gedenkbuch des Metzer Burger's Philippe de Vigneulles. Edited by Henri Michelant. Stuttgart: Bibliothek des Litterarischen Vereins, 1852.

Philippe de Vigneulles

Les Cent Nouvelles Nouvelles (4)

'MODICUM ET BONUM'

In order to add to the number of [stories], I now want to tell you one which is quite different from the one told just before, for instead of a partridge, a poor ignorant priest, through his stupidity, had his own donkey killed and eaten. And the said priest would rather have paid with a dozen partridges than with that donkey. But because of a misunderstanding, it happened as you will hear.

It is true and not long ago, as I heard it told by educated and trustworthy men, that in the see of Metz near Sainte Barbe, it was ordered by the prelates and princes of the church and by those who are charged with the administration of that office that visits be made to certain parts of the said see and most especially in that vicinity. With these said officers there came the archpriest of that region. And the above named went to many places and churches and took their meals and rooms in those quarters which seemed to them most commodious.

Now there lived in that area in a town whose name I do not know, a good, simple priest who was rather rich in material goods but lacking in education and less than a priest ought to be, for he neither knew nor understood any Latin at all. And the same priest had many animals, among them a donkey who bore all the burdens of the household, like carrying the wheat to the mill, bringing back the flour, and going after wood. And the said donkey did a hundred thousand useful errands for them. The priest or sometimes his servant even rode on him when they came to Metz. And they called this donkey Modicum.

Now the above-mentioned gentlemen decided to come the following day to take their food and dine with the said priest, because it seemed to them that he was well off and would receive them comfortably. But to give him due warning, they charged the archpriest to speak with him so that he might make his preparations in advance; not that it was their intention to put the priest to any great expense but only that they might have something tasty and appetizing and some light food, without his preparing large amounts or assuming any large costs.

And so the said archpriest came to notify and tell this poor simple preacher how the said gentlemen were all coming together tomorrow to dine at his home, at which the poor fellow was greatly amazed and astonished, not that he feared the expense but that it seemed to him he was not the man to serve properly gentlemen and the likes of these. And the archpriest, when he saw the look on his face and how apprehensive he was about the service which was being asked of him, comforted him by saying that he ought not to worry and did not have to do half as much as he thought he did.

"That may be," the poor simple priest said, "but I do not know how I should go about it, what foods I should prepare for them or what would be pleasing to their tastes."

"Ah, my God," said the archpriest, "you're a difficult fellow; they don't need much. Arrange it only that they have *modicum et bonum* and they will have quite enough without causing any great trouble."

"Modicum," said the poor simple priest.

"Of course, of course," replied the other, "let them have *modicum* and don't bother with anything else, since they're not starving."

"All right," said the poor priest, "I understand."

And at that point they took leave of one another; the archpriest returned to his friends and the poor priest, practically in tears, went back to his servant-girl and told her how they had to kill their poor donkey named Modicum in order to feast the officials who, as the archpriest had told him, were to dine there the next day. And his servant-girl began to cry with him out of pity for poor Modicum, hugging and kissing him all the while; but to no avail, for they had to do it, since it was the pleasure of his lordship the archpriest. And with great sorrow, they killed the said donkey, skinned and cut him into pieces. And the next day they put nothing over the fire in either pots or pans which was not Modicum and on the appointed day and hour when the gentlemen were to arrive, the table was set, the tablecloths spread and everything made ready.

Now the said gentlemen had some baggages on top of another donkey. They had hired a fellow from that region to drive it for them and he brought their said donkey along with the baggages to the place where they were to dine, that is to say, at the home of the above-mentioned good, simple priest. And no sooner had he come to the house, when the same gentlemen, after they had arrived, sat down to eat and were served such foods as had been prepared for them. But there wasn't a one among them who was not amazed as to what the devil kind of flesh it could be which their host was making them eat. And they could not eat or swallow it; and they began to complain and grumble against the archpriest who had had the responsibility of having something light and appetizing prepared. There was too much food, but it was worthless, for the said priest had put large chunks of the said donkey on the table in enormous portions as if it were for cartdrivers. And the lord archpriest, who was very much displeased, apologetically explained to them how this priest had not done as he had been told and ordered.

"For," he said, "I told him to prepare something good and moderate and that we would only have *modicum et bonum*, that it to say, a little something good and light."

And while they were talking, along came the good fellow who had been leading the gentlemen's donkey loaded with their bags, and when he had put the donkey into the stable, he came to wish them well. The good fellow knew about as much Latin as the poor simple priest, their host, as you will see by the answer he gave, for among these gentlemen there was one of the officials and subordinates who spoke marvellously good French and what is more was from France.

He began to speak to the good fellow saying: "My friend," he said, "abulaine auguet?"

And the good man took off his hat and said to him: "I don't know any Latin, sir." And the said official began to laugh.

Then he said to him: "I am not speaking Latin but am asking you if our donkey *ait bu au guet*, that is to say, if you gave him to drink while crossing the ford?"

And the good man who at first understood and answered: "Did you say *au wez*, sir? * Ay, I gave him drink *au wez*."

* The comic misunderstanding is based on the dialectical pronunciation of "wez" for *gué*, meaning watering-place. (See Godefroy,

For they had crossed a ford and he had let the donkey drink. And then everyone began to laugh at the good fellow's answer.

This finished, the man set himself to eating this food until he had enough and after they had drunken and eaten, for good or for bad, for which most were angry with the archpriest, they said grace and got up from the table. But my lord the archpriest who had not at all forgotten the matter, called his host, the simple priest and spoke to him plainly in front of the gentlemen.

"Come here," he said. "Host, why didn't you do as you were told, for the gentlemen are very displeased and I had clearly told you to prepare only a little and something good and you made enormous portions and the whole thing is worthless."

The poor fellow seeing that he had dearly paid with his unfortunate donkey, was equally unhappy with these words and said before all the gentlemen that if they had not been treated in the style to which they were accustomed, that the fault lay with the archpriest.

"For," he said, "I clearly asked him what I was expected to do and he told me several times over that you wanted nothing but Modicum. Thus you have killed my poor Modicum whose pieces you have eaten, and I assure you that I would have rather given you partridge to eat than my poor Modicum, for I made good use of him in all my chores."

Now when the gentlemen heard that they had eaten the donkey, you've never witnessed such laughter, but the few who had delicate stomachs, nearly vomited out their bowels and asked the said priest if it were true that he had killed his donkey.

"Indeed I did kill him," he said. And in order to convince them, he showed them her hide. And thus the gentlemen who had eaten the donkey Modicum took their leave and went their way, but God knows if they were laughed at for it and made the butt of jokes when the truth of the matter was known, that they had eaten the donkey. I know no more about it.

Dictionnaire de la langue française [Paris: E. Boullon, 1881–1902], 9: 733).

Les Cent Nouvelles Nouvelles (71)
Philippe de Vigneulles
'THE PEDDLER'

In a village near Metz which I do not wish to name, it happened still not too long ago, that a peddler who sold shovels, pots, and cauldrons was hawking his wares, as is the custom, throughout the city. And among his other goods he was selling combs for carding and dressing hemp or flax; it was an instrument with several iron teeth.

Now there lived in that village a very beautiful young woman recently married who, upon hearing the shouts of the peddler, came out of the house to see what it was he was selling and saw that he had combs and sorely wished to buy one, but did not have enough money. Nonetheless she called to ask him how much they cost.

"I make them," he said "for ten cents a piece."

"In faith," said the woman. "I would gladly take one, but for the moment I am very short of money."

The peddler, who was a clever man, looked over this lovely, young woman who was attractive, youthful, shapely, and in a perfect state for the lowly trade and was neither the cleverest nor the most experienced in the world. Thus, all at once, he was passionately attracted to her and said: "My sweet friend, do not fret over the money for if I have anything which suits your fancy, it is yours for the asking."

"Many thanks," she said, "my friend."

"Don't mention it," said our hero, "for I am the one who would like to please and serve you in every way and manner that I can and know how, sparing nothing."

And saying this and many other such words and sweet things he sat down alongside of her and moving closer, began to talk to her of this and that and told her his sad tales with more and more feeling until she, who was tenderhearted, was soon won over by the force of these sweet words and could not say no to him when he insisted that she accept, without paying, a comb for carding flax.

And as soon as our man saw that she was pleased, he closed the door, threw her onto a bed, and jumped on her in order to look into the matter further, and worked away until she was well pleased. This done, he took leave of her, kissed her, and set off for the other villages. But he was no sooner outside of town than he thought about what he had done and was already repenting it, thinking to himself that he would have done better to have been asleep than to have committed such a blunder and he lamented terribly his comb which he had thus stupidly lost without profit.

"Unhappy day," he said, "I amused myself with that woman; I don't earn in a week what she got from me. I would have done better to have gone and spent my money at a tavern than to have given up for so little pleasure the value of nine or ten cents." Then suddenly he thought it over and said: "By the body of Christ, if I can, I shall get it back some way or other or she will pay for it."

Things remained in this state for a time, while our peddler, whenever he remembered his comb, always suffered. And it happened one day as he was thus thinking about it that he had an idea; to tell the truth a wicked trick came to him, as you will hear. He immediately packed his bags and returned to wander through the village where this young woman lived and he kept a watch until he saw that the husband was at home. And as soon as he knew for sure that he was there, he went and knocked at the door and soon our bourgeoise came to see what it was and to ask: "Who is there?"

"It's me," he said. "And how is it that you refuse to pay me for my comb? Either you pay me my money," he said, "for my comb, or you give it back to me."

And he was yelling so loudly that the husband heard him clearly and the latter came and asked his wife if she owed anything to this peddler. The poor woman was so flustered she didn't know what to answer. She, however, replied in a low voice saying yes that she had bought a comb but she didn't have any money to pay for it.

"You bought it," said her husband. "Now give it back to him. May your body rot from a bloody, stinking plague! Do you have to buy things, if you do not intend to pay for them?"

The poor woman, completely ashamed, did not dare answer, and quite distressed, returned the comb to the said peddler who took it and left overjoyed. But for my part, I say it was a great shame for him to have deceived her in this manner.

Nicolas de Troyes

Le Grand Parangon des Nouvelles Nouvelles (1537)

Introduction

Nicolas de Troyes was a simple harness maker, a native of Troyes in the province of Champagne, who at the time he composed his work (May 1535–1537) was living in Tours. A brief paragraph at the head of the second volume of *Le Grand Parangon* contains this information along with an admission that many of the stories were taken from other sources, both oral and written. This is the only knowledge we have about the author. Scholars have conjectured that he may have been connected with the court of François I, who had several residences in the Loire Valley. Des Périers knew of the *Grand Parangon*, for he alluded to the sixty-second novella at the end of his sixty-first tale, and it is possible that the work and/or its author were also known to Des Périers's patroness, Marguerite de Navarre. The first volume of the manuscript has been lost. The second contains 180 stories, of which 59 were taken from the fifteenth-century *Cent Nouvelles* and 55 from the *Decameron*. The 55 novellas which have the greatest claim to originality were edited by Emile Mabille and published by Bibliothèque Elzévirienne in 1869. Many of the tales are narrated by persons having some connection with a bridge, which seems to provide a rudimentary frame for the collection.

Although saddlery was a highly skilled and much sought-after art, Nicolas's origins were undoubtedly among the most humble of all the French *novellistes'*; and it is perhaps for this reason that his stories seem closer to the sources of folk literature. He is unique, for instance, in his use of the supernatural, such an important element in most oral literature. In addition, he shows a concern for the poor people and a desire for social justice which is totally lacking in most of the other stories of the period. His language is simple, straightforward, and pure, and aside from a tendency towards run-on sentences, his prose style could have been studied with some profit by the king's own sister. Without pretensions or artifice, Nicolas lets the story speak for itself. Occasionally his candor slips into awkwardness, as at the end of the second episode of the "Good Judge of Troyes," but usually he is the born raconteur, with a natural instinct for bringing his tales to a humorous denouement and emphasizing all their droll possibilities along the way.

Dating back to the famous judgments of Solomon, the wise judge has always been a favorite subject of folk literature; and the method of narration used in this version is strongly reminiscent of that used by the old village storytellers in Noël du Fail's *Propos Rustiques*. The story is unusual in that it concentrates more on the illustration of certain character traits than on the perfection of the plot. We may account for this, however, by its origins in the *exempla*. The two central characters, the rich man, and the judge, confront each other on three separate occasions, and each time the judge has the perception and moral courage to see justice done to the poorer and weaker opponent and to unmask the ruthless hypocrisy of the cunning moneylender. The tale derives its narrative interest from the suspense arising out of each contest, as the rich man pits his wiliness against the judge's ability to outwit him and finally to turn the tables on him. As social criticism, the story makes a telling commentary on the jurisprudence of the time.

This righteous zeal for social justice did not, however, prevent Nicolas from engaging in the coarsest forms of pleasantry. Having undoubtedly read about the gigantic feats of Gargantua and Pantagruel, he recounts in the second selection a preposterous and highly gross sequence of events.

The story of Antoine contains, albeit in embryonic form, an archetypal theme—the loss of innocence—later to be developed so fully by the great French novelists of the nineteenth century. Antoine, the disinherited hero, goes forth to seek his fortune, loses his way, and falls into the clutches of a beautiful abbess whose sensuality is matched only by her avarice. Stripped of his capital, he returns to his father, who berates him but nevertheless gives him a second chance. It is at this point that his fairy godfather appears and gives him the means to triumph over the insatiable abbess, by investing Antoine with that superfluity of virility which can only have had its origin in the most exaggerated of Freudian fantasies. The subsequent fate of the ring and the bishop's misadventure may seem at first glance merely an irrelevant pretext for more crude humor, but in fact it serves to illustrate Antoine's new-found decisiveness. Whereas in the first half of the story, he is continually amazed or astonished, not knowing where to go or what to do, once possessed of the ring, he exhibits a rare presence of mind, not only outsmarting the abbess, but managing even to turn the bishop's misfortune to his own profit. By the last paragraph Antoine has demonstrated that he has thoroughly mastered the art of combining business with pleasure and has assured his future prosperity as well.

By no means the greatest among storytellers, Nicolas de Troyes nevertheless made a valuable contribution to the art by his adroit treatment of universal themes and by making of the still undisciplined French language a pure and clear vehicle for narration.

Texts Used

NICHOLAS DE TROYES. *Le Grand Parangon des nouvelles nouvelles*. Edited by Emile Mabille. Paris: Bibliothèque Elzévirienne, 1869. (For a review of the three editions prepared by Mabille, see Kasprzyk, *Nicolas de Troyes*, pp. 8–10. Miss Kasprzyk also prepared a typescript of *Le Grand Parangon*, which she deposited at the University of Paris in connection with her thesis.)

Selected Critical Bibliography

KASPRZYK, KRYSTYNA. *Nicolas de Troyes et le genre narratif en France au XVIe siècle*. Paris: Klincksieck, 1963.

Le Grand Parangon: Nouvella 116 (Mabille 22)*
'THE GOOD JUDGE OF TROYES'

There was once in the city of Troyes a very wise and careful judge, who judged the cases which came to his attention justly and laudably, according to the true facts, and without despoiling or robbing the poor people. Now it so happened that there was in the same town a rich man, a great moneylender who had a poor neighbor, and the latter had a house of no great value adjoining that of the rich man. Several times the said rich man had tried to buy it, but the other never wanted to sell it to him. Therefore he thought to himself that he would make him lose his house in a lawsuit, for he would try anything. Thus he came to the fellow and got him to rent him a cellar, and after he had rented it, the rich man put ten barrels of oil into the said cellar, half of which were filled only midway.

Some time later, the rich man wanted to have his oil and came to the cellar to draw it out and found the five barrels which were only half-full, although he knew very well what he had done. Therefore he had the fellow indicted, saying that he had stolen the oil which he had stored in his cellar.

The judge, being notified of the affair by the statement of the neighbor, who swore to him solemnly that he had never touched it, ordered that one of the full barrels and one of the half-full barrels should be emptied, in order to determine which one contained the most dregs, but he found more than half as many more in the full one as in the half-full one, whereby he knew the truth, that the said barrel had been brought into the cellar only half-full, as had the other four. For this he condemned the rich moneylender to pay all the expenses and damages with interest. But all judges do not do likewise.

This is what happened another time. The same rich man, about whom we were speaking, was a hypocrite, who pretended to be sanctimonious. He had a great reputation as an upright man, to the point that if someone gave him a treasure to keep he was thought to render a good accounting for it. Now one day, some one or other gave him a hundred ducats

---

* Mabille, who edited the second and only remaining volume of the *Grand Parangon*, renumbered the stories.

and went away to a foreign land, where he remained for some time, until upon his return he came to his house to withdraw his money, for he had necessary business to do with it. But when the rich man saw him, he refused to recognize him and said he had never seen him, at which the poor fellow was quite astonished and didn't know what to do, for he was in great need of money; but upon the advice of some honest man, he went to speak to the judge, who advised him exactly how he could get his money back.

Therefore the young fellow sent a man he trusted, whom he had instructed what to say. The latter came to the rich man and told him that he was the steward of some great nobleman who wanted to give into his keeping ten thousand ducats. At this the rich man was overcome with joy and received him warmly. And as the two were talking together, here came the young fellow who had given a hundred ducats into his keeping, and asked him for them in the other's presence. Immediately the rich man threw his arms around him and welcomed him. Then he went to get the ducats and gave them to him. Thus, thanks to the judge's advice, the man withdrew his hundred ducats, for the rich man did not want to deny him in front of the other, lest he would not give him the ten thousand ducats to keep. But it was only a trick, for he did not intend to give him anything.

One day it happened that this rich man was on his way to some business matter and had a purse containing five hundred ducats in his sleeve. He lost the purse and it was found by a townsman. Therefore the rich man had the announcement made by trumpeter that he had lost a purse full of ducats and that whoever had found it should receive a hundred ducats for his pains. When the said townsman who had found the purse containing the five hundred ducats heard this, he counted them, took a hundred ducats as his share and give the remainder to the rich man, telling him that according to his promise he was keeping a hundred for himself. The rich man did not want to accept this and said that there had been six hundred ducats in the purse he had lost and thereupon he had the fellow taken before the judge, where both of them appeared. When the judge heard them, he saw very well that there was some chicanery involved. Therefore he drew the fellow who had the purse aside and made him raise his hand to swear. After he had taken the oath, the judge said to him, "Now then, my friend, you promise to tell the truth!"

"Yes, my lord," said the fellow.

"How many ducats were there in the purse you found?"

"My lord," said he, "by the oath which I have taken, there were only five hundred."

"Very well," said the judge, "I believe you. Go and stand over there." Then he made the rich man come before him and made him swear like the other to tell the truth. "Now then, sir," said the judge, "by the oath which you have taken you will tell the truth."

"Yes, indeed, sir," said the rich man.

"How many ducats were there in the purse you lost?"

"Sir," said he, "I promise you by my faith that there were six hundred."

"And do you intend to maintain that?" said the judge.

"Yes," said the rich man.

Then he called to the fellow who had found the purse, and in the presence of the rich man and of several other personages, "Well now," said the judge, before them all, "Come here my good man. Didn't you swear to me that in the purse you found there were only five hundred ducats?"

"Yes, my lord," said the fellow.

"And you too," he said to the rich man, "didn't you swear to me that in the purse you lost there were six hundred ducats?"

"Yes, sir," said he.

"I believe," said the judge, "that neither you nor the townsman would stoop to perjure yourselves, for you are both honorable men."

Then he took the purse and told the fellow to keep it. And then he told the rich man that he should continue to announce the loss of his purse, for this one was not his, since both of them had sworn and neither of them would stoop to perjure themselves. But when the rich man saw himself caught in this way, he was very astonished and threw himself on his knees before the judge and begged him for mercy, saying that this was his purse and that he had perjured himself falsely and wickedly and begged the judge to have his purse returned to

172

him. This he did, but not without reproaching and denouncing him in front of everybody, which he had well deserved. And that is how the good judge acted, as many judges would not have done, but they would have seized the purse first and then made enquiries.

Le Grand Parangon: Novella 27 (Mabille 39)
'THE SPELL OF THE RING'

There was once a merchant who was both rich and honest. He had several children, among whom was a gay young fellow, a fine son of about twenty-five whose name was Antoine. One day his father took him aside in private and said to him, "Come here, Antoine, I must speak to you."

"What is it, father?" said the young man.

"You ought to know," said the merchant, "that you are my son, but you are illegitimate and are not my wife's son. Therefore I must warn you that if I should pass away, you would be put out of the house like a scoundrel and wouldn't receive a cent. And so while I am still alive, I want to help you, and if you will inform me what you want to do, I shall do everything in my power to help you succeed in your attempt."

The young man was surprised to learn that he was not the true son of the house and answered his father respectfully, "Father, since I am what you say, and you want to do me some service, I am in your debt. But if you please, I have decided to follow the merchant's trade, which in your generosity you have taught me from the beginning."

"Very well," said the father. "Here is what I shall do for you. You will go to Lyons to buy your stock. I have showed you how to do it. I shall give you five hundred ducats, as a gift outright. Invest them so well in merchandise that they will bring you a profit. I shall give you your own place where you can put your merchandise and there you will be able to buy and sell as much as you want, and that will remain yours. Now conduct yourself in such a way that you will be successful in the future."

"Thank you, Father," said the young man.

Then he gave him the five hundred ducats and had a good horse brought for him. Thereupon he took leave of his father and followed the highway to Lyons. After some days' journey, he drew near to Lyons, but by misfortune he got into a wood, when it was near the hour of vespers, and lost his way so that he didn't know where he was, but he rode across the wood until it was night and he didn't know where to go. Still he rode on a little farther and with God's help he saw a dwelling. Therefore he turned as best he could in that direction and arrived in front of a great door and knocked at the entrance as loudly as he could, but there was no answer. At last he knocked so loudly that someone came to the window, the portress of the place, and asked him what he wanted. Then he replied that he was lost. The said portress came down with a lighted candle and opened a little grill to speak to him and asked him what he wanted.

"Alas, lady," said the young man, "I am a poor gentleman on my way to Lyons, and I have lost my way and wandered about in these woods, and I do not know where to go. Please be good enough to give me lodging for the night and I shall pay you well."

"Oh, my friend," said the portress, "We do not take lodgers here. This is an abbey of cloistered nuns, and besides, men are not allowed to enter. If you were to give a thousand ducats, you could not sleep here."

When Antoine heard this reply, he was so astonished that he did not know which way to turn. On the other hand, he saw that this portress was very beautiful and it irked him to have to leave.

Thus he said next, "Lady, please be so good as to give me lodging for the night and I will pay you well."

"What, sir!" said she, "I am not the lady and have no authority at all. I am simply the portress of this place."

"Aha," said Antoine. "How is it that such a beautiful lady as you has been made the portress?"

"Aha, sir," said she, "you are making fun of me. When it comes to beauty, truly I am not worthy to be a simple chambermaid to my lady the abbess."

When he heard of the great beauty of the abbess, Antoine longed more than ever to lodge here. Therefore he said to the portress, "Madam portress, please be so good as to go tell my lady the abbess that a poor, lost gentleman is at her door and that he doesn't know where to spend the night and that if she would please lodge me for the night, I shall pay her well, and I promise to give you ten ducats for your pains."

Then the portress was overjoyed and went to tell this to the abbess, who, when she heard that he had given ten ducats to the portress, decided that he must be a gentleman and let him enter and put his horse properly into the stable and had him treated well. Then Antoine entered the abbess's chamber and greeted her politely as befitted her station and she returned his greeting. Then he began to tell her of his affairs and how he was going to Lyons and how he had lost his way in the forest. The abbess gave him a warm reception and treated him hospitably. The supper was made ready at once and while they supped they talked agreeably of many subjects, but Antoine did not take his eyes off the abbess, for she was beautiful to perfection.

After supper, the tablecloth was removed and it was a question of going to bed, but Antoine did not want to and continued to converse with the lady, speaking always of love and such things, until Antoine dared to say to her, "My lady, I cannot hide my secret from you any longer, but if you would please hug and kiss me a little, I promise to give you a hundred ducats, which I have here in a purse."

"What!" said my lady the abbess, "would you hug and kiss ladies who were nuns, in this way?"

"Oh, my lady," said Antoine, "it seems to me that I would be the happiest man in the world if I were in your good graces."

"And I promise you," said she, "that you are a little, but not too much."

Then he took out his purse and counted out one hundred ducats and gave them to her, after which he hugged and kissed her, but that was nothing to him if he didn't do something else to her. At last my lady the abbess said to him, "Sir, it is time to withdraw to your room and go to bed."

"What, go to bed!" said he. "My lady, it is not time. It's not the hour yet."

"Indeed," said the abbess, "but I want to go to bed."

Then Antoine did not know what to do, but kept gazing at the lady. At last he pulled out his purse and said to her, "My lady, I ask to be your lover, if you will permit it, and to sleep with you tonight. There are another four hundred ducats, which I give to you."

"What?" said she. "Sir, you are mad to want to sleep with me."

"Upon my faith, my lady, I intended to do you as many services as you did me, and therefore, I beg you not to hold back any longer."

Then he hugged and kissed her, and my lady kissed him too and held the money tightly. And so they went to bed together. And that is how the merchant made his purchases. He was with her for eight whole days, after which, when my lady the abbess saw that he could do no more, she told him that he must leave, lest someone should notice that there was a man inside. Thus he took leave of the abbess as politely as possible and sadly bid her farewell.

When he was outside he didn't know which way to go, for he had no reason to go to Lyons, since he hadn't a cent. Therefore he decided to return to his father's house and went there. When he arrived, his father made him welcome, asking him if he had bought a great deal of merchandise. He answered that he had spent all his money and more besides and that the merchandise would arrive one day soon. Some time passed and the merchandise did not arrive. Therefore the father made discreet inquiries of other merchants who had been to Lyons, but there was no one who said he had seen his son. Thus he knew immediately that Antoine had lost his money and called him aside and asked him what he had done with his money, demanding the truth, for he knew that he had bought nothing. Antoine was taken greatly by surprise and didn't know what to say, for he saw very well that he was caught and that he would have to tell the truth. Therefore he said to his father that he must forgive him, for he had gambled it away.

"Oh, wicked rascal," said his father. "You are a miserable wretch! How could you have gambled away all my money so wickedly? I promise you that you'll repent of it." And for a long time the father was vexed with his son.

Now it happened that some time later there was a fair in

Lyons and he called Antoine to him and said, "Come here, wicked rascal that you are. You'll never amount to anything, still I want to give you your fair share. Here, take five hundred more ducats which I'm giving you, but do you know something? Unless you bring plenty of goods back with you, never return, and never darken my door again."

Thus Antoine took the five hundred ducats, mounted his horse, and took the highway to Lyons. He rode so far that he arrived at the road leading to the abbey. Then he didn't know whether to go there or not, and as he was reflecting on it, always looking at the road which he ought to follow, he saw approaching a tall man, dressed as a hermit, with a long beard and white hair, who came up to him saying, "May God watch over you, my child."

"Good father," said Antoine, "May God grant you long life."

"Where are you going, my fine son?" said the hermit.

"I vow," said Antoine, "I don't know which way to go."

"And I vow," said the hermit, "that I know your desire very well. You would gladly go to see my lady the abbess for a bit, but because I like you, I want to make you a gift, for I like you a great deal."

Then Antoine was amazed at these words and didn't know what to think.

"Here now, Antoine," said he, "out of love for you, I am giving you a magic ring and with this ring you can easily recover the five hundred ducats you gave to my lady the abbess, at least you can if you are clever. This magic ring has this power: whoever has it on his finger and makes the sign of the cross will increase the size of his male organ by half a foot. Therefore take it. I give it to you with all my heart."

"I thank you in good faith, kind father," said Antoine, "and I don't know how to repay you. But truly now, tell me please, when one's organ has become so large, how is it possible to make it small again?"

"Oh, Lord, yes," said the hermit, "you must make the sign of the cross behind you."

Then Antoine took leave of the hermit, thanking him greatly for the good service he had done him. He took the road to the abbey and spurring on his horse, soon arrived. As soon as the portress saw him, she welcomed him, asking how he was. He told her he was well and inquired about my lady the abbess. She told him she too was well, then he went to see her immediately, and she received him hospitably, telling him he was welcome.

"My lady," said Antoine, "I thank you. Know that I have come here out of love for you and that I have another five hundred ducats. I have come to sleep with you with the greatest desire I have ever had. I shall give you another five hundred ducats, but I must enjoy you for the entire night and you must endure it till I get my fill. Otherwise I don't want to give them to you."

"Oh I promise you that I'm delighted," said the abbess, "and I'll go you one better. If I can't endure you one night I'll return what you gave me before."

"Upon my word," said Antoine, "that is a good arrangement."

Then he took out his five hundred ducats and showed them to the abbess, at which she went to get the others and they put everything together.

"Now," said the young man, "all that is for one man."

"By my faith," said the abbess, "it's mine."

Then they went to supper and enjoyed themselves and after supper they talked a bit and then went to bed. The young man, who was fresh and determined, broke three lances on the first try with his normal organ, which must have measured at least half a foot. He had the ring on his finger and now he made the sign of the cross and suddenly it grew longer by half a foot. Then he began the jousting for the fourth time, and the abbess found it wonderfully good, but her pleasure soon passed, for he doubled his signs of the cross until the poor abbess could endure no more. She began to shriek and jumped out of the bed, abandoning him. She gave him the one thousand ducats and asked him in amazement where in the devil he had fished up such an instrument, for he had not had it before. He wanted to keep at the job, but the abbess wouldn't permit him to touch her and thus passed the night until morning, when the young man arose and took leave of my lady the abbess, carrying with him his thousand ducats.

He took the highway for Lyons and as he went along he

came to a very beautiful spring and stepped down to refresh himself, and taking the ring from his finger, he laid it on a stone beside the fountain. Then after a while he mounted his horse and left, forgetting his ring, and took the highway to Lyons.

Now you ought to know that soon there passed by this fountain a bishop with his company, who stopped at the spring and seeing the ring on the stone, took it and put it on his finger without thinking, for it was not of great value. And besides he didn't know the power of the ring. After the said bishop had refreshed himself somewhat, he mounted his mule and went off with his company. Now you ought to know that this bishop was going to a small town in Auvergne to make his entrance, for he was bishop there and the entire town was waiting for him.

Thus, he rode on until he came to the outskirts of the town and all the men of the town came out to meet him. Immediately he began to make the sign of the cross, as was his custom, and his organ grew by half a foot. Then he rode on to the town gate and everyone knelt down for the benediction and he made the sign of the cross and again his organ grew until it stuck out between the mule's ears. He and his company were so ashamed that they didn't know what to do. They made hastily for the great church and from there carried him, distressed and angry, to his lodgings. When he had arrived, he began to pray to God and the Virgin Mary, continually crossing himself and that organ continually growing longer, until there was no more room for it in the chamber. The men of the town came to see him. Everyone was so greatly astonished by this event that soon the entire town knew of it and the news spread into the countryside and at last reached Lyons where Antoine immediately heard it. Then he knew that the bishop had found his ring. He asked where this bishop was and he was told. Immediately he mounted his horse and headed in that direction and when he had reached the town, he at once had notices made saying that a doctor who cured all maladies and many other things had arrived. As soon as the bishop knew of it, he ordered him to see if he could do something for him. When the doctor arrived, he looked at the organ which was more than ten yards long and was greatly amazed. Then he looked at his face and his hands and recognized his ring on his finger, but he gave no sign. At this, they asked him if he could really cure the bishop of having such a large organ. He replied yes, but that they must be willing to pay him.

"Alas, master," said the bishop, "it is not a question of payment. You shall have all you want, were it ten thousand ducats."

"Very well," said the doctor, "I promise you that before two weeks are up, I shall make your organ quite small, but first you must give me all the rings on your fingers."

Thus he gave them all to him and when he had them, he pretended to make him drink some potion, and then made the sign of the cross behind him. And that very day, he made it grow a foot shorter, for which they were all very glad. He could have made it small all in one day, but he did not want to, and he continued for two weeks until he had so shrunk his organ that he had only a very little one left, for which the bishop was wonderfully glad. Afterwards, he paid him well and gave him four thousand ducats, for which Antoine was very glad and returned to Lyons to amuse himself with good comrades and good ladies, with whom he worked a bit with his own organ, so that they were well satisfied. He managed to amass a great deal of money, for he was more than half a year in Lyons. Then afterwards, he bought a great deal of merchandise, which he sent to his father's house, who was greatly astonished, when he saw that his son had profited so well, and did not scold him again. But such adventures do not happen to everyone.

Noël du Fail (1520?–1591):
Baliverneries

Introduction

Noël du Fail was one of the few storytellers to interest himself in the lower classes. Himself a member of the lesser nobility, he lived much of his life as a gentleman among rustics in his native Brittany, where it was evidently his pleasure to participate somewhat condescendingly in the conversation and pastimes of the local peasantry or to sample their home-brewed refreshments within their humble dwellings.

Although he never attempted to bridge the social chasm which in the sixteenth century separated even a country squire from the common folk, he did study their habits, their simple pleasures, their dress, and their way of life with a quick eye, committing to memory all the details of their daily life.

By profession, du Fail was a jurist, first a judge, and eventually a member of the Parliament of Rennes, the author of a legal treatise entitled *Les Arrêts* (1579). As a young man he had been sent to Paris in the company of his tutor, Colin Brian, who later became the "Lupold" of his stories, and had received the standard classical education of the time. In the *Contes et Discours d'Eutrapel* (1585), he gave a lively account of the feuds, excursions, dissipations, and merry pranks of those student days. Seemingly the sojourn in Paris came to an end for want of money, induced no doubt by a penchant for gambling, and he followed the French army to Italy as a foot soldier in 1543, participating in the battle of Cérisoles, 14 April 1544.

There followed a period during which he pursued his legal studies before settling down in Brittany under the fond eye of his elder brother, François II du Fail, to whom he later gave the literary name of "Polygame." In 1547, he published his *Propos rustiques*, a collection of conversations between various rustic types, and in 1548, the *Baliverneries*, a loose series of narrative anecdotes, in which he introduced the characters who were later to be more fully developed in the *Eutrapel*. Strongly influenced by the style if not by the thinking of Rabelais, his stories display that writer's fondness for exaggeration, prolixity, and verbal pyrotechnics.

The story offered here, taken from the *Baliverneries*, begins with an oblique reference to an episode from Rabelais and echoes his style in the long, humorous description of the household articles the villagers attempt to save in their panic. Despite its burlesque tone, however, it offers a realistic glimpse into the possessions and activities of the common folk. The loosely constructed tale ends on the note of antifeminism which had become so much a standard part of the narrative tradition. The situation described was one unfortunately common throughout the period, when mercenary soldiers supported themselves in peacetime by forming into bands of brigands and plunderers.

Du Fail's language and style present a unique technical challenge, which we have tried to meet with all the scholarly resources at our disposal. Certain passages remain unclear even to the specialists consulted, however, and for these we must beg our readers' indulgence.

Text Used

NOËL DU FAIL. *Oeuvres facétieuses*. Edited by J. Assézat. 2 vols. Paris: Bibliothèque Elzévirienne, 1874.

Selected Critical Bibliography

DÉDÉYAN, CHARLES. "Noël du Fail et les femmes." *Annales de Bretagne* 51 (1944): 206–217.

PHILIPOT, EMMANUEL. *La Vie et l'oeuvre littéraire de Noël du Fail*. Paris: Champion, 1914.

———. *Essai sur le style et la langue de Noël du Fail*. Paris: Champion, 1914.

Baliverneries (3)

'A MAN'S BEST FRIEND'

"You must have noticed that town where you wanted to stop and drink, sir," said Eutrapel to Polygame.* "As we were going along, I called to mind something that happened there when I was a young boy."

"What was that?" said Polygame.

"Just this. When the wars between the Laringues and the Pharingues were ended,† the soldiers were expressly commanded to go home, each to his own woman, as quickly and honestly as possible, without devouring the peasantry. Nevertheless, though they had taken no oaths and received no pay, a company of men trained in warfare, all skilled in arms, mustered togther, and not being able to exercise their original profession any more, they were no less to be feared than was Spartacus, who was just such another organizer of abandoned men, and who put to flight Lentulus, the Roman, or the eleven thousand devils on the day of the wooden shoes.‡ Such were these soldiers, who were so numerous that since no one enforced the order, they could not only resist the village communities but lay siege to fortified towns. And because they had a provost or two at their heels, they were exceptionally provoked to wrongdoing for two reasons: the booty and plunder, which beckoned to them, and the ensuing death, if they failed to do as they should. Thus, having been heavy-handedly and without warning relieved of their duties, they despaired of their salvation. For this reason, they did a thousand wrongs, even to those poor priests, such as making them buy back their letters of priesthood for much more than they had cost. And this one poor soul they tied onto a bench and

* Eutrapel is generally believed to represent the author and Polygame his older brother, François II du Fail, seigneur de Chateauletard. François had been twice married and lived with several dependent female relatives. In the sixteenth century, the word "polygamous" was often applied to consecutive as well as simultaneous marriages.

† Cf. Rabelais's *Pantagruel*. These were two imaginary towns located in the giant Pantagruel's throat.

‡ The reference here is unclear.

there they auctioned his testes off to the last bidder before the candle went out.* Seeing which, the poor devil was obliged to make the final bid and outdo the others or there would have been less of him.

"It was rumored that on the next day they were to arrive at Mortagne and that the band was already beginning its approach. But oh good lord sir, how can I describe the fear, the astonishment, the fright, that the poor people thereabouts felt at this simple news? I am lost and no longer know where I am. One threw his spade, his trivet, and his hooked knife into the well. Another with his pot-hook attached to his belt, his kettle on his head, his washtub in one hand, his shoes crushed together in the other, ran with all his might towards the woods of Senne to hide his household there. Another, having loaded his chestnut roaster onto his shoulder, put his shoe horn into the patch on his doublet, sewn eight coins into his pocket, taken some sausage down from the chimney and tied them nicely to his sword, ran to the next parish saying, 'At least they won't get everything this way!' Another, having tied up with a cord his crock, his bottle, his awl, his sieve, his codpiece, his grease pot, and his scissors, ran breathlessly towards the vineyards of Bouillant. In the same way, I saw two of them, one laden with a double sack, which was full of apples on one side and sausages with a great deal of mustard on the other; the second carrying a wool basket, who ran, to give some idea, farther than from here to la Balletière. Others were driving in front of them their animals, laden down as the desperateness of the situation demanded. The oxen and cows carried between their horns numerous basins, lanterns, firearms, rakes, funnels, and two-ended fighting sticks. 'For,' they said to themselves, 'at least we shall not be caught losing these.'

"There was a dog who never stopped making a nuisance of himself; grovelling, fawning, wagging his tail, going from one to the other, and giving obvious signs that he wanted to help his master with some unusual service. He didn't stop, I say, until he had been loaded with half a dozen spindles, which gave rise to all the other dogs following his example and doing likewise, and those which they didn't want to burden took

* It was the custom to limit bidding at auctions to the time required to burn a certain length of candle.

some scythe or whip handle, so that they would not be taxed with ingratitude at home or accused of conspiring with the enemy.

"The women were busier than twenty packing their balls of yarn, sheathing their sheep shears, threading their needles, hooking together their pins, starching their headdresses, arranging their jewel boxes, hanging up their mustard pots, making themselves false bottoms,* arranging their collars, buckling their belts, tying up their packages, putting their shuttles into bags, getting their petticoats into place, rattling their money boxes, closing their chests, fastening the lead tips securely onto their spindles, filling up their blow pipes,† looking for their tools, wrapping up their distaffs, barricading their doors, looking to their kneading troughs, packing up their work, organizing their sabots, fastening their shutters. To sum up, it was a marvellous orgy, a desperate fury, a tragedy.

"Then they said, 'My cousin, my friend, please put that into your bundle for me. Upon my soul, neighbor, let us hurry, for if these soldiers once come and find us, we will be raped so often, that it will be impossible not to die of it.'

" 'You,' said one in her turn, who was wrapping up a scythe from Quentin, 'have you seen many die of that in your time?'

" 'I don't say it for that,' said another, 'but since it has to be done, I'd rather die from that cause than another.'

"Upon my faith, sir, they almost stayed behind, but oh the wickedness of the rabble! Here come ten or twelve old grannies who saw the trouble the younger women were preparing for their sons, nephews, and cousins. And they also knew very well that when it happened no one would take any more notice of them than of the old bags they resembled. Therefore, quickly and without delay, they informed their husbands, who, not happy about it, finished packing the rest of the stuff, reserving ampler judgment and punishment of the alleged treachery, more or less commited, until they should be in Orgières, where straightaway they beat their retreat

> Preferring to lose garden and grange
> Than commit their safety to the strange."

* Putting packages under their robes.
† Tubes through which small projectiles could be blown.

Bonaventure des Périers (1510?–1544?)

Les Nouvelles Récréations et Joyeux Devis

Introduction

Although there is far more conjecture than certainty concerning the details of Des Périers's biography, he was probably born in the little town of Arnay-le-Duc somewhere between 1510 and 1515. It is generally assumed that his formal education took place at the Abbey School of Saint Martin in Autun, where the Archdeacon Robert Hurault, Protestant sympathizer and former preceptor to Marguerite de Navarre, exercised considerable influence on his thinking.

Des Périers's first two adventures in publishing gave evidence of his humanistic training. In 1535 his name (Jo. Eutychus Deperius) appeared with that of Olivetan in the publication of the Waldensian Bible, a French translation from the Hebrew and Greek. Only one year later, at Lyons, Etienne Dolet acknowledged his help in the preparation of the first volume of his *Commentarii linguae latinae*.

By this time, Des Périers had already established something of a reputation in the literary circles of Lyons. In 1536 he became valet-de-chambre to Marguerite de Navarre and through her and his recent publications undoubtedly came to know other notable figures such as François Rabelais and Clément Marot. It was for the latter, in fact, that he published in 1537 his poem "Marot contre Sagon," in which he defended his poet-friend against the calumnious accusations of Sagon. That same year saw the publication in Paris of his *Prognostication des prognostications*, a satire on the predictions of astrologers.

In 1538 a series of enigmatic dialogues entitled *Cymbalum mundi* created a great commotion among Renaissance theologians. Though unsigned, the work was clearly Des Périers's.

What is less clear, however, is the precise significance of this curious Lucianic satire, which nonetheless earned its author the condemnations of not only the church but of Jean Calvin.

Thereafter the facts of Des Périers's life become sparser still. He apparently continued in the queen of Navarre's service until 1541. Sometime between that date, however, and the posthumous publication in 1544 of a Recueil, he died, if we are to believe Henri Estienne's testimony, by his own hand.[1]

If Des Périers is not one among a myriad of forgotten and obscure Renaissance humanists, it is in large measure because of his collection of stories, *Les Nouvelles Récréations et joyeux devis* published some fourteen years after his death in 1558.[2] Neither his verse nor even the admittedly interesting *Cymbalum mundi* could have saved him from oblivion. And yet, it is likely that the author himself attached less importance to these stories than to any of his other works. Unlike Rabelais, he does not ask his reader to seek out any *substantifique moelle*. His stories seem rather to be in the tradition of Boccaccio, told only to entertain and amuse:

. . . there is no allegorical, hidden or bizarre meaning. You'll not have the trouble of asking the significance of this or that. You'll need neither glossary nor notes. Take them [these stories] at face value. Open the book. If one story does not please you, go on to the next. They come in all shapes and sizes, but not for weeping.[3]

On the other hand, as in Rabelais, there is an implied lesson of optimistic good cheer. Although he peopled his world with the traditional cuckolds, sensual priests, and shyster lawyers, he does not bog down in weighty moralizing. His overriding tone is a gay lightheartedness, which seems to defy, in the manner of Rabelais's *pantagruélisme* the manifest evidences of dishonesty.

As distinguished from the more fulsome prose of most of his predecessors, Des Périers's narrative style is closer to the anecdotal tradition of the *facéties* in the manner of Poggio.[4] His stories are short and frequently strung together in some sort of associative pattern. To be sure, the sophisticated reader of today would find Des Périers's trailing postscripts, sometimes shallow and repetitious characterizations, and awkward transitions unpolished, but nonetheless, one is constantly aware of the artist who has given a definite form and a stylistic unity to his collection. To begin with, though he rarely penetrates beyond the surface of things, Des Périers does create through his candid dialogue a sense of immediacy and reality. The speech patterns of his characters lie somewhere between the extemporaneous prattle of Du Fail's peasants and the more cerebral exchanges of Marguerite de Navarre's courtly ladies and gentlemen.

Like his patroness, Des Périers seems to have collected anecdotes from friends and based his tales on true happenings. His taste ran more to the hearty jest than hers, however, and his ear was more sensitive to a regional turn of phrase or a bit of local dialect.

Above all it is his special use of verbal humor which gives to the stock situations and characters their originality and to the collection as a whole its stylistic coherence. In the story of the "Cantor's Stew" (3), though the author draws from tradition in his satire on church politics, he gives to his tale a new dimension with the cantor's waggish wit. In the end, the reader takes as much delight in his *bon mot* as in his material triumph.

Likewise the "Ear Specialist" (9) might have become just another reworking of a hackneyed theme were it not that Des Périers brings to the tired, old plot a brisk humor which does not rely on the situation alone. In the subtly contrived dialogue between the ingenuous wife and the overly solicitous neighbor, Sir André's falsehearted words of good will clash incongruously with those of the duped woman.

Linked to a long line of deceitful churchmen, the lecherous but delightful vicar of Brou amuses the reader with his quick and ready tongue. In the episodic "Vicar of Brou and his Bishop," the essential ingredient of the humor is nearly altogether verbal in nature. It is, in fact, the vicar's intentional overliteralness which makes for the comic situation and which in the end permits us to forgive him his sinfulness. As for the succinct "Holy Excommunition" (36), every detail leads up to the vicar's comic statement about a serious spiritual matter.

"In the Confessional" (40) is particularly characteristic of the story made up of a group of short, related anecdotes in the manner of the *facéties*. Though once again it depends essentially on verbal humor, it also uses caricature, in the person of the village priest who represents the kind of supercilious, half-educated cleric so distasteful to the humanist's mind.

One of the best-told stories in the collection is "Sister Thoinette" (62), which is a masterpiece of classical conciseness.[5] A definite departure, however, from the lighthearted tone of the preceding tales is the last story translated here, "The Italian Kiss" (78), for it begins by inveighing against certain inelegant Italian mores all too eagerly adopted by the French. It goes on to describe a woman who becomes victim of an uncouth Italian custom and her subsequent attempt to convict her aggressor in court. The poor defendant seems all but condemned when his witty retort to the judge saves him and turns a serious melodrama into farce.

Des Périers's own expressed intention to entertain his reader has led some to lump his work uncritically with writers of the Gallic tradition. A careful review of his art and of his themes would reveal that his stories represent, however, an important stage in the development of the novella, somewhere between the mirth-provoking tales of *Les Cent Nouvelles nouvelles* and the thought-provoking ones of the *Heptaméron*. Borrowing from the format of the *facéties*, Des Périers is, however, stylistically closer to Rabelais, with whom he shares the latter's predilection for wordplay. It might be noted, in concluding, that this taste for puns and amusing circumlocutions has discouraged to date a complete translation of his works.

Notes for Introduction

1. *Apologie pour Hérodote*, ed. P. Ristelhuber (Paris: Liseux, 1879), I, p. 403.

2. This is not the place to go into the complex question of the authenticity of Des Périers's authorship. We accept Sozzi's conclusions that, though there is no irrefutable proof, Des Périers is the author of the first ninety stories of the *Nouvelles Récréations et joyeux devis* (*Les Contes de Bonaventure Des Périers*, pp. 423–448).

3. See edition by Louis Lacour (Paris: Librairie des Bibliophiles, 1874), p. 9. The translation is ours.

4. Sozzi, *Les Contes de Bonaventures Des Périers*, pp. 418–419.

5. For an interesting reworking of the theme see La Fontaine's "Les Lunettes" (*Contes*, IV, 12).

Text Used

BONAVENTURE DES PÉRIERS. *Nouvelles Récréations et joyeux devis*. Edited by Louis Lacour. Paris: Librairie des Bibliophiles, 1874.

Selected Critical Bibliography

BECKER, PHILIPP AUGUST. *Bonaventure Des Périers als Dichter und Erzähler*. Vienna: Holder-Pichler-Tempsky, 1924.

CHENEVIÈRE, ADOLPH. *Bonaventure Des Périers, sa vie, ses poésies*. Paris: Piori, 1886.

HASSELL, JAMES WOODROW. *Sources and Analogues of the "Nouvelles Récréations."* University of North Carolina Studies in Comparative Literature. Chapel Hill: University of North Carolina Press, 1957.

SOZZI, LIONELLO. *Les Contes de Bonaventure Des Périers*. Turin: Giappichelli, 1965.

Les Joyeux Devis (3)
'THE CANTOR'S STEW'

There was once in the church of Saint Hilaire of Poitiers a cantor who sang bass and who, because he was a good fellow and a good drinker (as many of these people are), was well liked by the canons and often invited to dinner and supper. Since they treated him so well, it seemed to him that there was not a one among them who did not wish for his advancement; and so he would often say to one or the other of them:

"Sir, you know how long I have been serving this church. It seems time that I should be promoted. I beg you to bring it up in your chapter meeting. I do not ask for much; you gentlemen have all kinds of means at your disposal; I should be happy with the very least among them."

They listened to his request in good spirit and each one privately gave him an encouraging reply, saying that this seemed a reasonable thing. "And if the chapter is not able to reward you," they would say to him, "I shall reward you myself." In short, at every gathering of the chapter, where he would always remind them of his presence, they would say to him with one accord, "Wait a bit longer. The chapter will not forget you; you will have the first opening."

When it came time, however, there was always some excuse. Either the benefice was too large (yet one of them had accepted it), or it was too little and they did not want to make him so small a gift, or they had been obliged to give it to one of their brother's nephews.* But without fail he was to have the first opening.

And with these empty promises they would humor the bass. Thus time went by and still he served without receiving anything. Meanwhile, within his humble means, he continued to favor certain of these gentlemen whom he knew to be the most influential in the chapter with gifts such as fresh fruits, chickens, pigeons, or partridges, depending on the season, all of which the poor cantor bought at either the old marketplace or at the *regratterie*,† giving them to believe that he did so at no cost to himself. And they always accepted.

* Euphemism for a bastard child.
† Market for cut-rate or second-hand items.

Finally, seeing he was no better off and besides had lost time, money, and energy, the bass decided to wait no longer and to show them what he thought of them. And in order to do so, he managed to put aside five or six gold crowns. While he was saving (for it took time), he began to lavish even more attention on these gentlemen and to use greater discernment. When he saw that the moment was ripe, he approached the most prominent among them, asking them each whether they would do him the honor of dining Sunday next at his home and told them, speaking most respectfully, that in the nine or ten years he had been in their service the least he could do was have them once for dinner, and that he would treat them not as they deserved, but as best he could.

They accepted, but when the day came, each was prudent enough to have his customary meal prepared in advance, fearing they might be badly fed by the cantor, since they trusted more to his voice than to his cooking.

At dinnertime each sent his stew to the cantor, who said to the servants who brought them: "How is it, my friend, that your master does me this wrong? Is he so afraid of being mistreated? He shouldn't have sent anything."

Saying which, he took whatever was delivered and put everything all together into one large pot which he had especially prepared in a corner of the kitchen.

At that moment the gentlemen arrived and seated themselves in order of unworthiness. The cantor carried in the impressive entrée consisting of all the stews in the pot. God knows how appetizing they were, for one had sent a capon with leeks, another with saffron, another had sent a piece of salted beef with turnips, another a chicken with herbs, another a boiled chicken, and another a roasted chicken. When they saw this fine platter, they did not have the courage to eat; but each waited for the arrival of his own stew, never realizing that it was there before them. The cantor, going back and forth busying himself with serving them, kept watching their reactions at the table.

Seeing that the service dragged on a bit, they could not help but remark, "Take away this stew and bring our own!"

"But these *are* yours," he replied.

"Ours! They can't be!"

"But they are. Here are your turnips," he said to one, and to another, "Here are your cabbages," and to another, "Here are your leeks."

At that they began to recognize their stews and to look at one another. "We have certainly been taken in," they said. "Is this the way you treat your canons, bass?"

"The devil take him! I always told you this fool would get the better of us," one of them said. "I had the best stew that I've eaten all year."

"And I," said another, "had gone to a lot of trouble to prepare mine. I had a feeling I would have done better to eat at home."

When the bass had listened to them all, he said, "Gentlemen, if your stews were so good, how could they have gotten worse in so short a time? I kept them well covered near the fire. I don't see how I could have done any better."

"Indeed!" said they. "But who gave you the idea of mixing them all up together. Didn't you know they wouldn't be worth a thing like that?"

"In other words, what is good separately is not good together? In truth, I believe it," he said, "were it only for you gentlemen, for when you are each alone, no one is better than you. You promise heaven and earth. You make everyone wealthy with your empty promises, but put them together in your chapter house, you are all like your stews!"

They understood what he meant. "So that's what you have been driving at," they said. "You're quite right. But in the meantime, aren't we going to eat?"

"To be sure, to be sure. Better than you deserve," he answered.

Then he brought them what he had prepared and they ate heartily and left contented. Then and there they decided to promote the cantor, which they did. And so by means of a stew, he accomplished more than he had by all his former requests and supplications.

Les Joyeux Devis (9)

'THE EAR SPECIALIST'

It should come as no surprise that country girls are far from clever, since sometimes city girls foolishly allow themselves to be abused. It does not happen to them often, it is true, for it is in cities that women play wily tricks. But heaven only knows it does happen there, for I want to tell about a truly beautiful woman in the town of Lyons, who was married to a rather successful businessman. He had not been with her more than three or four months when his business called him away, leaving her only three weeks pregnant, which she realized because of faintings and other symptoms of pregnant women.

As soon as he had left, his neighbor, a certain Sir André, who by dint of neighbor's rights had taken to frequenting the house, came to see the young wife and began to jest with her, asking how she liked being a married woman. She answered that she liked it well enough, except that she thought she was pregnant.

"Is it possible?" he said. "Your husband couldn't have had the time since you have been together to make a child."

"I am certain of it, however," she said, "for I feel exactly the way Dame Thoiny did with her first child."

"Well," Sir André said to her without malice aforethought or any idea of what would happen, "believe me, I know about these things, and from the looks of you I suspect that your husband did not complete the child and that there are still some ears to be finished. Upon my honor, take care! I have known many women who have suffered the consequences, and others who, being more prudent and fearing misfortune, have had their child finished during the absence of their husband. The minute my friend returns, see that he finishes it."

"But he has gone to Burgundy," said the young woman, "and he can't possibly be back in less than a month."

"My dear," he said, "you're in a bad way. Your child will have only one ear, and moreover the others are in danger of having only one also, for more likely than not when there is some defect in a woman pregnant with her first child, the rest suffer too."

At this news, the young wife became terribly upset. "Oh my lord," she said, "I'm truly a wretched woman! I can't understand why he didn't think to do it before he left."

"I tell you," said Sir André, "there is a remedy for everything except death. For your sake, I shall certainly be happy to complete it for you, something I wouldn't do for anyone else, since my own affairs keep me busy. I wouldn't want any misfortune to befall you, however, because of lack of help."

For her part, she naïvely imagined that he was telling the truth, for he spoke brusquely and as if he wanted to make her believe that he was doing her a favor and that it was only a nuisance for him. As a result, she had the child finished, a service which Sir André graciously performed for her not only that once, but frequently thereafter.

On one such occasion, she said to him, "Yes but suppose you were to give him four or five ears? You'd better stop before you do more harm than good."

"Oh no," Sir André replied, "I'll only make one. But do you think it's done so quickly? It took your husband a long time to accomplish what he did! And besides, one can make less, but one can never make more, since once the job is done, it's done!"

And thus the ear was finished.

When the husband had returned, his wife said to him while she was caressing him during the night, "Upon my word, you're a fine maker of children! You made me one which would have had only one ear, and you left without finishing it."

"Come, come now," he said, "you're talking nonsense. Are children made without ears?"

"Indeed they are," she said. "Just ask Sir André, who told me that he had seen more than twenty who had only one ear because they were never finished and that the making of a child's ear is the hardest thing. If he hadn't completed it for me, think of what a fine child I'd have had!"

The husband was not too pleased with this news. "What sort of finishing is this?" he said, "and what did he do to you to finish it?"

"How can you ask?" she said. "He did what you do to me."

"Aha, is that so?" said the husband. "Have you played such a trick on me?"

Lord knows how badly he slept, he a man of short temper! Thinking about the completion of this ear, in his mind's eye he stabbed the completer more than a hundred times; and the night seemed longer than a thousand years, so eager was he to avenge himself.

And in fact, the first thing he did upon arising was to go to see Sir André, whom he denounced in a rage, threatening to make him regret the dirty trick he had played on him. His bark was worse than his bite, however, for when he had calmed down, he was mollified by a Catalonian coverlet * which Sir André gave to him, with the condition that the latter should no longer meddle in the making of his children's ears, a task which he could perform well enough without him.

Les Joyeux Devis (34)

'THE VICAR OF BROU AND HIS BISHOP'

This same vicar † had a chambermaid twenty-five years of age, who served him night and day, poor wench, and because of whom he was often called to the bishop's court to pay a fine. Despite this, the bishop seemed unable to reform him. On one occasion he forbade him to have any chambermaids less than fifty years old. The vicar accordingly hired one of twenty and another of thirty. Seeing that this was a sin *pejor priore,* ‡ the bishop ordered him not to have any chambermaid at all. The vicar had to comply or at least pretend to. But because he was a jolly fellow, he always managed to appease the bishop, who often visited him, in fact, for he gave him good wine and, on occasion, French company.

One time the bishop asked if he might come the following

---

* Woolen coverlets from Catalonia were highly esteemed.

† The vicar of Brou appears in several stories of the collection.

‡ Literally "worse than before." The phrase may refer to Matthew 27:64.

day to have supper with him; he wanted nothing but light foods, however, since he had not been feeling too well recently, and the doctors had ordered a light diet to settle his stomach. The vicar told him that he would be welcome, and thinking he would regale his bishop, he immediately went out to buy great quantities of calf and mutton giblets, which he placed to cook in a large pot.

Inasmuch as the bishop had forbidden it, he had no chambermaid at the time. How did he manage? While the bishop's supper was cooking, and about the time that the bishop was due to arrive, he removed his drawers and his shoes and carried out a load of laundry to a stream which ran along the road by which the bishop would pass. He went into the water up to his knees and, pail and paddle in hand, set to washing his linen with gusto, bobbing his front and back ends up and down like a crow cracking a nut.

About then, the bishop arrived, and those of his party who were ahead came upon our good vicar doing his wash, raising his rear and revealing everything he owned. They pointed him out to the bishop.

"Sir, would you look there at the vicar of Brou doing his laundry!"

When he saw him, the bishop was so astonished he did not know whether to laugh or be angry. He approached the vicar, who continued to beat with one arm after the other, pretending not to see anything.

"Well now, my good vicar, what are you doing here?"

And the vicar, as if surprised, said, "Sir, as you can see, I am doing my wash."

"Doing your wash!" said the bishop. "Have you become a launderer? Is this proper for a priest? Ha, I'll give you your fill of water in my prisons and I'll take away your benefice."

"But why, sir?" said the vicar. "You forbade me to have a chambermaid, and since I have no more clean linen, I have to do the work myself."

"Oh, you rascally vicar! Fine, fine, you'll get one, but what are we having for supper?"

"Sir, you'll eat well, God willing. Don't fret. You shall have light foods."

When it came time to eat, the vicar served the bishop and

as an entrée offered him nothing but the boiled giblets, at which the bishop remarked, "What's this you're giving me? You must be making fun of me."

"Sir," said he, "yesterday you requested that I cook nothing but light foods. I tried all kinds, but when I came to preparing them, they all dropped to the bottom of the pot, until I finally chanced upon these giblets which remained on the surface of the water. They were the lightest of all."

"You're good for nothing," said the bishop, "and always will be! You're well aware what tricks you're playing on me. Fine then, I'll teach you with whom you're dealing."

The vicar, however, had had a good supper prepared. He served foods of quite another sort and treated his bishop so well that he was very satisfied.

After supper they played at *flus* * for an hour, whereupon the bishop wished to retire. The vicar, who knew his habits, had prepared a tender young thing to go with his nightcap, and in addition, assigned to each member of the party a female companion, for this is what they were accustomed to when they came to his house.

When he retired, the bishop said to him, "Vicar, that will be all. I am quite pleased with you this time, but do you know what else you might do for me? My groom is nothing but a drunkard. I would like to see my horses treated like myself. See to this, please."

The vicar did not forget these words; he took leave of his bishop till morning and immediately asked throughout the parish to borrow a number of mares. In short order, he found as many as he needed and put them into the stable alongside the bishop's horses. What a neighing, stamping, and storming the horses created around the mares. It was really something to hear them. Having left the care of the horses to the vicar, the groom, who had gone out to curry his two-legged charge, heard this great din coming from the stable and quickly returned to quiet things, but he couldn't get back before the bishop had heard the noise.

The following morning the bishop wanted to know what

* *Flus* or *flux:* A game in which the winner is the one who holds the most cards of the same color.

198

had troubled the horses all night. The groom tried to pass it off as nothing, but the bishop insisted upon knowing.

"Sir," said the groom, "It was the mares who were with the horses."

Thinking it was another of the vicar's tricks, the bishop called him in and gave him a tongue-lashing.

"Miserable creature that you are, are you going to go on making a fool of me? You ruined my horses! Don't you worry, you. . . . . . ."

To this the vicar answered, "But sir, didn't you tell me last night that you wished me to treat your horses like you? I did the best that I could for them. They had hay and oats. They were up to their bellies in straw. All that was lacking was a female for each, and I had them sent for. Didn't you and your party each have yours?"

"The devil take you, nasty vicar," said the bishop. "You're always one up on me. I'll get even with you, and I'll pay you back for your kind treatment!"

In the end, however, he found no solution except to leave until the next time.

• • • • • • • • • • • • •

Les Joyeux Devis (36)

'HOLY EXCOMMUNICATION'

One Sunday during high Mass when it came time for the sermon, the vicar of Brou climbed up into the pulpit in order to preach to his parishioners. As is usual, the pulpit was located next to a pillar. While he was preaching, a clerk came from the vicarage and handed him some notes for letters of admonition, which were made public on Sunday, according to the custom. The vicar took these memoranda and stuck them into a hole which had been made expressly in the pillar to hold all the notes brought to him during the sermon.

When he had finished his preaching, he put his finger into the hole to take the papers out again, but they were too far in, probably because he had been deeply engaged in explaining some difficult point of the Gospel when he had put them there.

He pulled and twisted with his finger; he did everything that he could, but to no avail, for instead of pulling them out, he simply pushed them in farther. Finally, out of breath and seeing that he was making no progress, he said, "My parishioners, I stuck some papers in there which I can't get out, but I excommunicate everyone who is in this hole."

Les Joyeux Devis (40)
'IN THE CONFESSIONAL'

There was once a village priest who was very proud of knowing more than a bit of Cato, for he had read *De Syntaxi* and *Fauste gelida*.* And for that reason he convinced himself that he was a person of great elegance and spoke like one. In order to pass himself off as a great man of learning, he used words which filled up his mouth. Even during confessions he used terms which astounded the simple folk.

One day he was confessing a poor artisan whom he asked, "Now tell me, my friend, are you at all ambitious?"

The poor fellow answered no, since he thought that that word applied to great lords. He was almost sorry he had come to be confessed by this priest who, he had heard say, was such a learned scholar and spoke so loftily that nobody understood a thing, which he realized from this word "ambitious." For though he might have heard it used in the past, he had no idea what it meant.

After this the priest asked, "Are you a fornicator?"

"No."

"Are you gluttonous?"

"No."

"Are you prideful?"

Again he answered no. "Are you irascible?"

* Des Périers, who is mocking this half-educated cleric, is speaking here of two popular works of the period. The first is by the fifteenth-century grammarian Despautère and the second represents the beginning of an eclogue by the fifteenth-century, neo-Latin poet Baptiste Mantuan.

"Still less." The priest seeing that he continued to answer no was admirified.*

"Are you concupiscent?"

"No."

"Then just what are you?" said the priest.

"I am," he said, "a mason and here is my trowel."

There was another who answered his confessor in the same manner, but he was a little smarter. He was a shepherd whom the priest asked, "Now, my good fellow, have you kept the commandments of God?"

"No," replied the shepherd.

"That's very bad. And the commandments of the church?"

"No."

"Well," said the priest, "what have you kept?"

"I've only kept sheep," said the shepherd.

There is another story which is as old as the hills, but it's not possible that it's not new to someone. It's about a man who, after explaining his whole story to the priest, was then asked by the priest, "Have you anything else on your conscience?"

He replied that he had nothing else, except that he remembered having stolen a halter.

"Well, my friend," said the priest, "having stolen a halter isn't a big thing. You can easily make retribution."

"Yes," said the other, "but there was a mare at the other end of it."

"Aha," said the priest, "that's another matter. There's a big difference between a mare and a halter. You must give back the mare and then, the next time you return to be confessed by me, I shall absolve you for the halter."

Les Joyeux Devis (62)

'SISTER THOINETTE'

There was a young boy of about seventeen or eighteen who entered a convent of sisters one feast day and saw four or

---

* Des Périers coins a word to poke fun at the priest's pomposity.

five of them who seemed very beautiful to him. There wasn't a one among them for whom he would not gladly have broken his fast; and the idea so fascinated him that he thought about it all the time.

One day when he was discussing it with a good friend of his, this friend said to him, "Do you know what you should do? You're a good-looking fellow. Dress up like a girl and go to the abbess. She will no doubt agree to see you. You aren't known in these parts."

For he was a journeyman and went from place to place. He gladly took this advice, believing there was no danger he couldn't keep clear of, if he wished to. He dressed up like a rather poor girl and decided to call himself Thoinette.

Whereupon, believe it or not, she went to the convent, where she managed to be received by the abbess, who was very old, and as it happened, had no chambermaid. Thoinette spoke to the abbess and did a good job of telling her story, saying she was a poor orphan from a near-by village, which she named. Indeed she spoke so humbly that the abbess took a liking to her and out of charity wished to give her shelter, telling her that for a few days she was glad to take her in, and that if she wanted to be a good girl, she could stay there. Thoinette was on her best behavior and attended on the good abbess, whom she succeeded in pleasing. And soon thereafter she won the affection of all the sisters, and in fact in no time at all learned to do needlework, for perhaps she already knew a little, about which the abbess was so pleased that she immediately made her a nun of the convent.

When she had put on the habit, which was precisely what she wanted, she began to draw nearer to those whom she found the prettiest, and from one intimacy to another, made her way to the bed of one of them. She didn't wait for the second night to make known to her companion by honest and friendly diversions that she had a horned belly, explaining to her that it was a miracle and the will of God. In brief, she put her peg into her companion's aperture, and they both enjoyed themselves. He, I mean she, continued to do this happily for quite some time, not only with this one but with another three or four with whom she had become acquainted.

When something has come to the attention of three or four

persons, it is easy for the fifth to learn about it and then the sixth. Thus, there being among these nuns some who were beautiful and others who were ugly (Thoinette was less familiar with these), it is easy, through numerous suppositions, for the latter to think I don't know what. And they spied until they learned more certainly what was going on and began to whisper so that it came to the attention of the abbess; not that Thoinette was specifically named, for the abbess had brought her there and, since she liked her very much, would probably never have believed it. But in veiled tones, the sisters told her she ought not to trust in the habit, and that all those who were assembled there were not so pure as she believed, and that there was one among them who was doing a dishonor to the order and corrupting the sisters. But when she asked who or what it was, they told her that if she made them undress, she would learn all about it.

Stunned by this news, the abbess wanted to get to the truth of the matter the first thing and in order to do so, called all the sisters into the chapter house. Having been warned by those who loved her best of the abbess's intentions, which were to inspect each of them in the nude, Sister Thoinette tied the end of her peg with a string, which she held from the rear. She rigged up her little affair so well that for someone who did not look too closely, it seemed as though she had a split belly like the others. And she thought to herself that the abbess, who couldn't see beyond the end of her nose, would never be able to notice a thing.

All the nuns appeared. The abbess scolded them, explained why she had summoned them and ordered them to strip off their clothes. She put on her glasses to make the review and, examining them one after another, came to Sister Thoinette's row. She, seeing all these nuns bare, fresh, white, healthy, and plump, could not keep her peg from playing a nasty game. For at the very moment when the abbess was examining her the most closely, the string broke and the peg, bouncing back suddenly, banged against the abbess's glasses and sent them reeling two feet into the air.

The poor abbess was so surprised that she cried out, "Jesu Maria! Ah, without a doubt, it's you! Who would have ever believed it? How you have deceived me!"

What could she do, however, but handle the situation with calm, for she didn't want to create a scandal in the order; and after promising to protect the honor of the nuns, Sister Thoinette was asked to leave.

Les Joyeux Devis (78)

'THE ITALIAN KISS'

There was a newcomer to the town of Montpellier who found himself at a dance. Among the ladies present was a lovely young woman who was a widow. I think that they were dancing the Piémontaise, in which it is necessary to embrace. And it so happened that this gentleman had taken the young widow as his partner, and that when it came time to embrace, he, having been in Italy, wanted to kiss her in the Italian style. In kissing her therefore, he put his tongue into her mouth. This custom was then new in France, as it is even now, though it is becoming less so; for the French have begun to find everything acceptable, especially in such matters.

The lady was quite taken aback by such turtledoving, and though she did not complain, she nonetheless gave him a nasty look and was unable to resist talking about it; for shortly thereafter she told the story to a group in which a certain person, who in some way was connected with her, said, "How could you have allowed such a thing to happen? That's how they kiss courtesans in Rome and Venice!"

The lady became very irate, believing that the gentleman had taken her for something that she was not. Encouraged by this individual's persistence, she decided that if things remained as they were, she would do great damage to her reputation. Therefore, after considering the various ways of getting to the man, she decided that there was no better satisfaction than bringing him to court, so as to pay him back and re-establish her honor. In brief, she immediately obtained, through the help of connections in the town, a personal summons against the man, who never suspected a thing until the day it arrived. Since he was not from the town, although he lived close by, his friends advised him to leave for a few days, pointing out that he had little chance of winning the case, and that related as the lady was to judges and lawyers, she would otherwise pursue him to distraction; for there was no question of denying the deed, for he himself had probably confessed to it at several gatherings where he had been since. But feeling rather confident, he was not so concerned and said that he would not run away for such a matter and that he knew very well what he had to do.

When the day of the summons arrived, he appeared in court, where quite a large assembly had gathered to hear the debate on this much-discussed topic about town. He was asked one thing and another: whether on such and such a day he had been present at such and such a dance? He answered yes. Whether he knew the complainant well? He answered that he knew her only by sight and wished he knew her better. Whether he meant to imply that she was a woman of questionable reputation? He answered no. Whether it was true that on a certain evening he had kissed her? He answered yes.

"Well in fact, you did her a great dishonor for which she brings charges against you." This he denied.

"You put your tongue into her mouth."

"And suppose I did," he said.

"Such behavior," said the judge, "is reserved for women of ill-repute. You addressed yourself to the wrong party."

Seeing himself thus accused, he answered, "She claims I put my tongue into her mouth. As far as I'm concerned, I don't remember, but why, fool that she is, did she open her beak?" As if to say, "If she hadn't opened it, I wouldn't have put anything into it." For those who understand the local dialect it came out even better: *Et perche badave, la bestia?* That is, "And why did she open it, the stupid thing?"

Yes, but what did they decide in the end? They laughed and dismissed the case, on the condition that she should seal her beak the next time she allowed herself to be kissed.

Marguerite de Navarre (1492–1549)
L'Heptaméron

Introduction

Marguerite de Valois, duchess of Alençon and queen of Navarre, was one of the most influential and cultivated women of her time. As the favorite of her brother, François I, she presided over life at court for many years and was one of the first to introduce there the refinements which were to culminate in the elegant salon society of the seventeenth century. Her eminent situation, combined with her passionate interest in literature and ideas, made her the center of all the intellectual movements during the first half of the sixteenth century. Marot, Des Périers, Heroët, and Rabelais, as well as the Evangelical religious leaders of Meaux and even the heretical Jean Calvin, received her encouragement and protection.

Her own literary efforts were at first limited to poetry and drama, in which she sought to express her private spiritual struggles and the evolution of her religious and philosophical ideas. Storytelling and conversation had long been her favorite distractions, however, and she seems to have toyed for many years with the idea of putting together a French "decameron" [1] to be composed uniquely of *true* stories and narrated by a group of French aristocrats. The project seems to have been postponed until sometime after 1540, however, when she withdrew to her husband's estates in the Pyrenees. There she finally set down the stories she had collected over the years. The hundred tales were probably never finished. In any case, only seventy-two have survived, enough to complete seven full days and part of an eighth, forming a *heptameron*.

Whereas Boccaccio had used his art to divert his readers, Marguerite de Navarre chose rather to focus her efforts on realism and moralizing. The ten characters or *devisants* who tell stories to while away an enforced sojourn in a mountain monastery were all inspired by members of her own family and circle of friends. The wise Oisille was in reality her

The *Heptaméron*
Frontispiece from an original manuscript. In the
foreground are the storytellers; behind them, the monastery
Notre Dame de Serrance and the swollen waters of the Gave,
over which a bridge is being constructed.
[Drawing from ms. 242, reproduced by permission of the
Pierpont Morgan Library, New York.]

mother, Louise de Savoie, the irrepressibly Gallic Hircan was her second husband, Henri d'Albret, the idealistic Dagoucin was the Bishop Dangu, and the somewhat sententious Parlamente was none other than Marguerite herself.[2] Moreover, the historic veracity of many of the stories was intended to pave the way for firmly based philosophizing and moral judgments by the company.

Since she possessed to a high degree that form of sensitive and intuitive intelligence often attributed to woman-authors, Marguerite dealt foremost with the moral ambiguities of her society and the self-inflicted torments of love. Refusing to accept the medieval indictment of women, she protested against the promiscuous and even brutal sexual mores of the feudal nobility and probed the hypocrisies of the double sexual standard and the pitfalls of the arranged marriage. Courtly love and platonism which glorified the woman and insisted upon the sacred character of love seemed to her to offer some alternative, but she was never able to reconcile either doctrine completely with her strong theological beliefs.

Thoroughly imbued with the pessimism of evangelism and the reform, she believed mankind to be sinful, violent, and even depraved when left to its own devices and systems. The tantalizing possibility of platonic love remained, however, one of her recurrent themes and the subject of endless debates between the dialoguists.

In general, Marguerite tended to see life in terms of paradox and contradiction, and the dialogues following her stories are an attempt to interpret human experience from several different points of view. This openminded and enquiring attitude is perhaps the most modern aspect of the *Heptaméron* and saves it from becoming tiresomely moralistic.

The fourth novella is often brought forth as proof that the queen of Navarre was sincere in her promise to tell only true stories, for according to literary tradition, its heroine is none other than Marguerite herself. It serves as an interesting documentation of the dangers to which court ladies were exposed.

In more than one story, one hears the mocking accents of Des Périers, who must have amused his patroness with many an impudent yarn. Such a story is the twenty-ninth novella, in which the self-possesed country priest is a spiritual descendent of the vicar of Brou. The exchanges on the morality of the lower classes enlarge the story's import, however, as the assembled courtiers grope towards a comfortable and pious justification of their own higher standard of living by eulogizing the simple pleasures of the poor.

Both the twenty-sixth and the fortieth novellas deal with the dilemmas of women unable to love according to the dictates of their hearts. The heroine of the twenty-sixth, a spiritual ancestress of the princesse de Clèves, proves equal to the ruthless cunning of her would-be lover, only to succumb to the inner torments of unrequited love. The fortieth, based on a true event, deals frankly with the problem of clandestine marriages, which under the reign of Henry II were decreed illegal. Following the story, a spirited debate explores the pros and cons of such matches and attempts to arrive at a sensible compromise for the contracting of marriages. The wise and witty final page of dialogue reveals not only the lighter side of the author but also her humanity. More pessimistic than Rabelais and more attuned to the sufferings of the heart, she was nevertheless capable of evoking the joyous earthiness so characteristic of the Renaissance.

The fifty-sixth novella returns to the theme of the wicked priest, but behind its conventionalized mockery, the reader senses the influence of the reform. It mocks not only the shameless avarice of the two Franciscans, but also the idea that priestly intervention has been allowed to replace scriptural meditation and personal piety.

As a stylist, the queen of Navarre had decided weaknesses, and in an age when syntax had not yet been taken in hand by the Academy, some of her sentences tended to be both rambling and ungrammatical. Tradition holds that the stories were dictated, while traveling, to a lady-in-waiting, a fact which may account for some of their prolixity. We have tried to retain their aristocratic and somewhat stilted flavor while still transposing them into readable English. In order to do this, it has been necessary to separate long run-on paragraphs and even to tamper with sentence structure. It is our hope that the end result justifies the seeming infidelities and that we have enhanced the text without detracting from its true meaning. Since the conversations between the stories are one of the queen's major contributions to the art of short fiction, we have included in our translations those portions of the "devis" which deal with the preceding stories.

Notes for Introduction

1. Antoine Le Maçon, one of her protégés, published a French translation of the *Decameron* in 1545. The work is dedicated to Marguerite, who mentions it in her prologue.

2. The other *devisants* have been identified as follows: Longarine—Aimée Motier de La Fayette, Saffredent—Jean de Montpezat, Nomerfide—Françoise de Fimarcon, Ennasuite—Anne de Vivonne (mother of Brantôme), Simontault—François, baron de Bourdeille, Geburon—le seigneur de Burye.

Text Used

MARGUERITE DE NAVARRE. *L'Heptaméron.* Edited by Michel François. Paris. Garnier, 1960.
(Yves Le Hir published with Presses Universitaires de France in 1967 a new edition, entitled *Marguerite de Navarre, Nouvelles* but the unorthodox numbering and lack of critical notes make the Garnier edition still preferable.)

Selected Critical Bibliography

DELÈGUE, YVES. "*L'Heptaméron* est-il un anti-Boccace?" *Travaux de linguistique et de littérature.* vol. 4, no. 2. Strasbourg, 1966, pp. 23–37.

FEBVRE, LUCIEN. *Autour de l'Heptaméron. Amour sacré, amour profane.* Paris: Gallimard, 1941.

FESTUGIÈRE, JEAN. *La Philosophie de l'amour de Marsile Ficin et son influence sur la littérature française au XVIᵉ siècle.* Paris: Vrin, 1941.

GELERNT, JULES. *World of Many Loves. The Heptameron of Marguerite de Navarre.* Chapel Hill: University of North Carolina Press, 1966.

HARTLEY, K. H. *Bandello and the Heptameron.* Melbourne: Melbourne University Press, 1960.

JOURDA, PIERRE. *Marguerite d'Angoulême, duchesse d'Alen-*

çon, reine de Navvare, (*1492–1549*). Paris: Champion, 1930. Reissued 1966.

KASPRZYK, KRYSTYNA. "La Matière traditionnelle et sa fonction dans '*L'Heptaméron*'." In *Mélanges de littérature comparée offerts à M. Brahmer*, pp. 257–264. Warsaw: Editions scientifiques de Pologne, 1967.

KROMER, WOLFRAM VON. "Die Struktur der Novelle in Marguerite de Navarres *Heptaméron*." *Romanisches Jahrbuch*, Hamburg 18 (1967): 67–88.

LEBÈGUE, RAYMOND. "Les Sources de l'*Heptaméron*," *Comptes Rendus de l'Académie des Inscriptions et Belles Lettres*. 1956: 466–472.

————. "Réalisme et apprêt dans la langue des personnages de l'*Heptaméron*," Actes du colloque de Strasbourg: *La Littérature narrative d'imagination*. Presses Universitaires de France (1961): 73–86.

————. "*L'Heptaméron*: un attrape-mondains," *Mélanges Marcel Raymond: De Ronsard à Breton*. London: University Park, 1967, pp. 35–42.

LEFRANC, ABEL. *Les Idées religieuses de Marguerite de Navarre d'après son oeuvre poétique*. Paris: Fischbacher, 1898.

————. *Grands Ecrivains de la Renaissance*. Paris: Champion, 1914, p. 63: "Le Platonisme dans la littérature en France à l'époque de la Renaissance" and p. 139: "Marguerite de Navarre et le platonisme de la Renaissance."

SAULNIER, V.-L. *Marguerite de Navarre: Théâtre profane*. Paris: Droz, 1946. 2nd ed. 1963.

STONE, DONALD, JR. "Narrative Technique in '*L'Heptaméron*.'" *Studi Francese*. Turin 2 (1967): 473–476.

TELLE, EMILE. *L'Oeuvre de Marguerite d'Angoulême, reine de Navarre et la Querelle des Femmes*. Toulouse: Lion et Fils, 1937.

Heptaméron (4)
'A BEDTIME STORY'

In the country of Flanders, there was a woman of such high birth that there was no higher, the widow of her first and second husbands, by whom she had had no living children.* During her widowhood she lived in retirement with a brother of hers, by whom she was greatly loved. And he himself was a very noble lord and the husband of a king's daughter.

As is natural in youth, this young prince was a great lover of pleasure and enjoyed hunting, amusements, and women. He had a very disagreeable wife, who did not approve at all of her husband's pastimes, so that the nobleman always brought along in addition to his wife, his sister, who was the best and most joyful companion possible, but remained all the while a woman of virtuous behavior.

There was in the nobleman's household a young man whose grandeur, good looks, and pleasing ways surpassed those of all his companions.† Seeing that his master's sister was so joyful and quick to laugh, this gentleman decided that he would attempt to find out whether the proposal of an "honest friendship" ‡ would displease her. This he did. But he found her reply at variance with her countenance.

Now although her answer befitted a princess and a truly virtuous woman, nonetheless, seeing him so handsome and courteous, she easily forgave him for his audacity. And she showed him that he had not fallen from her favor by reminding him often, when he spoke to her, that he should not renew

---

* According to Brantôme, this lady was Marguerite herself. He claimed to have received this information from his grandmother, a lady-in-waiting to the queen of Navarre and supposedly one of the ten *devisants* of the *Heptaméron*. The brother is of course François I and his wife Claude de France, daughter of Charles VIII and Anne de Bretagne. Pierre de Bourdeille, seigneur de Brantôme, *Les Dames Galantes,* ed. Maurice Rat (Paris: Garnier, 1960), pp. 422–423.

† Brantôme identifies this gentleman as l'Amiral de Bonnivet, Guillaume Gouffier de Bonnivet. Bonnivet was killed in the battle of Pavia, 24 February 1524. The events in the story probably took place around 1520. *Ibid.*

‡ "Honneste amitye": a courtly love affair.

his proposal. This he promised, so as not to lose the privilege and honor of conversing with her.

Still, as time went on, his affection grew so strong that he forgot the promise he had made her, not that he undertook to try his fortune with words, for against his will, he had had too much experience with the wise replies she knew how to give. But he thought that if he could find her in an advantageous position, seeing that she was a widow, young, well formed, and in good health, she might take pity on him and on herself at the same time.

To arrive at his ends, he told his master that there was some very fine hunting near his home and that if he were willing to go there and take three or four deer in the month of May, he had never yet seen anything so amusing. As much for the love he bore the gentleman as for the pleasure of the hunt, the nobleman granted him his request and went to his home, which was fine and well ordered, as befitted the richest gentleman in the countryside.*

He lodged his lord and lady in one wing of the house, and he put the one he loved more than himself on the opposite side, in a room which he had so well fitted out with rugs and tapestries, that it was impossible to discern a trap door, which was in the space between the bed and the wall, and which led down into his mother's room. She was an old lady, somewhat afflicted by catarrh; and fearing that the noise of her coughing might disturb the princess directly above her, she exchanged rooms with her son.

In the evening, this old lady brought preserves to the princess for a light meal, at which the gentleman was present, for being so loved and favored by her brother, he was never barred from her rising and going to bed, at which he always found the means of increasing his affection. As a result, one evening, after he had kept this princess up so late that her drowsiness had at last forced him to leave her room, he went to his own, and there he put on the most gorgeous, perfumed nightshirt he owned and such a well-trimmed nightcap that,

* The château of Bonnivet was reputed to have been one of the most beautiful of those built during the Renaissance. Unfortunately, only a few pieces of the ornamental stonework remain in museums.

admiring himself, he thought that no woman in the world could refuse his beauty and grace. Therefore, promising himself a happy outcome for his undertaking, he got into his bed, where he did not plan to spend much time, for he had the wish and certain hope that he would find a pleasant and more honorable one.

And as soon as he had sent away all his servants, he got up and closed the door behind them. Then he listened for a long time to see if there were any noise in the princess's room above him, and when he was assured that all was quiet, he wanted to begin his pleasant labor, and little by little he opened the trap, which was so well made and fitted with cloth that it made not a single noise. And through it he climbed into the room to the bedside of his lady, who was just falling asleep.

Then, without taking into account the obligation he owed to his mistress, or to her family, and without asking her leave or paying his respects to her, he got into bed beside her; and she found herself in his arms before she even realized he was there. But she was so strong that she slipped from his grasp, and demanding who he was, she began to hit and bite and scratch so that he was obliged to try to stop her mouth with the coverlet for fear that she might call out. This he found impossible, however, for when she saw that he was not sparing all his strength to shame her, she spared none of hers to protect herself and called out as loudly as she could for her lady-in-waiting, who was asleep in her room. She was as wise an old woman as could be found,* and still in her nightdress, she came running to her mistress.

When the gentleman saw that he was found out, he was so afraid of being recognized by his lady that he climbed back down through the trap as quickly as he could, and all his desire and self-assurance were now changed into despair at returning in such a sorry state.

He found his mirror and his candle on his table, and looking at his face which was bloody with the scratches and bites she had given him, and his beautiful nightshirt, which was so stained that it was more bloodied than gilded, he began,

"Oh, my handsome face, now you have received your just

* Brantôme identifies this lady as Madame de Chastillon. Cf. Brantôme, *Dames galantes*, pp. 422–423.

deserts, for on your vain promise, I undertook an impossible deed, one which instead of increasing my happiness will probably redouble my unhappiness, for I am sure that if she knows that in spite of the promise I made her, I undertook this folly, I shall lose the enjoyment of the honest moments which I, more than any other, have shared with her. But by my vainglory, I have deserved it, for in order to show off my beauty and grace, I should not have hidden them in the shadows to gain her heart. I should not have tried to take her chaste body by force. I should have waited with long service and humble patience until love was victorious, for without it all the virtue and strength of man are powerless."

Thus passed the night in such lamenting, regrets, and sorrowing as cannot be recounted. And in the morning, seeing that his face was disfigured, he pretended to be very sick and unable to face the light of day, until the company was out of his house.

The lady, who had been victorious, knowing that there was no man in her brother's court who would have dared to undertake such a strange deed, except the man who had had the effrontery to declare his love to her, was certain that it was her host. And when she and her lady-in-waiting had searched everywhere in the room to find out who it might have been and had no success, she said to her in great anger, "You may be sure that this could be none other than the lord of the house, and in the morning, I shall report this to my brother in such a way that his head shall be a witness to my chastity."

Seeing her so angered, the lady-in-waiting said to her, "My lady, I am very glad that you love your honor so much that to increase it you would not spare the life of one who has risked so much on the strength of the love he bears you. But very often when one thinks he is increasing his honor, he diminishes it. Therefore, I beg you, my lady, to tell me the whole truth of the matter."

When the lady had told her the whole story, the lady-in-waiting said to her, "You can assure me that he got nothing from you but scratches and blows?"

"I assure you," said the lady, "that he did not, and if he does not find a good surgeon, I think that tomorrow the marks will be quite evident."

"Then, if that is how it is, my lady," said the lady-in-waiting, "it seems to me that you should be praising God rather than thinking of revenge, for you can be sure that since his heart is big enough to undertake such a deed, he now feels such disappointment at having failed, that you could not offer him any death which would be easier for him to bear. If you want to revenge yourself on him, let love and shame do their work. They will be able to torment him better than you. If you are doing it for your honor, be careful my lady, not to fall into a trouble like his, for instead of finding the greatest pleasure that he could have had, he found the greatest pain that a gentleman could suffer. Thus you also, my lady, thinking to increase your honor could diminish it, and if you make the complaint, you will make known what no one knows, for on his side you may be sure that nothing will ever be revealed. And when my lord, your brother, hands down the punishment you ask of him, and the poor gentleman is dead, the rumor will be heard everywhere that he did what he wished with you; and most people will say that it is unlikely that a gentleman would have done such a thing if the lady had not given him plenty of opportunity. You are young and beautiful and you enjoy pleasant company. There is no one in this court who doesn't see the favor you show to the gentleman you suspect, which will make people think that if he tried to do such a thing, it was not without some fault on your side. And your honor, which has let you go about with your head up, will be called into question everywhere that this story is told."

Hearing the good reasoning of her lady-in-waiting, the princess knew that she was right and that she would be blamed very rightly, in view of the encouragement and favors she had always given to the gentleman. Therefore she asked her lady-in-waiting what she should do.

She replied thus, "My lady, since you are pleased to accept my advice, considering the affection which inspires it, it seems to me that in your heart you ought to rejoice that the handsomest and most well-bred gentleman I have ever seen in my life was not able either by love or by force to divert you from the path of true virtue. And for that, my lady, you ought to humble yourself before God and recognize that this was not due to your own virtue, for many women who have led a more austere life than you have been brought low by men less worthy of being loved than he. And you must fear to accept proposals of friendship more than ever, for there are many who have fallen prey the second time to dangers they avoided the first. Remember, my lady, that love is blind, and this blindness is such that when you think the path is safest, at that hour it is the most slippery. And it seems to me, my lady, that you should not make any sign to him of what has happened to you, and if he should try to say something about it, you should pretend not to understand him, to avoid two dangers: first that of pride in the victory you have won, and the other that of remembering things so pleasant to the flesh that the most chaste have difficulty in not feeling some of their sparks, even though they avoid them as much as possible. But also, my lady, so that he may not suppose by some chance that what he did was agreeable to you, I am of the opinion that little by little you should withdraw from him the affection you have shown for him, so that he may realize how much you despise his folly and how great is your goodness, since you have been content with the victory God granted you and asked no other revenge. And may God give you grace, my lady, to continue in the virtue he has placed in your heart, and knowing that all good things come from him, may you love him and serve him more than was your wont."

The princess decided to take the advice of her lady-in-waiting and went to sleep as joyfully as the gentleman was wakeful with sorrow.

The next day the nobleman wanted to leave and asked for his host. He was told that he was sick and could not face the light of day or speak to anyone. At this the prince was very surprised and wanted to go to see him, but knowing that he was sleeping, he didn't want to wake him, so he left his home without saying goodbye and took with him his wife and his sister. Hearing the gentleman's excuses and the fact that he had not wanted to see the prince and his company depart, the latter was convinced that he was the cause of her grief and did not dare to show the marks which she had made on his face.

And although his master often sent for word of him, he did not return to court until he was quite cured of all his wounds aside from the one which love and disappointment had made in his heart.

When he did finally return and found himself before his victorious enemy, it was not without blushing, and this man, who was the most daring of the entire company, was so abashed in her presence that he often lost all his composure. And for this reason, she was wholly assured that her suspicion had been correct, and little by little, she grew estranged from him, not so subtly that he was not very well aware of it, but he did not dare to show it for fear of worse still, and he kept this love patiently in his heart at the distance which he had merited.

"Now, ladies, this should put fear into those who take as their due what doesn't belong to them; and ladies should take heart at the virtue of this young princess and the good sense of her lady-in-waiting. If one of you should find herself in the same situation, the remedy has already been given."

"It seems to me," said Hircan, "that the gentleman of whom you have spoken was so lacking in heart that he does not deserve to be remembered, for when he had such an opportunity, he should not have given up for young or old. And you must admit that his heart was not full of love, since there was still room in it for the fear of death and shame."

Nomerfide replied to Hircan, "And what should the poor gentleman have done, since he had two women against him?"

"He should have killed the old woman," Hircan replied, "and when the young one saw herself without aid, she would have been half won."

"Kill her!" said Nomerfide. "You want to make a lover into a murderer now? If that is how you think, I'd be afraid to fall into your hands."

"If I had gotten that far," said Hircan, "and the young woman found herself without help, I would consider myself dishonored if I didn't finish what I had set out to do."

Heptaméron (26)

'THE WISE AND FOOLISH LADIES'

In the days of King Louis the Twelfth, there was a young nobleman known as the Lord of Avannes. He was the son of the Lord of Albret and the brother of King John of Navarre,* with whom he ordinarily made his home. At the age of fifteen, the young gentleman was so handsome and charming that he seemed destined for nothing but to be loved and admired, which he was by all those who saw him, and especially by a certain lady who lived in the city of Pampeluna in Navarre. She was married to a wealthy man, with whom she lived very honorably. And although she was only twenty-three and he was going on fifty, she dressed so conservatively that she looked more like a widow than a wife. She was never seen at weddings or parties without her husband, whose goodness and virtue she placed higher than the charms of all other men. For his part, her husband had found her so irreproachable that he trusted her completely and put all the affairs of the household into her charge.

One day, this rich gentleman and his wife were invited to a family wedding which the young Lord of Avannes had honored with his presence. As could be expected, no one in his generation loved dancing more than this young nobleman, and after dinner when the dances began, the rich man begged him to dance. The Lord of Avannes asked him in turn whom he should take as his partner, and he replied, "My lord, if there were anyone here more beautiful or more at my command than my wife, I should introduce her to you, and beg you to honor me by inviting her to dance."

The young prince did as he was asked, but he was so young that he took greater pleasure in leaping and dancing than in admiring feminine charms. His partner, however, paid more attention to the gracefulness and good looks of the said Lord of Avannes than to the dance, even though very prudently she revealed nothing by her demeanor. Finally, when it was supper time, the Lord of Avannes said goodbye to the other guests and returned to the château, accompanied by the rich man on his mule.

As they were going along, the latter said to him, "My lord,

* This is Gabriel d'Albret, fourth son of Alan the Great, Sire d'Albret. Marguerite was related to the Albret family by her second marriage. It is probable, however, that the incidents of the story took place under the reign of Charles VIII. Gabriel died a bachelor in 1504.

you paid such a great honor to my relatives and me today that it would be ungrateful of me not to put myself and all that I have entirely at your service. I know, my lord, that young gentlemen like yourself, who have stern and miserly fathers, are often in greater need of money than we who by living modestly and managing well think of nothing but amassing wealth. Now this is how it is, God gave me the wife I wanted, but He didn't want to let me have my paradise entirely in this world, so he deprived me of the joy that a man derives from having children. I know, my lord, that it is not my place to adopt you, but if you will accept me as your servant and confide your petty debts to me, I shall not fail to help you when you need it, at least as far as I can stretch a hundred thousand crowns."

The Lord of Avannes was delighted with this offer, for he had just such a father as the other had described. And thus, after having thanked him, he named him his father by adoption.*

From that time on, the rich man took such an interest in the Lord of Avannes that from morning to evening, he never stopped asking if he needed anything, nor did he hide from his wife his zeal for serving the young nobleman, for which she loved him even more. Henceforth, the Lord of Avannes lacked nothing that he wanted. He often went to see the rich man and ate and drank with him, and when he didn't find him in, the wife gave him all that he asked. In addition, she spoke to him so wisely, urging him to be honest and virtuous, that he feared and loved her above all other women in the world.

Keeping God and her honor ever before her, however, she contented herself with seeing him and talking to him, which is the only satisfaction possible for true and virtuous love.† Thus she never gave him any reason to suspect that she had any affection for him other than that of a sister and a Christian.

Throughout this secret friendship, the Lord of Avannes,

* In the sixteenth century, it was the custom to adopt informally someone with whom one was on especially intimate terms. This relationship was known as an "alliance." A celebrated example was the "fille d'alliance" of Montaigne, Mlle. de Gournay.
† The love referred to here is of course the unconsummated passion advocated by the traditions of courtly and platonic love.

with the aid of these people, was very elegant and well dressed. He was approaching the age of seventeen and beginning to seek out the company of ladies more than before. But although he would have preferred to love the wise lady more than any other, his fear of losing her friendship if she heard such a proposal, made him hold his tongue and seek amusement elsewhere.

He addressed himself, therefore, to a gentlewoman who lived near Pampeluna and had a house in the town. She was married to a young man who loved horses, hawks, and hounds more than anything else. For her sake, the Lord of Avannes began to organize all sorts of pastimes—tourneys, races, wrestling matches, masques, parties, and other games, to all of which came this young woman. But because her husband was extremely jealous, and her father and mother knew her to be beautiful and flirtatious, they all guarded her honor jealously and kept such a close watch on her that the Lord of Avannes could have nothing but a brief word with her in the midst of a ball. After a very few such exchanges, however, he perceived that nothing stood in the way of a closer relationship but the time and the place.

Therefore, he went to his adopted father the rich man and told him that for reasons of piety he wanted to make a pilgrimage to Our Lady of Monserrat.* And since he planned to travel alone, he asked him to let his retinue stay in his house. The rich man readily agreed, but his wife, in whose heart was Love, who is always an accurate prophet, suspected immediately the truth behind the trip and couldn't refrain from saying to Monsieur d'Avannes, "My lord, my lord, the Our Lady whom you worship is not beyond the walls of this city. I beg you therefore to take care of your health before anything else." At these words, he who feared and loved her blushed so hotly, that without speaking, he confessed the truth to her. And with that, he left.

Having purchased a pair of fine Spanish horses, he disguised himself as a groom and made up his face so that no one could recognize him. When the foolish lady's husband, who was

* Famous monastery near Barcelona which houses an ebony statue of the Madonna said to have been carved by St. Luke.

passionately fond of horses, saw the two which the Lord of Avannes was leading, he immediately decided to buy them. And after the transaction, he observed the groom, who was handling them very well and proposed that he come to work for him. The Lord of Avannes agreed and told him that he was a poor groom, whose only trade was caring for horses, in which he would do all he could to please him. The gentleman was delighted and put him in charge of all his horses. Then returning home, he told his wife to keep an eye on his horses and his groom while he went to the château.

The lady, as much for want of anything better to do as to please her husband, went to inspect the stable and look at the new groom. To her he seemed to have a nice appearance, but she still did not recognize him. Seeing that she didn't know him, he came to make his bow to her, as is the Spanish custom, and kissed her hand. And while doing this, he pressed her hand so tightly that she recognized him, for when they were dancing together, he had often done the same thing. From that moment the lady did not cease to look for a chance to get him aside.

That same evening, she did so, for having been invited to a festivity to which her husband wanted to take her, she pretended to be ill and unable to attend.

Her husband did not want to disappoint his friends so he said to her, "Since you don't want to go, my love, take care of my dogs and horses and see that they want for nothing."

The lady found this assignment very much to her liking, but without giving herself away, she answered that since he had nothing better for her to do she would show him in small ways how eager she was to please him.

Her husband was hardly out the door before she went down to the stable and found something amiss. To remedy it she gave orders left and right to the stablehands until she remained alone with the head groom.

Then for fear that someone might come in, she said to him, "Go down into the garden and wait for me in the pavillion at the end of the walk." He obeyed her with such diligence that he didn't even take time to thank her.

And after she had put the whole stable into order, she went to the kennels, where she was just as conscientious to see that the dogs were well treated, until it seemed that she had been transformed from mistress into chambermaid. And afterwards she returned to her room so tired that she went to bed, saying she wanted to rest.

All her maids left her except one she trusted, to whom she said, "Go into the garden and send me the person you find at the end of the walk."

The maid went and found the groom, whom she brought back immediately to her mistress. The latter then made the servant go out to watch for her husband's return.

Seeing himself alone with the lady, the Lord of Avannes took off his groom's habit, his false nose, and his beard. Then, not as a cringing groom, but as a handsome nobleman, without asking the lady's permission, he lay down next to her, and was received as the finest youth of the day should be received by the most beautiful and foolish lady in the land. He remained with her until her husband's return, whereupon he resumed his disguise and left the place he had usurped by cunning and malice.

As soon as he entered the courtyard, the gentleman heard how diligent his wife had been in obeying him, for which he thanked her heartily.

"My love," said the lady, "I was only doing my duty. It is true that if someone didn't keep an eye on these good-for-nothing boys, you wouldn't have a single dog that wasn't mangy or a horse that wasn't skin and bones. But since I know their laziness and your good intentions, you'll be served better than you have ever been before."

The husband, who thought he had certainly hired the best groom in the whole world, then asked her what she thought of his choice.

"I must confess," she said, "that he does his job as well as any servant you could have chosen, but still he needs to be kept after, for he's the laziest boy I've ever seen."

Thus for a long time, the lord and his lady lived on better terms than before. He lost all his suspiciousness and jealousy of her, because she who had loved parties, dances, and gatherings grew attentive to her housekeeping. Now she was content to wear a simple gown, whereas before she had been accustomed to spend four hours attiring herself. For this she was praised by her husband and everyone else, who did not realize that a greater devil had taken the place of a lesser. Thus this young woman lived hypocritically in the guise of a respectable wife, when in actual fact she was so voluptuous that reason, conscience, order, and moderation had ceased to exist for her.

The youth and delicate constitution of the Lord of Avannes could not support this life for very long. He began to grow so thin and pale that even without a disguise he was unrecognizable. But his insane love for this woman had so dulled his wits that he abused a strength that even Hercules would have lacked. The result was that finally, forced by illness, and at the urging of the lady, who did not love him as much sick as well, he asked his master's permission to return to his parents. He gave it to him very regretfully, making him promise that he would return to his service when he was well.

Thereupon, the Lord of Avannes set out on foot, for he had only to walk down to the next street. When he arrived at the house of his adopted father, he found only the wife, whose virtuous affection had not been diminished by his voyage.

When she saw him looking so thin and pale, however, she could not refrain from saying, "I don't know about your conscience, my lord, but your body hasn't benefited at all from this pilgrimage, and I strongly suspect that the distance you traveled by night did you more harm than that you traveled by day, for if you had gone to Jerusalem on foot, you would have been more tanned, but not so feeble and thin. Learn a lesson for once and don't serve such idols any more, for instead of reviving the dead they kill the living. I would say more, but your body has sinned, it has taken so much punishment that it would be a pity to torment it any further."

When the Lord of Avannes heard these words, he was as sorry as he was ashamed and said to her, "I have heard in the past, madam, that repentance follows sin, and now I am experiencing this truth at my own expense. I beg you therefore to excuse my youth, which could not be punished except by experimenting with the evil which it refused to believe in."

The lady put an end to this discussion and made him get into a fine bed, where he remained for two weeks, living on nothing but clear broth. The husband and wife kept him such good company that he always had one or the other near him; and although, as you have heard, he had acted foolishly and contrary to the desire and counsel of the wise lady, nevertheless she did not love him any the less sincerely, for she always hoped that after having sowed his wild oats, he would reform and learn to love honorably and in this way be entirely hers.

Thus, during these two weeks when he was in her house, she preached to him so often about the love of virtue that he began to despise the folly he had committed. And as he gazed upon this lady, whose beauty surpassed that of the foolish one, and came to know better and better the charm and purity of her character, one day when it was rather dark, he mastered his timidity and could not keep from saying, "Madam, I don't see any better way to become as virtuous as you would like, unless I devote myself body and soul to the love of virtue. And I beg you, madam, to tell me if it wouldn't please you to give me all the help and encouragement you could."

Overjoyed to hear him talking in this way, the lady replied, "I promise you, my lord, that if you want to love virtue as a gentleman of your caliber should, I shall help you to succeed with all the powers that God has given me."

"Very well," said the Lord of Avannes. "Remember your promise and understand that God, unknown to man except by faith, deigned to take on flesh similar to that which sins in order that by drawing our flesh to the love of his humanity, he could also draw our souls into love for his divinity, for he wanted to use visible means to make us love by faith those things which are invisible. In the same way, this virtue which I want to love all my life is invisible except by its external effects. That is why it needs to take on some sort of body to make itself known to mankind, and this it did when it clothed itself in your person which is the most perfect it could find. Therefore, I recognize and confess you to be not only virtuous, but the only virtue, and I, who see Virtue emanating from beneath the veil of the most perfect body that was ever created, want to serve and honor her all my life, forsaking for her all other vain and pernicious loves."

The lady, who was not only delighted but astonished by these words, concealed her happiness so well that all she said was, "My lord, I won't undertake to reply to your theology, but as one who fears evil more than she believes in good, I want to beg you to stop making remarks in my presence which show so little respect for those who have believed them. I know very well that I am a woman, not only like any other, but very imperfect, and unless Virtue wants to go unnoticed in this world, she would do better to transform me than to assume my shape, for disguised like me, Virtue could never be known as she really is. Because of my imperfections, therefore, I shall not cease to feel for you only such an affection as befits a woman who fears God and her dishonor. Nor shall I declare my feelings until your heart is ready for the patience which virtuous love requires. At the right time, my lord, I shall know what to say, but you may be sure that you do not love your own person, welfare, and honor as much as I myself love them."

Fearfully and with tears in his eyes, the Lord of Avannes then begged her earnestly to prove her words by giving him a kiss, but she refused, saying that she would not break the local customs for him.

During this debate, the husband arrived and the Lord of Avannes said to him, "Father, I feel myself so attached to you and to your wife that I want you to consider me your son forever." To this the good man readily agreed.

"And as proof of this friendship, I beg you to let me embrace you." This he did also.

Following this, the lord continued, "And if I weren't afraid of offending against the laws, I would do the same with my mother, your wife."

Upon hearing this, the husband ordered his wife to embrace the nobleman. She did as she was told without seeming to have any strong feelings one way or the other about carrying out the order. But because it had been sought so desperately and denied so cruelly, this kiss only caused the fire which words had already kindled to burn more fiercely in the poor lord's heart.

Immediately after this, the Lord of Avannes went to the château to see his brother the king, and there he told many fine tales about his voyage to Monserrat. At the same time, he learned that the king his brother was planning to go to Olite and Taffalla.* Realizing that the journey would be long, he

---

* Towns in Spanish Navarre. Olite was the ancient seat of the kings of Navarre, who had summer palaces in both towns.

grew so despondent that he began to turn over in his mind a scheme which would determine before he left whether or not the wise lady was really better disposed toward him than she pretended to be.

Accordingly he took lodgings on the street where she lived in a house that was old, in bad condition, and made of wood; and around midnight, he set fire to it. The fire caused such an uproar that it could be heard throughout the town, and the noise soon reached the house of the rich man, who called out the window to ask where the fire was. When he heard that it was in the house of the Lord of Avannes, he went there at once with all his servants and found the nobleman standing in his nightshirt, so pitiful-looking that he immediately put his arm around him and wrapped him in his robe. Then he led him back to his house as quickly as possible.

"My love," he said to his wife, who was in bed, "I am entrusting this prisoner to you. Treat him as you would me."

As soon as he had left, the Lord of Avannes, who would have been only too glad to be treated as her husband, jumped blithely into the bed, hoping that the circumstances and the place would make this wise lady change her mind. He learned just the opposite, however, for as he jumped into the bed on one side, she got out on the other and put on her robe.

Then when she was dressed, she approached him at the head of the bed and said, "My lord, did you think that a chaste heart would alter with the circumstances? Believe me, just as gold is refined in the furnace, so a chaste heart becomes stronger and more virtuous through temptations. You can be sure that if I had not wanted to act in accordance with my words, I would not have failed to find the means to realize my desire. But since I didn't want to use such means, I ignored them. Therefore, if you want me to continue in my affection for you, I ask that you rid yourself forever of not only this desire but of the very thought that whatever you might try to do, you would ever find me anything except what I am."

While she was speaking, her women servants arrived and she ordered them to bring him something to eat, but for the time being he was neither hungry nor thirsty, so full of despair was he at having failed in his enterprise, and so full of fear that because of this manifestation of his passion, he would no longer be on intimate terms with her.

Having seen to the fire, her husband returned and insisted that the Lord of Avannes spend the night in his home; but there the latter passed the night in such a state that he used his eyes more for weeping than for sleeping. Early in the morning, while they were still in bed, he went to tell them good-bye and when he kissed the lady, he knew that she bore him no grudge for his offense, but rather felt sorry for him—which only heaped coals on his love for her.

After dinner, he left for Taffalla with the king, but first he returned to say goodbye once more to his adopted father and his wife, who since her husband's command no longer raised any objection to embracing him as a son.

You may be sure, however, that the more her virtue prevented her eyes from revealing her hidden flame, the more it intensified and became unbearable, with the result that this woman, unable to endure the struggle in her breast between love and honor, and having sworn never to reveal her true feelings, when she had lost the consolation of being able to see and talk to the person she lived for, fell into a continuous fever caused by her melancholy humour. Her extremities grew ice-cold and her entrails burning hot. Alarmed by an obstruction, which made her extremely melancholic, the doctors, who do not hold the good health of mortals in their hands, advised her husband to warn his wife to look to her conscience, for she was in the hands of God (as if those who are in good health were not).

Her husband, who was devoted to his wife, was so sad at these words that to console himself he wrote to the Lord of Avannes, begging him to take the trouble to visit them in the hopes that the sight of him might make her better. When he received the letters, the Lord of Avannes did not delay, but came post haste to his adopted father's house. At the doorway, he found the women and servants wailing for their mistress as she deserved. The nobleman was so astonished by this that he stood in the entry as if in a trance until he saw his adopted father, who embraced him and fell to weeping so hard that he was unable to speak. At last he led the Lord of Avannes to the sickroom.

Turning her languid eyes upon him, the poor lady recognized him and taking his hand pulled him to her with all her might, embracing and kissing him, while she wailed and lamented in an astonishing way, saying, "Oh my lord, the time has come when all dissimulation must cease and I must confess to you the truth I tried so hard to conceal. I want you to understand, my lord, that God and my honor never allowed me to declare this to you, for fear that I should increase in you what I was trying to diminish, but you can see that the refusal I gave you so often did me such harm that it was the cause of my death. I am glad of this, for God had the grace to let me die before the violence of my love could sully my conscience and good name—and lesser fires than mine have destroyed greater and stronger edifices. Now I am leaving the world happy, since before dying I have been able to tell you that my affection is equal to yours, save only that in men and women honor is not the same thing. And I beg you, my lord, not to fear to pay court from this time forth to the greatest and most virtuous ladies you can find, for the strongest passions inhabit such breasts and are the most wisely conducted; and with your grace, beauty and virtue, your efforts will certainly bear fruit.

"I shall not pray to God for myself, for I know that the gates of Paradise are never closed to true lovers. Love is a fire which punishes so well in this life that lovers are exempt from the harsh flames of Purgatory. Thus I bid you adieu, my lord.

"I leave your godfather, my husband, in your care. I want you to tell him what I have just told you, so that he will know how much I loved God and him. Now leave me alone. From this time on I want to think of nothing but going to receive the promises which God made to me before the creation of the world."

And saying this, she kissed him and embraced him with all the strength left in her feeble arms.

The nobleman, whose heart was as heavy with compassion as hers was with suffering, hadn't the strength to say a single word, but withdrew from her sight and fell onto a nearby bed in a swoon.

Then the lady called her husband and after having spoken very virtuously to him, left the Lord of Avannes in his care, assuring him that next to him, he was the person whom she had loved most in this world. Then when she had embraced her husband, she bid him adieu.

At this moment, the holy sacraments and extreme unction

were brought to her from the altar, both of which she received with the joy of one who is sure of his salvation; and seeing that she was losing her sight and that her strength was failing, she began to say aloud the *In Manus*. Hearing this, the Lord of Avannes revived and watching her with pity, saw her give up her glorious spirit with a soft sigh to Him from whom she had come.

When he saw that she was dead, he ran to the corpse, which he had approached fearfully when it was living, and began to kiss and embrace it so passionately that he could hardly be separated from it. At this the husband was quite amazed, for he had never thought that the lord had felt such an affection for her. And saying, "My lord, this is too much," they drew away.

After he had wept for a long time, the Lord of Avannes related the whole story of their friendship and how until her death, she had never given him a single sign of anything but the most rigorously correct conduct. At this, her husband, more content with her than ever, redoubled his grief and sorrow at having lost her. He continued all his life to serve the said Lord of Avannes, but soon after, the young gentleman, who was only eighteen, went away to court, where he remained for many years without wanting to speak to a woman of the world because of his regret for his lady. And for more than ten years he wore nothing but black.

"Now ladies, there you have the difference between a wise lady and a foolish one, which goes to prove the different effects of love. One suffered a glorious and praiseworthy death for it, while the other shamed and defamed herself, prolonging a worthless existence. For although the death of a saint is precious in the sight of God, the death of a sinner is just the opposite."

"Truly Saffredent," said Oisille, "I don't think you could have told us a more beautiful story. And whoever knew the hero, as I did, would have enjoyed it even more, for I have never seen a man more handsome and well-bred than the Lord of Avannes."

"Think of it," said Saffredent, "here was a wise woman who, in order to appear more virtuous than she was in her heart and to hide a love inspired by Nature for a true gentleman, went so far as to let herself die by depriving herself of the pleasure which she secretly desired."

"If she had really wanted to," said Parlamente, "she had enough opportunities to manifest her desire, but she was so virtuous that her passion never got the better of her reason."

"You can depict her any way you want," said Hircan, "but I know very well that a worse devil always replaces the first one and that neither fear nor the love of God has such a voluptuous hold on women as sinful pride. In addition, their gowns are so long and so woven through with dissimulation that no one can know what is underneath. If it were not more to their dishonor to admit it than it is to ours, you would find that Nature has forgotten to give them nothing that she has given to us men; but because of the constraint which keeps them from daring to take the pleasure they long for, they have transformed this vice into an even greater one, which they consider to be more virtuous: the vainglorious cruelty, by which they hope to acquire an immortal reputation. Thus they glorify themselves by resisting the vices of Nature's law (if Nature is truly vicious) and turn themselves not only into cruel inhuman beasts, but into devils, from whom they get their pride and their malice."

"It is a shame," said Nomerfide, "that you have a virtuous wife, since you not only have no esteem for virtue, but want to prove it is a vice."

"I'm very glad," replied Hircan, "to have a wife who does not act scandalously, as indeed I do not want to act scandalously myself, but when it comes to the purity of the heart, I believe that she and I are children of Adam and Eve. And that is why if we see ourselves as we are, we don't need to cover our nudity with fig leaves but rather to confess our frailty."

"I know very well," said Parlamente, "that we all stand in need of God's grace because we are enslaved by sin. But if it is true that our temptations are not the same as yours and that we sin through pride, at least no other person is harmed, nor do our hands and bodies remain sullied. Your greatest pleasure, on the other hand, lies in dishonoring women, and your honor lies in killing men on the battlefield, both of which are absolutely forbidden by the law of God."

"I admit that what you say is true," said Geburon, "but God said, 'Whoever gazes lustfully at another woman is already an adulterer in his heart, and whoever hates his neighbor is a murderer.' In your opinion, are women more exempt from this than we are?"

"God who judges the heart will give the verdict," said Longarine, "but it is already a great step forward when men cannot accuse us, for the goodness of God is so great that without an accuser, he will not judge us at all. Furthermore, he knows the frailty of our hearts so well that he will still love us for not having acted upon our evil impulses."

.   .   .   .

Heptaméron (29)
'THE PRIEST AND THE PLOWMAN'

In the county of Maine, in a town called Carrelles, there lived a rich plowman who in his old age married a beautiful young woman by whom he had no children. She, however, made up for this lack by having a good many friends; and when she ran out of gentlemen and people of quality, she turned to her last resort, the church, taking for her companion in sin the one who could absolve her from it, namely, her priest, who often came to visit his lamb. Her husband, who was old and dull-witted, never suspected a thing. But because he was hale and hearty, his wife acted out her mystery play as secretly as possible, fearing that if her husband became aware of it, he would kill her.

One day when he was out working, his wife, believing he wouldn't be back very soon, sent for the priest to confess her. While they were enjoying themselves together, her husband arrived so suddenly that the priest didn't have a chance to leave and had to look for a place to hide. Upon the advice of the wife, therefore, he climbed into the attic and covered over the hole with a winnowing basket.

The husband entered the house and she, for fear he might suspect something, regaled him lavishly at dinner, nor did she spare the wine, of which he drank such a quantity that what with his fatigue from ploughing in the fields, he was overcome by a desire to sleep in his chair by the fireside. Growing tired of staying so long in the attic, and hearing no noise in the room, the priest approached the opening and stretched his neck as far as he could. He saw that the old fellow was sleeping. While he was watching him, he leaned inadvertently so hard on the winnowing basket that winnowing basket and man came tumbling down in front of the sleeping husband, who was awakened by the noise.

The priest scrambled to his feet before the other saw him and said, "Here is your winnowing basket, neighbour. Many thanks!"

And with that he departed.

Astonished, the poor plowman said to his wife, "What's this?"

"My friend," she answered, "it's your winnowing basket which the priest had borrowed and which he came to return."

"That's a fine way to give something back," he grumbled. "I thought the house was falling down."

Thus the priest saved himself at the expense of the old fellow, who found fault with nothing except the rude way in which his winnowing basket had been returned.

"Ladies, the Master whom he served saved him this time in order to hold on to him and torment him longer." *

"You mustn't think," said Geburon, "that simple people of humble birth are any more exempt from wickedness than we are; they are even worse, for look at the thieves, murderers, witches, counterfeiters, and all the others like them, from whom we never have a moment's peace; they are all poor working people."

"I do not find it at all strange," said Parlamente, "that they are more capable of wrongdoing than the rest, but I do find it strange that they suffer from Love, considering all the other things they have to do, or that such a genteel passion could find a place in an ignoble heart."

* Spoken by the narrator, Nomerfide.

"Madam," said Saffredent, "you know that Jehan de Meung * has said,

> Aussy bien sont amourettes
> Soubz bureau que soubz brunettes.†

and besides the love of which the story speaks is not the kind which constrains one to wear a harness, for although poor people do not have wealth and honors, they have the comforts of nature more easily than we. Their food is not so fancy, but they have better appetites and are better nourished by coarse bread than we are by our delicacies. They do not have beds as fine or as well made as ours, but they sleep better and have more peace of mind. They do not have the painted and be-jewelled ladies whom we idolize, but they have the satisfaction of their pleasures more often than we and without fear of commentary, except that of the birds and the beasts who see them. What we have they lack and what we do not have, they have in abundance."

·   ·   ·   ·   ·   ·   ·   ·   ·   ·

Heptaméron (40)
'A LOVE MATCH' ‡

Rolandine's father, who was a nobleman named Count Josse-belin,§ had several sisters, some of whom were married to rich husbands and some of whom had become nuns. One, however,

---

* (1240? to 1305?) author of the second part of the *Roman de la Rose*. His antifeminism led him to satirize the exaggerated position of woman in the courtly-love tradition.
† Cf., *Le Roman de la Rose*, ed. Ernest Langlois (Société des Anciens textes), verses 4333–4334: "There are as many love affairs under homespun as under fine cloth."
‡ This story is based on the marriage of Catherine de Rohan to dom Morice, René de Kéradreux, murdered by her brother Jean II, vicomte de Rohan in 1478. He was arrested in November of that year by the duke of Brittany and not freed until February 1484.
§ Rolandine (Anne de Rohan, a lady in waiting to Anne of Brittany) is the heroine of the twenty-first novella.

remained at home unmarried. Without any doubt she was more beautiful than all the others, and she loved her brother so much that he in turn preferred her to his own wife and children. Many distinguished houses had proposed matches for her; but because he was afraid of being separated from her, and also because he was very attached to his money, he would never hear a word of it. For this reason, she spent most of her life unmarried, living very virtuously in her brother's home.

There was a handsome young gentleman who had been raised in that household and who had grown up to be so honest and good-looking that in a quiet way he ruled over his master. For instance, whenever the latter had anything to ask of his sister, he always sent this gentleman. In fact, he gave him so much authority and put so much trust in him that he sent him every morning and evening to visit her. As a result of these frequent visits, a serious attachment developed between the two. But since the gentleman feared for his life if he should offend his master, and the woman feared for her honor, they expressed their love only in words.

Count Jossebelin began to tell his sister repeatedly, however, that he wished this gentleman had been wealthier and that had he come from a family equal to hers, he would have preferred him above anyone else as a brother-in-law. He repeated this so often that when she had discussed it with her suitor, the two of them decided that if they were to marry they would easily obtain his forgiveness. And Love, who so readily believes whatever it wishes to, made them think that nothing but good could come of it. On the basis of this expectation, they concluded a marriage without the knowledge of anyone save a priest and a few women.

After several years, during which they enjoyed the pleasures to which marriage entitled them, Fortune, who was envious at seeing two people so happy (for they were the most beautiful couple in all Christendom and the most perfectly in love), did not want to let them continue thus and raised up an enemy against them, a spy who noticed how happy she seemed, while remaining ignorant of her marriage. This person, therefore, informed the Count Jossebelin that the gentleman he trusted so much was going too often to his sister's room at hours when a man had no right to be there.

The first time that the count heard this, he did not believe it because of his confidence in the gentleman and his sister. But the other repeated the accusation so often that out of concern for the reputation of his household, he posted a watch on them. Thus the poor things, who had no evil intentions, were surprised together. For one evening, when the count was informed that the gentleman was with his sister, he swiftly broke in upon them and found the two of them, blinded by love, in bed together. So angry that he was speechless, he drew his sword and ran after the gentleman to kill him, but the latter, being very quick on his feet, fled in his nightshirt, and since he was unable to escape by the door, he jumped from a window into the garden.

Half undressed, the poor woman threw herself on her knees before her brother and said to him, "Sir, spare the life of my husband, for I am married to him, and if there is anything wrong in it, punish no one but me, for what he did was at my request."

Beside himself with rage, the brother answered only this, "If he were your husband a hundred times over, I would still punish him as a faithless servant who has deceived me."

And so saying, he went to the window and called out loudly for him to be killed, which was done promptly, as he had commanded, before his eyes and those of his sister.

Seeing this pitiful sight which no prayer had been able to forestall, she spoke to her brother like a woman out of her mind: "Brother, I have neither father nor mother, and I am old enough to be able to marry whomever I please. I chose the man whom you told me over and over again you wished I could marry. And because I took your advice and did what legally I could do without you, you have put to death the man you loved more than any other. Since my prayers were not able to save him, I beg, for the sake of all the love you ever felt for me, to make me in this same hour his companion in death, as I was the companion of all his fortunes. In this way, by satisfying your cruel and unjust anger, you will put my soul and body to rest, for I cannot and will not live without him."

Despite the fact that he was insane with anger to the point of losing his reason, the brother felt pity for his sister and without denying or acceding to her request, he left her. Later, when he had thought over what he had done and learned that the man had really married her, he regretted having committed such a crime. Still, for fear that his sister might demand justice or vengeance, he had a castle built for her in the middle of a forest. There he kept her and forbade her to speak with anyone.

After some time had gone by, in order to set his conscience at rest, he tried to win her back and mentioned marriage to her, but she replied to him that she had had such an unappetizing dinner that she had no desire to eat the same thing for supper, and that she intended to live in such a way that there would be no need to murder a second husband. For since he had done such an ignoble thing to the man he loved most in the world, she could hardly believe that he would forgive any other. In addition, she went on, although she was weak and powerless to avenge herself, she trusted in the True Judge who lets no sin go unpunished. And His love being the only one she wished to share, she would spend the rest of her life as a recluse.

This she did, for until her death, she never faltered, living in such patience and austerity that after her death everyone flocked to her grave as if she had been a saint.

After her passing, her brother's house went completely to ruin. Of his six sons, not one survived; all died miserably. And in the end the inheritance came down, as you heard in the other story, to his daughter Rolandine, who also inherited the prison he had built for her aunt.*

"May our Lord grant, ladies, that you learn a lesson from this and that none of you ever have the least desire to marry for your own pleasure without the consent of those to whom you owe obedience, for marriage is an estate of such long duration that it should never be entered into lightly and without the approval of our best friends and relatives. Furthermore, no one can marry so well that he doesn't experience at least as much pain as pleasure." †

* Rolandine was imprisoned by the count for her refusal to abjure a clandestine marriage contracted between her and an illegitimate nobleman.
† Spoken by the narrator, in this case Parlamente.

236

"By my faith," said Oisille, "if there were no God and no law to teach young girls to act wisely, this example should suffice to give them more respect for their relatives than to try to marry to suit themselves."

"All the same, madam," said Nomerfide, "whoever enjoys one good day in a year is not unhappy all his life. For a long period of time she had the pleasure of seeing and speaking to the man she loved more than herself; and she experienced the joys of marriage without the pangs of conscience. In my opinion this happiness was great enough to make up for what she suffered."

"Do you mean to say," asked Saffredent, "that women enjoy sleeping with their husbands more than they dislike seeing them killed before their eyes?"

"That was not what I meant," replied Nomerfide, "for that would go against what I know about women. What I meant was that the unaccustomed pleasure of marrying the man one loves best must be greater than the sorrow of losing him by death, which is a common occurrence."

"Yes," said Geburon, "that is true of natural death, but this death was so cruel that I find it incredible that the lord in question dared to commit such an outrage, considering that he was neither her father nor her husband, but merely her brother, and that she was of an age when the laws permit girls to marry without consent."

"I don't find it at all strange," said Hircan, "for he didn't kill his sister, whom he loved so much and against whom he had no just grievance; he killed the gentleman whom he had raised as a son and loved as a brother, whom he had honored and enriched in his service, and who in turn had sought to marry his sister, which he had no right to do."

"Still," insisted Nomerfide, "it is not usual nor common for a woman so highly born to have the pleasure of marrying a gentleman-servant for love. If the death is strange, the pleasure is also a new one, and even greater because all wise men oppose it. In its favor it has the fact that a heart full of love is contented and that the soul can rest easy since God is not offended. As for the death, which you claim is cruel, it seems to me that since it is necessary to die, the quickest way is the best, for everyone knows that the passage is inevitable, but I consider happy those who do not have to linger on its outskirts and who leave the only bliss that can be considered such in this world to fly to one which is eternal."

"And what do you mean by the outskirts of death?" asked Simontault.

"Those who have had many spiritual tribulations," replied Nomerfide, "or those who have had a long illness and who have been in extreme physical or mental pain have come to long for death and to think its coming too slow. I say that those are the ones who have been on the outskirts of death, and they can tell you of the inns in which they spent more time weeping than resting. This lady couldn't avoid losing her husband by death, but her brother's anger spared her from seeing him spend long years in illness or spitefulness. And by converting the peace that she had known with him into the service of our Lord, she could truly call herself happy."

"Don't you take any account of the shame that she suffered," asked Longarine, "or of her imprisonment?"

"I believe that the person who loves perfectly," Nomerfide replied, "with a love joined to the commandment of God, never knows shame or dishonor unless he commits a fault or diminishes the perfection of his love. The glory of loving well knows no shame; and as for the imprisonment of her body, I believe that due to the freedom of her heart, which was wedded to God and to her husband, she did not feel it at all, but found great liberty in her solitude, for a person who can't see the one he loves has no greater joy than to think of him unceasingly, and no prison is so small that thoughts cannot wander where they will."

"Nothing is more true than what Nomerfide says," put in Simontault, "but the man whose fury caused this separation should be considered a miserable creature, for he offended against God, love and honor."

"Truly, I am amazed," said Geburon, "at the different kinds of love to be found among women, and I see very well that the more they love, the more virtuous they become, while those who are not in love pretend to be virtuous in order to hide the truth."

"It is true," said Parlamente, "that the heart which is as it should be towards God and man loves more strongly than the heart which is filled with vice, nor does the former fear to reveal the depth of its feeling."

"I have always heard it said," commented Simontault, "that men should never be restrained from pursuing women, for God gave man the love and courage to ask and woman the fear and chastity to refuse."

"But it was hardly fair," said Longarine, "to have praised the man so often to his sister. And it seems to me that it is either foolish or cruel for the man who guards a fountain to praise the quality of his water to one who is gazing at it and perishing of thirst, and then to kill him when he wants to take some."

"It is true," said Parlamente, "that the brother was responsible for igniting the fire with such sweet words, and he shouldn't have extinguished it with sword blows."

"I'm amazed," said Saffredent, "that you should think it is wrong for a simple gentleman, using only his own powers of persuasion and no external pressure, to be able to marry a woman of high birth, since the wisest philosophers hold that the least man is worth more than the greatest and most virtuous woman."

"The reason for this," replied Dagoucin, "is that in order to keep peace in the public domain, only the rank of the family, the ages of the parties, and the ordonnances of the laws are considered, without weighing the love or virtue of the parties, in order not to disturb the monarchy.* And from this comes the fact that marriages which are made between equals, in accordance with the judgment of relatives and men, are often between two people so different in heart, temperament, and tastes that instead of entering into an estate which leads to salvation, they start on the road to Hell."

"Indeed," said Geburon, "it has been seen time and again that those who, being alike in heart, temperament, and tastes, have married for love, without consideration of their lineage or family, have often sorely repented of it later, for their great, unconventional passion often turns into jealousy and rage."

* This was a sore point with Marguerite. Her only daughter, Jeanne d'Albret, was twice forced to marry against her parents' wishes for reasons of state, once by François I and later by Henri II.

"It seems to me," said Parlamente, "that neither one way nor the other is praiseworthy, but that two people should submit themselves to the will of God without concerning themselves with glory, avarice, or lust, and seek only a virtuous love and the consent of their parents, desiring to live in the married state as God and Nature command. And although no estate is without its tribulations, still, I have seen such people live without regret and we are not so unfortunate in this company that none of the married people here can be numbered among them."

Hircan, Geburon, Simontault, and Saffredent swore that they had married in just such a spirit and that they had never regretted it. And whatever the facts of the matter may have been, those concerned were so delighted to hear this that nothing they could have said would have pleased them more. Therefore they arose and went in to give thanks to God, the monks being ready to say vespers.

At the end of the service, they went to supper, continuing to discuss their marriages throughout the evening and telling about the events which had occurred when they were courting their wives. Since they were constantly interrupting each other, however, it would be impossible to retell these stories in logical order, though they would have been no less interesting to set down than those they had told in the field. They took so much pleasure in this and enjoyed it so thoroughly that bedtime arrived before they were aware of it. Lady Oisille took leave of the company, which then went so joyously to bed that I suspect that those who were married slept less than the others, what with recalling their past loves and demonstrating those of the present. And thus the night passed agreeably until it was morning.

Heptaméron (56)

'THE TONSURED HUSBAND'

A French lady passing through the city of Padua was told that in the bishop's prisons there was a Franciscan; and when she asked the reason, for she saw that everyone joked about him, she was told that this aged Franciscan had been the confessor of a very honest and devout lady, who had been left a widow. She had an only daughter, whom she loved so much that she spared no pains to amass a goodly sum for her and find her a good match.

Now when she saw that her daughter was growing up, she worried continually about finding her a husband, who could live with the two of them in peace and harmony, that is to say, a person of good conscience, as she considered herself to be. And because she had heard some silly preacher say that it was better to do evil on the advice of doctors of theology than good by the inspiration of the Holy Spirit, she spoke to her good father confessor, a man already advanced in years, who was a doctor of theology and thought to lead a good life by everyone in the town. With his advice and goodly prayers, she assured herself, she could not fail to secure peace for herself and her daughter. And when she had earnestly begged him to choose for her daughter a husband such as a woman who loved God and her honor might wish for, he replied that first they must seek the blessing of the Holy Spirit through prayer and fasting, and then as God guided his understanding, he hoped to find what she asked for. And thus the Franciscan went his way, thinking about his own affairs.

Since he understood from the lady that she had amassed five hundred ducats in order to give a husband to her daughter and would undertake to feed the two and supply them with a house, furniture, and accessories, he decided that he had a young companion, who had a fine build and handsome face, to whom he would give the girl, the house, the furniture, and the guarantee of room and board, while the five hundred ducats would come back to him to satisfy his burning avarice; and after he had spoken to his young companion, the two found themselves in agreement.

He returned to the lady and said to her, "I believe that without a doubt God has sent me the angel Raphael, as he did to Tobias, to find the perfect husband for your daughter, for I can guarantee that I have in my house the most honest gentleman in all Italy. On occasion, he has seen your daughter, and he is so taken with her that today, while I was in prayer, God sent him to me, and he declared to me that he wishes to marry her. I know his house and family and that he comes from a well-known line, and I have promised him to speak to you. To tell the truth, there is only one drawback which I know about him. That is, that wanting to save one of his friends, who wished to kill another, he drew his sword, trying to separate them, but as luck would have it, his friend killed the other, so that although he himself struck no blow, he is a fugitive from his city, because he was present at the murder and had drawn his sword.* Now, on the advice of his parents, he has withdrawn to this city in the disguise of a student and is staying here incognito until his parents can settle the case, which he hopes will be soon. For this reason, it is necessary to perform the marriage secretly, and you must be willing to let him attend the public lectures during the day, and every evening he will return to eat and sleep here."

The good woman answered at once, "Sir, I find what you say very much to my liking, for at least I shall have near me what I desire most in this world."

Then the Franciscan went and brought him to her in fine shape, wearing a doublet of crimson satin, with which she was quite satisfied. And after he had come, they were betrothed, and right after midnight Mass was said, they were married. Then they went to bed together until the break of day.

Thereupon, the husband said to his wife that to avoid being recognized, he was obliged to go to the school. And taking up his doublet of crimson satin, and his long gown, and not forgetting his black silk cowl, he came to bid farewell to his wife, who was still in bed, assuring her that every evening he would return to eat supper with her, but that they shouldn't expect him for dinner. Thus he got up and left his wife, who considered herself the happiest woman in the world for having found such a mate. And the young Franciscan returned to his old father, bringing with him the five hundred ducats, as had been agreed between them, according to the marriage contract. In the evening, he did not fail to return to have supper with the woman who believed he was her husband; and he maintained himself

* It is possible to explain the obvious parallel with the terms of Romeo's banishment in *Romeo and Juliet* by the fact that the author of the original story, the Italian Bandello, was well known to Marguerite de Navarre. Cf. K. H. Hartley, "Bandello and the Heptameron."

so well in her love and her mother's that they would not have wanted to exchange him for the greatest prince in the world.

This life went on for some time, but because the goodness of God pities those who are deceived in good faith, through his grace and goodness, it happened that one morning this lady and her daughter had a most devout desire to hear Mass at the church of St. Francis and to visit their good father confessor, who, so they thought, had helped one to acquire such a good son and the other such a good husband. And fortunately, not finding the confessor or anyone else they knew, they were obliged to hear the high Mass, which was just beginning, and wait to see if he would appear.

Now as the young woman was watching the divine service and its mystery with great attention, the priest turned around to say *Dominus vobiscum* and this young wife was completely taken by surprise, for it seemed to her that it was her husband or someone very like him. But for all that, she didn't say a word, but waited until he turned around again to where she could get a better look at him; and there was no doubt that it was he.

Therefore she pulled at her mother, who was lost in contemplation and said to her, "Alas, my lady, what do I see?"

"What?" asked the mother.

"That is my husband who is saying Mass, or it is his double!"

The mother, who had not been paying attention, said to her, "My daughter, please don't get such an idea into your head, for such a thing is quite impossible. These holy people would never do anything so dishonest. You would be committing a great sin against God if you put any faith in such an idea."

Nevertheless, the mother did not quit looking at him, and when it came to *Ite Missa est,* she knew truly that never had two brothers from the same womb been so alike. Nevertheless, she was so simpleminded that she would gladly have said, "My God, keep me from believing what I see!"

Because it concerned her daughter, however, she did not want to leave the thing unexplained and she resolved to know the truth. When evening came and the husband, who had not noticed them, was supposed to return, the mother came to her daughter and said, "If you wish, we shall know the truth now about your husband, for when he is in bed, I shall go up to him, without his realizing what is happening, and you shall pull off his cowl from behind. Then we shall see whether he has the same shaven crown as the man who said the Mass. Thus they did as they had decided, for as soon as the wicked husband was in bed, the old woman came in and playfully took both his hands. His wife pulled off his cowl, and he was left with his handsome shaven crown, at which the mother and daughter were utterly astounded.

They called their servant at once and had him seized and tied up until morning; and no excuse or fine talk did him any good. When day came, the woman sent for her confessor, pretending to have a great secret to tell him, and when he arrived in all haste, she had him seized like the young man and reproached him for the way he had deceived her. Thereupon she sent for the officers of the law and turned them both over to them. We can assume that if they had honest men for judges, they were not allowed to go unpunished.

"There now, my ladies, that goes to show that those who have taken the vow of poverty are not exempt from the temptations of avarice, which is the cause of so much evil-doing."

"But also of so much good!" said Saffredent. "For with the five hundred ducats, which the old lady wanted to make into a treasure, there was a great deal of merrymaking, and the poor girl, who had been waiting so long for a husband, was able to have two by this means, and truly knew better how to speak of all the hierarchies."

·   ·   ·   ·   ·   ·   ·   ·   ·   ·   ·   ·   ·